RACING WITH
CORNELIUS SHIELDS

CORNELIUS SHIELDS

RACING WITH CORNELIUS SHIELDS AND THE MASTERS

REVISED EDITION

PRENTICE-HALL, INC., ENGLEWOOD CLIFFS, N. J.

Photo Credits:

Dan Nerney—Frontispiece

Morris Rosenfeld & Sons, Inc.—Pages 2, 38, 45, 51, 54, 73, 76, 123, 174, and 231

Yacht Racing Magazine, Rowayton, Conn.—Pages 84, 98–99, 172, and 197

Yacht Racing Magazine, Rowayton, Conn., photos by Boatfoto by Howey Caufmann—
Pages 79 and 167

Long Beach News Bureau—Pages 152 and 313

Burt Richner—Page 12

Bahamas Tourist News Bureau—Page 238

Yonkers, New York, *Herald Statesman*—Page 298

New York Times—Page 43

Gerald W. Ford (photo reconstruction by John Sutphen, Jr.)—Page 5

Peter N. Smith—Page 15

Robert Allan Jr.—Page 310

Printed in the United States of America
Prentice-Hall International, Inc., London
Prentice-Hall of Australia, Pty. Ltd., Sydney
Prentice-Hall of Canada, Ltd., Toronto
Prentice-Hall of India Private Ltd., New Delhi
Prentice-Hall of Japan, Inc., Tokyo

Library of Congress Cataloging in Publication Data
Shields, Cornelius
Racing with Cornelius Shields and the masters.

"Revision of Cornelius Shields On Sailing."
1. Yacht racing. 2. Sailing. I. Title.
GV826.5.S53   1974   797.1′4   74–9744
ISBN 0–13–750224–9

Guest chapters by   ROBERT ALLAN, JR.
ROBERT BAVIER
BRITTON CHANCE, JR.
TED HOOD
BUDDY MELGES
BUS MOSBACHER
OLIN STEPHENS II
RODERICK STEPHENS, JR.
TED TURNER
STEPHEN VAN DYCK

*Then: To Do Do, with love and appreciation
for her great patience*

*Now: To Do Do, with more love and appreciation
for her even greater patience*

Acknowledgments

To express my gratitude to all those who contributed to my life in racing would take almost as many pages as this book contains. I would especially like to thank my ten friends for their kindness and cooperation in sharing their sailing knowledge, without which I would not even have attempted this new edition. For their invaluable help, I am also grateful to Donald Graul, Managing Editor of *Yacht Racing,* for his aid in preparation of the written and visual material; Owen Torrey of Charles Ulmer, Incorporated, for editorial assistance, and Peter R. Smyth of *Motor Boating and Sailing* for his part in the preparation of one of the guest chapters.

Contents

Introduction

BY CORNELIUS SHIELDS, JR.

When the publisher asked me to write this introduction I was honored, but immediately realized the impossibility of conveying my father's influence on sailing. A few personal memories will have to suffice in order to encourage the reader to learn more about my father in the chapters that follow.

When I was a child, we lived in a house on the water, and I would watch for hours from shore until the sail of International One-Design #25 appeared in the little cove at the end of each racing day. I would watch my father lower the sails and gently coast to the mooring—he never seemed to miss. His judgment was always perfect. I learned later how difficult a feat this was. Then he would put the boat away, and row ashore with his crew. After dinner, I delighted in the stories of the day's racing, which he shared in detail with me.

Before long, I was able to go with him. Our first sails together were in his beloved 12-foot dinghy, *Patience,* which he sails to this day. Those were wonderful adventures for me but they must have been exasperating for my father. My first lessons, at age two, were spent learning to steer the boat. The concept of the tiller was very confusing at first and I can remember nearly ramming several prominent yachts in the harbor.

It wasn't long before I was crewing for him in the Interclub class frostbite races. My job was to hike, work the centerboard, and keep the tell-tales clear. When I was about fourteen, Dad gave me an Interclub. He felt I was old enough to strike out on my own. Since my sister's sailboats were both called *Whim,* I decided to christen mine *Whimsy.* My father had always stressed the importance of having a compatible, well-trained crew—an essential ingredient for winning in these small, sensitive little boats. In those days, I didn't always take racing as seriously and would choose my female crews for their attractiveness rather than their sailing ability.

When I was in high school, Dad gave me a 110 class boat, which I named *Iris.* The first few years racing her were difficult and frustrating, since I was not placing well. In 1955, I began my third season as a 110 sailor. In one of the early races, Dad sailed with me to look at my new genoa. My father had been working with the technical aspects of his boats since I can remember. He would argue with a sailmaker about the shape of a sail and have it recut time and time again until he was satisfied with its performance. On *Iris,* he knew at a glance that the sail was not quite right. I explained that I was going as fast as the other boats, but *Iris* was not pointing nearly as well as I thought she should. He said my genoa should be flatter forward and taken up on the luff wire a bit. The sail was perfect after the sailmaker corrected these faults, and I went on to win the 110 World Championship that year. His sail knowledge and advice proved invaluable.

Dad and I would practice against one another in Interclub dinghies, International one-designs, and in Shields class boats. We would take turns being the "constant." In these sessions, we always learned something about sail trim, jib leads, or boat speed. For many years, I crewed for him in the International one-design class on his *Aileen.* Here I learned about his perfectly timed starts, a key factor in his racing success from dinghies to J-Boats. In my preparation for the 1962 America's Cup trials as skipper of my Uncle Paul's 12-meter *Columbia,* I practiced match-race starts with Dad for hours, each of us sailing an International. I learned from experience that my father was a tireless perfectionist.

His complete drive and desire for excellence in sailing was matched in his business life. He shared both his business and sailing with his brother, Paul. It was a fine partnership and a winning combination through the years.

My father's philosophy of competition included a constant readiness to match his ability against all challengers, and he always sought opportunities to do so. On flukey days, when the season's leaders were staying home, he was out racing. I am convinced that he lost many championship series by risking the title when he was ahead. He wanted to win by competing, not by "playing the percentages."

One of his firmest racing principles was perseverance. "No matter how bad a race looks," he would say, "keep giving maximum effort, keep fighting even if you are far behind." Another principle he applied to series racing was consistency. A steady average of thirds or fourths is the way to win trophies. I experienced this myself in the 1965 Mallory Cup series. I never won a race, but I did win the series with a consistent record of thirds and fourths. Dad always says that no one wins every race, but with 100 percent effort you will usually be right up there in the fight for first place.

A race for him begins long before the starting gun. He is always on the boat early, checking the gear and giving the boat's bottom a final cleaning. He gets out to the starting area early to time some practice starts, check the tide, plan weather-leg tactics, and chart compass courses for the downwind legs. He works with the crew to finalize their assignments before the start. Smooth organization has always been an essential part of his racing plan. This certainly applied to his ocean-racing successes on *Good News, Stormy Weather,* and *Bolero.* He is often a winner because of his dedication—he just works harder. He disciplines himself to be a bit better at every aspect of sailing. Of course, he would never admit this when he won. His explanation was simply, "It was just my day."

One race I shared with my father and will never forget was the 1961 International One-Design Alumni Race. After his heart attack in 1956, the doctors told him there was to be no more racing. Despite that warning, he successfully took the helm of *Columbia* in the 1958 America's Cup trials, and now in 1961, another challenge, the Alumni Race, was impossible for him to resist. To race once more against his regular competitors offered the chance to relive the many challenges of the past. Bob Bavier, Bus Mosbacher, Bill Cox, Arthur Knapp, George Hinman—all the former top skippers were entered in the Alumni Race.

We assembled a fine crew. We cleaned the boat's bottom, tuned the rigging, and checked every piece of equipment—everything was ready. The day provided a 25- to 35-knot rainy northeaster. Dad got the best start and built up a 200-yard lead by the time we reached the weather mark. We rounded, set the spinnaker in seconds, and then our troubles began. The halyard was not well-cleated and let go after the sail filled. We sailed over the spinnaker and ripped it—that mistake cost us the race.

There are many sailing experiences my father treasures, but none more meaningful than his Mallory Cup win for the North American Men's Championship in 1952, the first year it was contested. I crewed for him and in his comments when accepting the trophy he expressed the wish that someday I would win the Mallory. His wish became a reality in 1965 when I won the exciting series on Lake Pontchartrain in New Orleans.

Dad always likes to point out record performances, like Buddy Melges' three consecutive Mallory Cup wins or Carleton Mitchell's almost unbeatable three straight Bermuda Race victories and even our own three-championship family. My sister Aileen's Adams Trophy for the North American Women's Championship in 1948, Dad's Mallory win in 1952 and mine in 1965 set a father, son, and daughter record that will be difficult to match.

I will always be grateful to my father for introducing me to the wonderful sport of sailing. The best part of winning a race for me has always been the sight of his beaming face at the finish. I was only one of the many young people who benefited from his help and encouragement over the years and with whom he shared his great love of sailing.

Introduction

BY BUS MOSBACHER

This is the first time that Corny Shields has ever invited me to precede him. This covers quite a period of time, too, as some of my earliest memories and most indelibly inscribed lessons in tactics and strategy were learned from the "Gray Fox of Long Island Sound," as he has been affectionately called for many years. I am flattered and delighted at the opportunity for our lifelong (for me) friendship ashore and competitive jousting afloat (on the golf course, too, but that's another story) has been most meaningful and rewarding.

There have been a sizable number of keen students of the boat racing game—Harold Vanderbilt, Arthur Knapp, Bill Luders, Bill Cox, Briggs Cunningham, Herman Whiton, Ted Hood, George O'Day, Albert and Ernie Fay, my brother Bob, to name just a few—but none who have made a more thorough study of all the many facets. There is little, from the hull and sails through crew and rig or tactics and weather, that Corny has not given careful thought and attention. This devotion to detail and masterful dedication to achieving the maximum possible results is famous.

The greatest testimonial to Corny Shields and what he has stood for must necessarily be the manner in which he ran the International One-Design Class, and the Sound Interclub Class before it, during his active years. He was obsessed with keeping these fine arenas competitive on a man to man basis at the highest possible level. The strictest control was maintained over sails, gear, haul-outs, and the like so that no one could buy an advantage. He also waged a perpetual campaign to bring to this battlefield men or women, young or old, who were of championship caliber. As soon as such a sailor won an important series or title in good competition, a most persuasive phone call from Corny was soon to follow. Incidentally, lack of a boat or of the financial ability to obtain and campaign one was never an obstacle to this type of prospect. When necessary, Corny could always form a syndicate for the purpose or persuade some elder statesman to help out a deserving youngster.

With all his dedication to the one design principle, however, when Corny turned his hand to the cruising boats or the open design six or twelve meter classes, he was as resourceful and ingenious as anyone—to this I can attest, with scars to show. Many have also said over the years how much he has contributed to both the frostbite fleet and the junior sailing program at the Larchmont Yacht Club. These I have not had the opportunity to witness personally, but their records speak most eloquently.

I think back over my happy years in sailing, and find so many of the great memories intertwined with the Shields family. Aileen Shields sailing Bob's and my International *Susan* in her first try at a "big" boat in "big" competition and winning by a mile; Aileen crewing for me on *Susan* in Bermuda in my first try at international team racing abroad; playing golf with Corny while Doe Shields visited and shopped with my Patricia during our honeymoon; the hard fought *Vim-Columbia* duels during the 1958 America's Cup Trials; a friendly foursome in a driving rainstorm at the climax of that series with George Hinman and Bubbles Havemeyer, members of the selection committee; his experienced hand helping Corny, Jr. and *Columbia* in 1962 during the trials; the appreciation for the way the *Weatherly* crew turned out to a man—designer, engineers, and all, to lend a hand when *Columbia's* rig went over the side.

I've wandered afield, though. All who read this book will profit therefrom as I have, for, as Corny stresses, there isn't a day when we can't learn something new about this wonderful sport. I wish it had been written twenty-five years ago so that it might have been a little easier to learn many of the secrets that Corny reveals here. I know you'll enjoy this most fascinating and informative volume, which while it has come a bit late for me shall be required reading for my three young sons.

BUS MOSBACHER

Part One

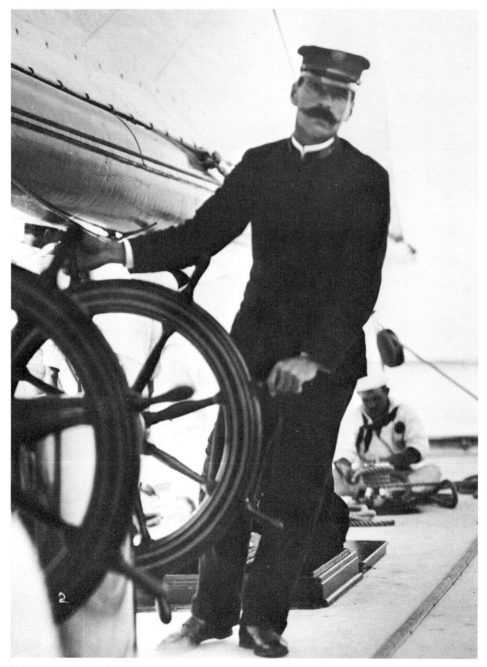

The legendary skipper, Captain Charles Barr, at the unique double wheel of the *Reliance*. Barr was undoubtedly the most successful and famous of the professional racing skippers.

1. Ten Years After the Last

My sailing career started at the advanced age of six years in Sydney, Nova Scotia. As in the age-old success story of the corporation president's son, I started at the top—really at the very top, as I sailed the J-Boat *Columbia* against the legendary skipper Captain Charlie Barr at the helm of the famous *Reliance*. These two America's Cup yachts were over 140 feet long, drew 19½ feet, and carried 16,000 square feet of sail. The club topsails stood 180 feet above the waterline. In these match races, I rather regularly beat Captain Barr, as my clever tactics seemed to outwit him.

I very much want you to read this book, so before you close the covers in exasperation with the foregoing boastful account of my achievements, I must confess that my *Columbia* and Barr's *Reliance* were merely chips of wood a few inches long. I raced them in a beautiful stream that ran through our property. In my childhood imagination, they immediately became the real boats I heard my older brothers talking about and saw pictured in their magazines. This was in the spring of 1903, just prior to the America's Cup series against the British challenger *Shamrock*. I would spend hours starting the small chips evenly, as if they were on a starting line, and watching them as they "sailed" down the stream. There were eddies and currents in the stream that made the little chips do curious things. One boat might gain as it rushed along close to shore, and another time it might go faster as it sped down the center of the stream—examples of what I learned years later sailing in tricky tidal currents.

The entire course those chips sailed was only about 100 yards, but never failed to provide me with an endless amount of fun.

In *Cornelius Shields on Sailing* (Prentice-Hall, 1964), I described, with some emphasis, the phenomenal ability a youngster has to build or do anything he desires with his imagination. What a wonderful gift. If adults were more conscious of it, they would forget buying expensive and elaborate gifts for children. The child, instead of playing with a toy or present, very often enjoys the box it arrived in more than the gift. That package or box becomes anything he wants to make it: a car, boat, airplane, truck, and so on. Don't ever discourage this in a child in spite of your disappointment at his disinterest in the gift. That act of imagination on his part can be the beginning of important things. Great inventions, industrial development, and artistic creations can often be traced to the dreams of early childhood.

I haven't done any active racing during the past ten years, but I have had the benefit and the surprise of learning a great deal about tactics by merely observing. Watching others race has brought to my attention many mistakes I made over the years. It's a good idea to observe a top fleet instead of waiting until you are sailing against them. As an observer, you often see things that, as a helmsman, you might not think of until hours after the race, because you are too close to the decision-making process. While watching a race, you can see such things as skippers going all the way to the lay line, then getting a lift and losing it all; tacking short of the mark, then later being met at the mark by a number of competitors on starboard tack. For this reason, it is a good idea to make one knowledgeable member of the crew act as an "on board" observer, in charge of double checking all the simple things such as marks, distant breeze changes, competitor positions, and other essential happenings that a helmsman may neglect as he sails the boat.

Observing is also a most enjoyable way to sail since you have the benefit of never losing a race, just as the fan in the bleachers is always right and the Monday morning quarterback never calls a bad play. The first time I thought of having an observer assist me was in a Bermuda series with the late Sir Eldon Trimingham, one of the keenest helmsmen I ever knew, who also had a delightful sense of humor. He once described a particularly dumpy, low-performance boat by saying, "The boat was so slow she hit the same wave three times!"

Eldon was watching the race from a spectator boat. I had just taken

Reliance, the famed Herreshoff sloop, heading for the finish line under full sail during her successful defense of the America's Cup in 1903.

up golf and was amazed at what a teaching pro could observe and correct during a lesson. I knew it would help me if Eldon would observe throughout the day and review the racing with me in the evening. He didn't think that sailing lent itself to the same approach as golf, but agreed to make the attempt and watch with extra care the next day. I knew that would be fine for me, as I could trust his judgments. It worked out wonderfully. His comments were productive on almost everything I did. He would notice times that I should have stayed on a tack a bit longer and other instances when I should have short-tacked. There were sail-trim observations and many other ideas as well. It was a very helpful session, and one I really appreciated.

Two reasons that so many college sailors are such good competitors are the coach's constant attention and days filled with multiple races. The increase in popularity of college sailing over the past ten years is one of the many marvelous and healthy developments in our sport.

Observing your opponents before, during, and after a race also can be instructive. I remember racing an International one day in a strong breeze when one boat was doing very well. The skipper was not particularly experienced and I wondered what was making the difference. At the end of the day's racing, I congratulated him on his fine performance. He remarked that it was quite surprising to him, since he had left his brand-new, full-cut jib at home and had to sail with an older one. He said that the old sail was much too flat to be very fast. That explained his speed in the strong air—the flatter jib was the answer. The full sails that the remainder of the fleet had used were not as fast in heavy air. He gave me a valuable piece of information that he didn't even know he had. The moral of the story is that you can always learn something from everyone, often from the inexperienced. Perhaps this is because, in his innocence, he will try something that turns out successful, which the more experienced would have rejected as contrary to his greater store of knowledge.

The neophyte can learn even more from examining the winning boat and listening intelligently to the dockside replay of the race by the top finishers. That generous and sportsmanlike sharing of techniques and analysis is one thing that makes our sport so worthwhile.

One of the best things about junior sailing is the open-minded approach that the youngsters have. Exposing them to competition often teaches them more than any amount of instruction could. Little League baseball and Pop Warner football, AAU age-group swimming, and junior sailing all illustrate this point. Such competition encourages a young person's development, and a coach can refine this development into valuable skills. Young people are eager to listen and learn while adults are over-confident and too knowledgeable to benefit from instruction and group-learning situations.

It seems to me that during the past ten years there have been more racing equipment innovations and refinements than in any other decade of my racing life. The variety and efficiency of the new winches, the development of rod rigging, the sophisticated blocks and travelers—especially the new jib traveler systems—and Ted Hood's slotted headstay are just a few examples of what has been happening. The fantastic sail developments such as deck-sweeper jibs and the variety of spinnakers of every size, shape, and weight are simply amazing. The plethora of gadgets to increase the speed and simplify the handling of racing yachts is almost overwhelming. The startling new computer which calculates the speed of a boat to windward, automatically accounting for sea and current conditions, indicates the degree of sophistication of modern racing equipment.

All these marvelous advances fascinate me, but also cause me to wonder about future helmsmen. Maybe they will control their boats by radio from deck chairs on the yacht-club porch, observing the maneuvers through space binoculars—a big-boat version of the model yacht regattas held on the small lakes of city parks. I know this is a bit exaggerated, but it helps to explain why I am so pleased when an event like the revival of 6-meter racing in San Francisco occurs. I am aware that I have a soft spot in my heart for the 6's, having raced them regularly against the British, the four Scandinavian countries, and the Italians from 1920 through 1937. In spite of this, such revivals, as well as continued observance of one-design control, are, in my estimation, also very beneficial to the future of racing.

Later in the book, I tell of the role played by the 6-meter *Saga* in the formation of the International one-design class. The recent series in San Francisco between Australia and the United States has confirmed my opinion of the durability of good basic design and racing concepts. The U.S. boat, *St. Francis V*, designed by Gary Mull, won the series over the Australian's *Pacemaker*, designed by Olin Stephens. In an open series following the main event, 20 boats were entered. *St. Francis V* won the open series also, but *Saga* finished seventh. Quite a respectable showing for a 40-year-old boat!

Hopefully, the revived 6-meter series will be continued. Perhaps changing the 6-meter rule to allow the use of aluminum hulls might encourage the Scandinavians, Italians, Canadians, and others to participate.

I do hope the ready availability of the marvelous racing equipment described above does not stifle the creative experimentation of the average skipper. Good ideas for making a boat sail faster are often pioneered by the ordinary sailor out on the race course. Necessity is still the mother of invention. For example, I recall one of my own "inventions" back in 1920. The Victory class was launched that year. It had been founded by Harry and Junius Morgan, sons of the legendary J. P. Morgan. This class was probably the first of Harry's countless contributions to yachting. Through the kindness of Drake Sparkman, I became the skipper of one of these fine boats which were designed by William Gardner, who was also the creator of *Atlantic,* the J-Boat *Vanitie,* and many other famous craft.

The Victory was the first class to use the Marconi rig. While sailing her, I soon noticed that the upper 25 percent of the main luffed first. In my experience with gaff rigs, the luff had never seemed so pronounced aloft. I was rather puzzled at this new phenomenon. I also noticed that when the main was eased, the boom lifted appreciably. I should have realized that the release of the strain on the main leech was causing the boom to lift. I still couldn't understand why the whole luff was not breaking at the same time. I tried an experiment to see if I couldn't make that happen. I had a heavy crew member hold the boom down. This eliminated the upper main from luffing! Now, how could I devise a permanent remedy, eliminating the need to trim the sheet to correct the upper luff? I solved the problem with a tackle placed about six feet aft of the forward end of the boom. Two small wooden wedges secured on each side of the boom prevented the tackle from sliding forward under strain. The forward block of the tackle was secured at the mast at deck level. It worked well and I was delighted. The mainsail now swung like a door on a hinge and the entire luff broke simultaneously when the main was eased. I also found I could ease the main further on a reach without a break aloft. Best of all, my tackle increased the speed of the boat on a reach.

I went along with my competitors' explanations for my increased speed. They theorized that my sail was fuller or that my mast was raked forward or maybe that it was the hard Mitchell green bottom paint I used, and so on. No one paid any attention to my boom tackle. Most thought it was merely to keep the sail full when the wind was very light.

I really don't know if I was a pioneer, but for years I never heard of or saw a boom tackle like mine. To this day, I don't know who coined the name "boom vang"—mine was simply "tackle."

One characteristic of the tackle I didn't learn of until years later was its effectiveness in heavy windward work without a traveler. It is not as effective as a wide traveler, but to some extent does produce the same result. The boat does sail flatter with better speed because of the vang, which flattens the entire mainsail.

There is an interesting illustration of a designer pushing a rule to its natural limits in the 6-meter *Rebel*, designed by Bill Luders for my brother Paul in 1937. The sail measurement rule specified the size of the genoa based on the position of the sheet lead block, much like the present rule for the Flying Dutchman. Bill thought of taking a very large sail, cutting off the corner at the clew, and adding a wooden club, sheeted with a bridle to the legal deck lead. Thus, we had the benefit of the large sail's long overlap and full leech while staying within the rules. I certainly thought it was a most original idea, until I finally noticed a jib of the same design on a print which had been hanging over my fireplace for years. The print depicts the America's Cup boat *Vigilant* sailing in 1893 with this device!

Offshore racing is nearly a science today as crews drive the boats constantly from start to finish. It wasn't always that way, and I remember my first preparations for a Bermuda Race in 1946. Drake Sparkman had arranged for me to sail the *Good News*, the famous 61-footer designed by Olin Stephens. I had the impression that in most offshore races there was considerable laxity in sailing the boat hard after the first day when few competitors were in sight to spur maximum effort. I was convinced that if an ocean racer were sailed as hard as the one-designers around a 10-mile triangle, better results would be obtained. With this in mind, I selected a group of young, very capable crew members, whose experience included one-design racing. I like to sail with young people. As a rule, they are joyful and pleasant to be around and not apt to create feuds—a most unhappy condition on any boat, or anywhere else for that matter.

My only uncertainty concerned seasickness, which can always put a dent in an offshore performance. I had a chance to test for this on a three-day practice sail on the open ocean. We went through every possible maneuver: jibing in hard breezes, reefing, man overboard, jib and spinnaker changes, and so on. I also tested for possible relief helmsmen. I had the wheel during my watch and "Ducky" Endt, the other watch of-

ficer, took it during his. We learned a lot during that session, and as it
turned out no one was sick in the severe weather of early June.

To prepare our eager group for possible disappointment, I stressed the
fact that the Bermuda Race was a real lottery. You could be well out in
front within a few miles of finishing and run into the normal flukey
weather and end up losing. And that is exactly what happened! We were
only about five miles from the finish, well ahead of *Baruna,* our nearest
competitor, when we were becalmed. *Gesture* came over the horizon in a
small squall and went miles around us to win the race. We did manage
to grab a second, however. The practice session and constant 24-hour attention to racing paid off handsomely.

I never tire of thinking of the enjoyment I have had during my lifetime of sailing. A few weeks before I wrote this, I was out in my little
Patience, sailing for three straight days in a beautiful fall northeaster. It
was some of the best and most exciting sailing I have ever had. Curiously
enough, even though I am not allowed to race, I believe I am getting
more enjoyment from sailing that 41-year-old 12-foot dinghy than I did
from some of the largest yachts I ever sailed.

I suppose that some who read this will think I am exaggerating, but
that little boat never fails to give me delight and genuine pleasure. It's
probably impossible for anyone who is not a sailor to understand, but
when I feel her go through the seas and respond to my every touch, it
means everything to me. Think of the golfer playing his last game in the
fall or the hunter sitting in his blind and waiting for the fowl. Every
sport has those special moments—that last day of the season.

One of the most exciting developments during the past ten years has
been the continued great expansion of sailboat racing. The sport is growing and spreading more than almost any other. Sailors are racing on
man-made lakes that didn't even exist when the first edition of this book
was written. There are boat builders and sailmakers in Colorado, Texas,
Utah, Iowa, and Kansas, and sailors are using their products in areas that
we coastal residents might call landlocked! This is the future of racing;
these are the helmsmen who will be in the big classes and top competition during the next decade.

Many people have taken up sailboat racing without a great deal of
experience and have done very well. They haven't had the traditional
junior sailing programs or early racing as crew, but they get to college or
in an area where sailing is popular and in a short time become top skip-

pers. We had a sailor in the International class who didn't start to race until he was 45 years old. He was very bright, an electrical engineer, and in three years had won the season championship. He was not a traditionalist, but he was a dedicated and smart fellow who made up his mind that he was going to sail and win. He represents an exception to the rule of youth succeeding. I am sure that many of the sailors on Carlyle Lake near St. Louis, and Lake Roy Hubbard in Texas are going to be heard from in the future of yacht racing, along with helmsmen from many other areas that are not widely known but provide exciting sailing in Colorado, Kansas, Arizona, and other "landlocked" states.

A spectacular development in the sailboat-racing world is the emergence of the smaller cruiser-racers. The Midget Ocean Racing Club (MORC), Midget Ocean Racing Association (MORA), and the International Offshore Rule (IOR) level-rating classes of Quarter Ton, Half Ton, and Three-Quarter Ton all have put 20- to 30-foot boats into the hands of a huge number of adept skippers. These younger sailors can race at the top level on a modest budget. The MORC and MORA boats are measured to their own rules and hold their own races, while the level-rating classes can compete in many important offshore-racing series, in addition to their special sort of regatta. The level-rating regatta usually consists of three-course races and a long and medium distance race. This schedule puts an emphasis on consistent performance rather than specialized design.

In all of these classes, a family man has a boat that he can use for family cruising as well as to introduce his wife and children to casual racing. A young man who couldn't rationalize the capital expenditure or the time involved in campaigning an all-out racing dinghy or keelboat can now own a recreational and racing boat combined. At the Fall MORC Series in Detroit, there were 60 boats on the line; similar turnouts are common for these boats. That is why the 20- to 30-footers are increasing in popularity. An interesting sidelight is the fact that many of the far-out designs that have been attempted in the IOR classes have not had any great success. The boats that seem to be winners are the all-around fine performers such as Ron Holland and Gary Carlin's *Eyghtene,* which won the 1973 World Quarter-Ton Championship; the *Ganbare,* designed and skippered by Doug Peterson, which nearly took the One-Ton World's; and the 1973 MORC National Champion, Tony Johnson's Southern 21, *Foot Loose.* All are sensible and proven designs available in production

Ganbare, designed and owned by Douglas Peterson, took a second in the 1973 One-Ton World's in spite of the fact that she was only beaten once across the finish line in the five-race series.

versions at reasonable prices. MORC has been that way since Bill Shaw's *Trina* started it all, and the IOR level-rating classes show the same promise for the future.

The future does look bright with the many young designers, sailmakers, and skippers all taking a major role in national and international competition. I look forward to the next decade with as much enthusiasm as I did the last.

In addition to a look at the racer-cruiser situation, we should also examine the direction of small-boat racing. The importance of the modern high-performance planing dinghy is obvious, but what of its one-design characteristics, which to my mind make racing a true test of the sailor and not his pocketbook or the time he can give to rig and boat development? As a new class develops, it seems to gradually cost more for a sailor to stay competitive. Seemingly innocent, small changes are gradually introduced that make the boat less than one-design. These changes may expand the class, though I'm not too sure about that, but even one change destroys the purpose of the one-design concept. I think the outstanding characteristic of one-design racing is the focus on skipper and crew against skipper and crew with the boat merely the vehicle. Even if they are not the best boats, not the fastest, not the most difficult to tune, the fact that they are one-design and identical makes all the difference.

The Sunfish class, which was designed by Alexander Bryan and now numbers more than 100,000, and the Laser class, which has grown to nearly 20,000 boats in three years, are examples of what a class can do if it maintains the strict policy of one-design sails, rig, and hull, thus protecting an owner's investment. Both these classes deserve an honorable mention for bringing so many people to sailing. Compare them with the more open classes of one-designs like the Flying Dutchman, Soling, and Star. Spars, sails, and hulls change with regularity as one designer plays with the rules and another has his chance to make his boat or rig just a little bit faster. This is an error. How can a young person keep up in a class that requires such high upkeep costs? You must have boats available that a sailor can get into with a small investment but without sacrificing top competition. Such a class gives a young sailor the opportunity to learn the most from racing while having the most fun. He will not be able to blame his boat or equipment for his defeat, nor credit them for his success. His racing performance will be his alone. The greatest thing you can do for a youngster is to expose him to those things at which he can become proficient and enjoy throughout his life. That is a sad thing abut playing football, baseball, and track: They disappear from your life so quickly. Tennis, golf, fishing, and sailing are sports that last throughout a person's life and are enjoyable at many levels of competition.

One of the things that has pleased me most during the past ten years is the acceptance of the Shields class sloop at colleges and universities. So many young people have written commenting on the class and the fun of racing a mini-12-meter. The class is dedicated to the one-design principle which insures even racing for all the colleges, schools, and marine institutions that own the boats. The fleet now numbers 206.

Another wonderful quality of racing is that you don't have to sail constantly to be able to perform. It is such a natural talent that a good sailor can come back and win after a long layoff. Once the basic skills are acquired, you never have to relearn them. Perhaps it is this natural aspect of sailing that seems to attract a very wholesome type of boy and girl, more so than any other sport that I know.

As the years pass like the marks of a race, I think of several things that younger people should be aware of and make a part of their lives. One of these is to have a real interest in something other than one's profession or job. It would be fine if this were sailing, as that would please me, but it should be something that dominates your leisure time—good examples are golf, painting, tennis, raising flowers, cards, civic affairs, or photography. It should be an activity that can take over all of your thoughts and concentration. Even now, yacht racing interests me more than ever. I read all I can, talk to as many people as possible, and I am sure that it keeps me actively involved and really enjoying myself in my serious effort to learn.

I think a lot about the problem we all have of being concerned, sometimes overly so, with what other people think of us. We are afraid of saying things or doing things because of what someone else's reaction might be. That can be a personal handicap. Each of us has a distinct personality and must be true to it. If we don't develop our personality, it's our own fault. If we try to please everyone we meet, we become chameleons and nonentities. All of us, no matter how strong we are, can be caught not expressing ourselves candidly, and that's wrong. It is futile to be concerned with pleasing everyone else. To paraphrase Lincoln, "You may please all the people some of the time; you can even please some of the people all the time; but you can't please all of the people all the time."

People who work at their jobs to the exclusion of their families are also missing a lot. Working to support your family, then not having any fun with them isn't good. Making "X" number of dollars and then thinking that you had better make twice that much is a frightful disease. No fun, no hobbies, and what do you have—money? To a certain degree,

The author at the helm of *Do Do,* his Shields class sloop.

ing. In sailing, you are out there alone or with your crew, and the others are friendly enemies. You give them a nice hail before the start while, under your breath, you are saying, "I'm going to lick you!" I could never help feeling that way, even when my competitors were good friends. After the race, the boats disappear to all the different clubs so you might only see your competition across the water. But on the golf course, you are with your fellow players and the same animosity doesn't seem to develop. There are also many opportunities to make new friends, picking up an afternoon foursome with three new faces.

Temperament is a real handicap to any sport; if you can't control your behavior, you are really lost. It gets down to fundamentals. If you can't take a beating and come back, you don't belong in any sort of sports activity. At the least, it is a serious handicap.

Since my first book came out some ten years ago, I have had many comments on it. One of the first came from Roy Alexander, publisher of *Time* magazine. He told me that he thought it was a good book, and added that he was saying so because he sat down and read it straight through and not because he was a friend. It was on *Time*'s recommended list for eight weeks, which Roy emphasized was an editorial decision, not his.

With this new edition, there is added material from some of the best sailors in the country. When I thought of each one and contacted them, they all said the same thing: "I would love to do a chapter . . . but I just don't have the time." Then I would explain that the book depended on their contributions, which is a fact, and that I wouldn't do it without them. Well, in my opinion, the result is well worthwhile, because each is an excellent piece of work which will prove interesting and instructive. Everyone can profit greatly from the experience presented by the various masters.

I can't pose as an expert in this book, because everyone who sails regularly is an expert. I can only expect to remind sailors of things they may have forgotten, and recall some of the errors I made due to lack of preparation or that extra bit of thought. I have directed the book more toward the novice sailor than the so-called sophisticates. I hope, however, that even the best racing helmsmen will find something interesting and useful.

Something that amazes me about the book is its popularity among some golfers! My daughter knows one and asked me to autograph his copy for him. I wrote that I hoped the book wasn't good enough to take him away from his wonderful game. I get many letters from golfers who feel the same way about their game as I do about sailing, but they haven't managed to convert me to their tautness and high pressure game. Of all the letters that have come in, the one from young Brian Porter of Elgin, Illinois, stands out in particular. He wrote to me and a note from his mother was included. It seems that in a school classroom they were talking about saints and when they came to the patron saint of weather, water, and wind, or something like that, Brian popped his hand up. His answer was, "Oh, I know about the water. That's St. Cornelius!" That has always amused me.

This new edition comes out in 1974, which is an America's Cup year, and that always brings back pleasant memories of *Columbia* and the 12-meters, J-Boats, and match racing.

A match-race start is one of the greatest thrills yacht racing has to offer. Although a match race series is great once in awhile, I wouldn't want to make a commitment to that sort of racing exclusively. I think that fleet racing is much more interesting on the whole. Match racing is exciting because it offers a real chance to show your talent, courage, ability, and competitive spirit. You are out to beat your opposition fairly in every way you possibly can, and his intentions are the same. Match racing is like chess with its devious patterns of maneuvering. It is far ahead of an open start with 15 or so boats, which is more like checkers, because in a match race you are all alone and you must control that other boat. In a fleet start, you can always find a place on the line because nobody else is trying to prevent you from starting. In a match race, the other skipper is actively trying to keep you from starting. It is a real life battle of wits and skill.

The biggest problem in an America's Cup 12-meter campaign is the importance of developing a schedule that allows plenty of time for the unexpected. Active preparation starts early in the year. In spite of the fact that you are in Newport for three months or more, you can't afford any major time lost on any aspect of the program, including boat modifications and rig or crew changes. It's hard to believe how much time is consumed. The 12's are not like small boats which allow you to try out sails, rig, and trim in an afternoon. You have to have 11 top men present whenever you want to make a move. Any single aspect turns into an all-day affair. That's why it takes all summer and that's why planning and scheduling are so important.

In addition, there is the human equation to the Cup: The boat is problem enough, but the supply, crew, equipment, and shoreside activities are even more involved. Under the stress of the trials, any potential feuds or ill will quickly become major problems. In spite of, or maybe because of its complexity, I am looking forward to viewing the international excitement that is the America's Cup.

I tried to think of a key idea to start off this edition and I have come up with one that might be amusing and instructive to you. Think of the similarities between saving money, losing weight, and sailing a yacht race. How could there be any connection, you think? Well, here is my idea: Making money is certainly not easy, but saving it is even more difficult. Preserving and protecting his security after he has earned it must be one of man's toughest tasks. Weight is hard to lose, but it is even harder to keep it off once you have reduced to your proper level. Now how about sailing? The weather leg is a complex problem in wind, tactics, strategy, and technique, and a lead at the windward mark is one of racing's greatest rewards. Hanging on to that lead around the rest of the course, though, is the mark of the real champion.

My advice: Work hard to make it and then twice as hard to preserve it in all the races of life. My wish: That each of you cross his own finish line, champion in his class.

2. A Look Astern

I was born in St. Paul, Minnesota, in what turned out to be a good yachting year, 1895. It was the year that *Defender* beat *Valkyrie III* and kept the America's Cup in the United States, and it was also the year that the beautiful little sloop *Ethelwynn*, designed and sailed by W. P. Stephens, beat England's *Spruce IV* in the first race for the Seawanhaka Cup. There is some sort of prophetic coincidence here, for both of these famed yachting prizes were to play an important part in my life.

My father, who had started working as a waterboy on James J. Hill's Great Northern Railroad and had risen to become its vice-president, moved the family to Bristol, Tennessee, where he became president of the Virginia Iron, Coal, and Coke Company. Fortunately for my future as a sailor, we didn't stay long in landlocked Bristol, but in 1900 moved to the lovely harbor city of Sydney, Nova Scotia, where my father became president of the Dominion Iron and Steel Company.

We lived a little to the west of Sydney, where two bays form a "Y" that cuts into the Sydney Peninsula. The house was set back a few hundred yards from the water and had an immense lawn running down to the water's edge. We had several boats, I remember: a canoe, some rowing boats, a launch, and my father also had an interest in a big cruising cutter, the *Dione*.

It was a wonderful place for a boy to learn to love the water, for the tradition of the sea was very strong in Nova Scotia. My older brothers, Paul and Lou, became fond of sailing while we lived there. My father first bought them a little 18-foot ketch-rigged sailboat, something like the Block Island boats, and then later commissioned Herick Duggan, who designed boats as a hobby, to do the drawing for a lovely little fin-keeled sloop about 28 feet overall. She had a gaff rig and mahogany hull, and was christened *Virginia*. We took delivery of her after we moved to Sault Ste. Marie, Ontario, where my father had gone to become president of the Lake Superior Corporation.

In Sault Ste. Marie, we lived on the St. Mary's River, which links Lake Superior to the other Great Lakes. The river was two or three miles across and lay between low, sparsely populated banks. I was a child just old enough to wander around by myself, and I used to spend hours exploring the water's edge, watching the great 400- and 500-foot ore boats steaming down the river.

One morning, down at the water's edge, I found a log two or three feet long that had been sawed lengthwise, leaving a kind of ship's deck. I doubt that anyone else would have given that log a second look, but it was to become my first "boat."

I hauled it out of the water and shored it up as I had seen real boats shored at the shipyard. I cleaned it, painted it, and put masts and little liferails on it. I spent hours admiring it, and came to love it. With my child's imagination, I could transform it into the beautiful America's Cup racer *Reliance,* or into the magnificent ocean liner *Majestic,* on which my mother and older sisters had just returned from Europe. Most of the time, though, it remained simply my boat. Children have always found magical delight in their own simple objects—broken boxes or sticks that become, for them, racing cars or airplanes. The strongest impressions are those of childhood, and in my own case the kind of feeling I had for that first "boat" has stayed with me all my life. The boats have changed, but the emotion has remained basically the same.

From a child building a toy, I've moved through an active, rewarding lifetime on the water: an apprenticeship in the fundamentals of sailing; the first tentative steps in racing; then years of active campaigning against the keenest rivals in the world of yachting. I've been racing boats for over half a century, and I'm certain there's no one who has received more pleasure than I from my sport.

In Sault Ste. Marie, I didn't spend all my time on shore, building "boats." I also went sailing when Lou and Paul took me. The memory of one such sail is still very much with me.

On a lovely, clear day in July 1903, when I was eight years old, Lou and Paul took their sloop, *Virginia*, out on the St. Mary's River. We left the mooring and beat upwind. I was sitting on the weather quarter, watching the sails and the sky and the water. The breeze began to make up, and Paul, who was steering, didn't ease her at all, but let her have her head. She heeled over until the lee rail was buried. The weather side, with me on it, rose higher and higher until I was looking straight down into the water, sliding to leeward and grabbing desperately for a hand-hold.

I knew the boat was going over, and I was afraid. Though I had only heard the words used by the grown-ups, and barely understood what they meant, I muttered under my breath, over and over, "Luff her, you damn fool, luff her!"

I can hear those frightened words as if I'd spoken them today. They must have eased her eventually, because they sailed back to the dock, where they unceremoniously dumped me and left me to walk home. Probably they were disgusted with my chicken-heartedness, but in truth I was badly scared in that hard breeze. I have fond memories of *Virginia*, though, for it was aboard her, some years later, that I acquired a true awareness of the beauty of sailing and developed a passion for boats.

In 1904, my father died. Because I was only nine, I had never been as close to him as my older brothers and sisters; my feeling for him was rather one of great respect and admiration. This was partly because of the times: the father of that era wasn't as free and easy with his children as the father of today. Also, because of the large size of our family (there were seven of us), he had little time to spare. Without question, parents are more conscious of their children as personalities today than when I was a boy, and we parents are luckier for it. I know I've gained immeasurably from the sharing and interchange with my children, and have learned a great deal from them.

After my father's death there was no reason for us to stay in Ontario. My oldest sister, Katherine, was married and living in New York, so in 1906 my mother bought a house in New Rochelle, where she could be close to family and friends. My other two sisters, Alice and Cornelia, assisted my mother in bringing me up. They couldn't have been better "guardian angels." My appreciation, love, and affection for them continue to this day. *Virginia* was shipped down, and we found a mooring place for her in New Rochelle Harbor. Paul and Lou were occupied with their careers, so the boat spent most of her time at the mooring.

New Rochelle was a wonderful place for a boy to grow up, and I spent my time swimming in Long Island Sound, tramping along the harbor shore, and doing the thousand things that interest a boy. I sailed only once or twice with Paul on *Virginia,* and a few times I crewed for Fred Gade or Bob Mahlstedt in their Bugboats, the predecessors of the Star class. I loved the water, but there were many other things I liked to do just as well as sail. I was certainly not prepared for the radical change that would soon come over me. I was to undergo an experience that would make sailboats a part of my life forever.

One day I was sailing off New Rochelle Harbor with Sterling Mac-Kintosh aboard his Larchmont Interclub. It is over half a century since that day, but I've never forgotten it. It was about eleven o'clock, and the weather was clear and beautiful. The wind was blowing 10 or 15 knots from the northwest, and we were beating into it. I was preoccupied and interested in what was going on around me.

"I've been steering all morning," Sterling said. "Would you like to take the helm for a while?"

This was the first time I'd ever been offered a helm. I'd never asked to steer either, for I'd simply never felt the inclination—I was content just to look on while others did the actual boat handling.

But we changed places, and it didn't take twenty seconds before I was hit by a welling-up of emotion so strong that it's almost indescribable. It was like a theater curtain going up. Suddenly, I was tremendously happy. Perhaps what I experienced is similar to what happens to a glider pilot when he's set free from the tow and soars for the first time. Transmitted through that tiller was the feel of having control over a living, energetic thing. The emotion was far more exalted and complex than the simple thrill of command. I felt a great exhilaration, and for the first time really sensed the full joy of sailing, rather than the mere motion of the boat.

It was one of the greatest experiences of my life, and I will be forever grateful to Sterling for having given it to me. Never, before or since, has anything opened up to me so spectacularly.

I kept the helm for the balance of the hour. Then we went about and came in for lunch. Food was the last thing in the world I cared about: I couldn't wait to pick up the sails and get out to *Virginia*. I sailed her for the rest of that day, and for years after, until I sold her; it was a rare day when I missed the delight of sailing her all day long. From the first time I took the tiller, I never again worried about capsizing. When you handle a boat yourself, you learn instinctively what she'll take, and your confidence grows.

During the next few years, I came to love the water in the way that's natural to a sailor. Occasionally, I crewed for local skippers during races, but for the most part I spent my time aboard *Virginia*, absorbing all she could teach me. My mother, who hadn't sailed much in the past, often went out with me. While I handled the sheets and tiller, she would sit up on the forward deck, leaning against the mast, and she would sing. This always made me nervous, for she wasn't the world's best swimmer. (She'd taught herself to swim—in an unusual and frightening way. She always said she knew she could do it, and one day, when I was in my early teens, she simply jumped off the end of the dock into 15 feet of water and proved her point.) I remember one sail when we ran into a thunderstorm. My mother persuaded me not to go back into the harbor. She was sure we'd be perfectly safe, and she assumed that I could handle a boat in rough weather. When the storm broke, I discovered her down under the deck, taking her shoes off—"just in case we go over," she said.

Without my realizing it, those days were preparing me for the time when I'd be a racing skipper. And racing is the aspect of sailing that has gripped me the hardest.

I sailed my first race as a skipper in 1909, and from the start it was a comedy of errors. The race was held off Stamford, Connecticut, and I had to sail the 12 or 13 miles up there from New Rochelle. Some friends had said they would crew for me, but when they didn't appear on the morning of the race, I left without them. The *Virginia* was a sizable boat for one person to race, especially one with my limited experience, but I was all fired up and vowed I'd take part, no matter what.

My trip up the Sound went badly from the outset. The wind was from the northwest, and it was strong, hitting 20 knots in the gusts. As I was leaving the harbor, the battens in the mainsail broke. A few miles further on, off Larchmont, the bobstay fitting let go; then the backstay parted and the tiller broke off at the rudderhead.

The last was too much; I knew I wouldn't be able to race without repairs. I patched things up, sailed back to the harbor, and rowed to the shipyard. The man at the yard fixed the tiller, and I rove a new back-stay, repaired the bobstay with wire, and borrowed a set of battens. Two hours later, I was reaching back up the Sound. There was a wonderful breeze, and late or not, I was determined to compete.

Virginia and I came up to the committee boat and went roaring across the starting line, ready for a battle to the death. *Virginia*, though noble and proud, was past her maidenhood, and though I would have fought the man who said so, with strain she tended to weep at the seams. She had been lightly built to save weight, and the years had dealt somewhat harshly with her. Because I loved the boat so, she and I kept the secret between us. My habit was to steer with one hand and bail her out with a bucket with the other.

The course was a reaching start east to the "Cows," the light buoy off Stamford, then a jibe with another reach out into the middle of the Sound, and finally a beat home to the weather mark. Well ahead, I could see the group of boats that had started on time. *Virginia* was fin-keeled and flat-bottomed, which made her fast on a reach. Crouched low in the cockpit, I strained my eyes ahead. It looked as though we were gaining on the fleet—perhaps we could still beat one of the stragglers.

Turning the last mark, I trimmed the sheets for the beat to windward. A race is not lost till the finish; on we sailed, intent on catching someone.

The author's gaff-rigged sloop, *Virginia* (on the right with sail number R2), running before the wind on Long Island Sound.

Then, suddenly, I realized that *Virginia* was almost half-full of water. Bucket in one hand, tiller in the other, it was a question of keeping her going while at the same time keeping her from swamping.

If we had roared across the starting line, we more or less wallowed across the finish line, nearly awash like a rock at half-tide. "Who won?" I shouted to the race committee as I went by. "How did the race come out?"

"What class are you in?"

"Special Class 'R.'" I answered the hail as proudly as Commodore Perry signaling, "We have met the enemy and they are ours."

"There are no other class 'R' boats out today," they called. "You're the only one."

The ignominy of it! The shame of it! I had won my first race by a sail-over. I was broken-hearted, but nonetheless the sail had been glorious, and now I was blooded, after a fashion. I set to work with the bucket. Ten minutes later, *Virginia*'s bilges were dry and I started for home.

Between 1910 and 1913, I went away to school at Loyola in Montreal. I was always an indifferent student, and like most boys of fifteen I couldn't wait for classes to end so I could go outdoors and find something interesting to do. I lived only for the summer holidays, when I could get back to sailing. Long before, probably from the time of my first race, life had taken on an important meaning for me, and I was impatient with anything that interfered. My drive to excel had found its natural expression—I was convinced that some day I'd be a champion racing skipper.

Having found my element, I wanted to sail constantly, to learn all I could about the tremendously pleasurable and intricate business of racing. I soon realized the poor *Virginia* had to go. I needed to get into a really active, competitive class, where I could test myself against top skippers.

In 1913, feeling like a traitor, and with horrible pangs of nostalgia, I sold *Virginia*. The Larchmont Interclub one-design boats were my ideal class. I happened to think of a family friend who lived in Niagara Falls and owned such a boat, which he kept in Larchmont but sailed very little. I got in touch with him and asked if he'd be willing to charter his craft. We made a deal; I would care for the boat and race it, and he would have it when he came to Larchmont to race. In the latter event, I would serve as his crew. There would be no charter fee.

She was everything I expected, and I was proud to be a member of this popular class. I did not do well, but it was always the equivalent of winning in my opinion if I could be in the first five or maybe occasionally beat some of the top skippers at the start or across the finish line.

The following season, I bought a Larchmont Interclub and named her *Barbara,* after Paul's little daughter. The next three years were spent learning from good men in good boats. At that time, the club was running only one race a weekend, and I didn't feel that was sufficient. I was able to persuade several of the Interclub skippers to come out on Sundays for informal races so we could sharpen our techniques. Also, some of the younger members of the class held scrub races on weekdays. These informal races were invaluable to all of us. For my part, they built up a feeling of confidence and helped me to go on the offensive instead of sailing purely defensively. I soon learned that in certain tactical situations it's preferable to sail a defensive race—for instance, when you have the highest point standing in the fleet and choose to cover the rival nearest you in standing. But as a general rule you can't sail tentatively and defensively if you want to win. You must sail purposefully, with a spirit of attack. Your competitors must always be aware of your threat, and the only way they'll remember your boat and name is if you sail against them aggressively.

During the first two years of my ownership of *Barbara,* I won a few races and lost many more, but eventually the rigorous training paid off. In 1916, sailing *Barbara,* I won the championship of the Yacht Racing Association of Long Island Sound. The same year, I sailed Gordon Hammersley's Herreschoff New York 30, *Okee,* in the annual New York Yacht Club Cruise. This was the first time I'd competed outside the Sound, and the *Okee* was the biggest boat I'd raced. (The 30's, one of the great classes in yachting history, measured 30 feet at the waterline and 44 feet overall.) We finished the cruise with the highest point score.

Every day I went out sailing. The beach at New Rochelle was a fine place to swim, and I used to moor *Barbara* there and swim to shore. Once in a while I would take friends out, and we'd spend an afternoon lazily poking around the Sound.

On one of these trips, I met a young girl with lovely brown hair and a wonderful sunny disposition. Her name was Josephine Lupprian—her friends called her "Doe." When I first saw her, I said to myself, "I'd certainly like to get to know her better." But that looked impossible, because she was always surrounded by many admirers. "All the same," I thought, "perhaps luck will come my way."

The years 1914 to 1916 were fateful ones for a youth passing from boyhood into manhood—but I suppose this time of transition is fateful no matter what the years. The world, too, was going through its own period of upheaval. When, on April 6, 1917, the United States went to war, I was twenty-two.

Like everyone, I wanted to serve—and I wanted to serve at sea only. I enlisted in the naval reserve, and was sent to Seagate, near the Bensonhurst section of Brooklyn, where I became a chief petty officer. A short while later, competitive exams for officer's training were announced, and I was lucky enough to pass. After training, I was commissioned an ensign in the naval reserve.

At about this time, the United States decided to increase the complement of the regular Navy. The regulars were already on active duty, and most of us felt we stood a better chance of getting into things if we were regulars. (As it turned out, this wasn't the case: The reserves saw as much action as the regulars.) There was also a matter of prestige involved—it was considered a mark of honor to wear the silver anchors of the regular Navy.

Nothing is done in the service without an examination first, so the reserves from all over the country were tested, and four hundred of us were chosen to attend the U.S. Naval Academy at Annapolis.

During the following four months, I worked harder than I ever have in my life. My indifferent scholarship caught up with me, and I had to keep at my books from the first light of morning until late at night. Seamanship and boat handling were easy for me, but my lack of grounding in mathematics made navigation extremely difficult and gunnery seemingly impossible. I worked with the other cadets, especially one fellow—Al Wolf—whenever I could, until my mind was a seething tangle of mathematical formulas, gun-laying tables, intercepts, trajectories, and equally esoteric terms. Unfortunately, firing a gun in the Navy isn't just a matter of drawing a bead and pulling the trigger.

The day our grades were finally posted, I felt like a king. I had scored 100 percent in boat handling, 3.8 out of a possible 4 in navigation, and had done well in the other subjects. Somehow, by the grace of God, I had scraped by in gunnery. Now, silver anchors and all, I was an ensign in the United States Navy. (Such is the irony of life that a year after I earned these coveted symbols, they were issued to all officers, regardless of branch.)

The tension and anxiety weren't over yet; we still had to sweat out our assignments. We were all afraid that we'd be saddled with desk jobs, or else assigned to battleships or service ships. We didn't want battleships, because the Navy had few of them, and they were kept moored so far up the York River, in Virginia—out of reach of enemy attack—that we were sure the war would be over before they could put out to sea.

When our orders were finally issued, I'd worked myself into such a state that my hands actually shook as I tore open the envelope. Again, I was lucky. I had been assigned to the armored cruiser *Montana*.

Although everyone wanted to draw destroyers—the most gloried and dashing of ships—an armored cruiser was the next best thing. The *Montana* subsequently became one of the most active ships in the Navy. Armored cruisers were used as capital ships-of-the-line, and the *Montana* made sixteen trips across the North Atlantic escorting the troop ships that carried the American Expeditionary Force to France. We would assemble at Hampton Roads, Virginia, at Halifax, Nova Scotia, or at New York, and steam eastward to within 100 miles of the Irish coast, where we would turn our sea-weary charges over to the British escort destroyers.

Although their forays had lessened somewhat as Germany became hard pressed by the Allies, German U-boats were still a constant threat in the North Atlantic.

In order to avoid exposing our vulnerable troop ships to attack, the convoys usually kept to the more northerly routes. There, the weather was our greatest enemy.

My introduction to convoy work was an eye-opener. On the very first trip, we went through the worst storm to hit the North Atlantic coast in years. We were off Halifax harbor, and slowly, majestically, our convoy came into sight, ship after ship, steaming into the fairway. There were about 40 altogether, and among them was a beautiful, new, 30,000-ton Dutch liner. She passed us as we fell back to take up our station at the rear of the convoy, and I read the name *Justicia* on her stern. She was the biggest ship I'd ever seen, and was really an impressive sight.

About the third day out of Halifax, the wind and seas made up. Everything movable aboard the *Montana* was secured, and all the hatches and ventilators were battened down. As the day passed, the seas got worse, and the ship got sloppier and sloppier. The majority of the crew was laid low with seasickness, and the ship was so crowded that ratings and messboys were sleeping in the companionways. With the ventilators battened down and the blowers off, not a breath of air moved below decks, and the smell was overpowering.

The World War I armored cruiser, U.S.S. *Montana,* aboard which the author served in 1918–19.

As a boy, I'd had trouble with severe headaches and delicate stomach. When I mounted the ladder to the bridge to take over my first trick as a junior watch officer, I hoped I wouldn't get sick. I was so preoccupied with the problem that I forgot the pride of standing a junior bridge-watch on an armored cruiser. I wasn't sick, however, and managed to keep functioning.

By evening, conditions had worsened, and all attempts at maintaining stations were abandoned. The convoy scattered, and each ship was left to slog it out alone. At one point, I spotted what appeared to my inexperienced eyes to be a little Navy steam-launch rolling her bottom out and making very heavy weather of it. I couldn't imagine what a vessel that small would be doing out there, and took a look at it through the glasses. It wasn't a launch, of course—it was the huge *Justicia.* She was dwarfed by those monstrous seas.

After battering us for three days, the storm finally moderated. It had blown full hurricane strength, with winds up to 100 miles per hour recorded at the height. The *Montana* bore the scars of the struggle. Her forward deck had been sprung, and the forecastle metalwork was a mass of twisted wreckage.

Oddly enough, I was never again bothered by seasickness.

I was lucky to have good friends aboard the *Montana.* One of them was Drake Sparkman, with whom I'd grown up in New Rochelle. (Drake later became head of the noted design and brokerage firm of Sparkman & Stephens, and was instrumental in getting many fine yachts for me to sail.) Another was a chap named Thomas Kilkenny, a true Irish wit, a marvelous storyteller, and one of the most popular men aboard.

I recall one of Kilkenny's stunts with particular vividness. Every fourth day, as an exercise, the junior watch officer had to turn in a number of positional reports, called the "day's work," to the navigating officer. Some junior officers resented the task, for it left them little time for themselves. Kilkenny got into the habit of slipping into the chart house before 8:00 A.M. and copying the navigator's positions from the charts, altering the latitudes and longitudes a little. His "day's work" consisted of the time it took to steal the positions.

One day, he changed the figures a little more than usual. The navigating officer was a bristly little fellow with a toothbrush mustache. He stepped out of the chart room and sent up a shout. Kilkenny came running, imagining, I suppose, that he was going to be shot for treason or for stealing military secrets.

"Kilkenny," the navigating officer said severely, "what's the matter with you? You're two minutes out in your noon fix, and two miles in error."

"Oh, hell, sir," Kilkenny said with relief, "you can see that far."

Kilkenny had a natural aversion to work and was somehow able to make a living doing the things he liked. After the war, he built a beautiful junk in Hong Kong and sailed it through the Mediterranean and Red Seas. Later, in Hong Kong, he built the famous schooner *Safong* to a Sparkman & Stephens design and sailed her to this country. He was a wonderful, free-and-easy fellow with a great zest for living.

When the war ended, I was as eager to get out of the Navy as I had been to get in. For one thing, I wanted to get started in business. I was also eager to resume my racing. Most important of all, I feared that if I stayed in the Navy, I might be shipped to China or some place equally distant from New Rochelle, where Doe was still living. She and I had been seeing a good deal of each other, and I wanted that pleasant state of affairs to continue.

For the time being, however, the Navy had other ideas. The reserve officers were released within two weeks of the Armistice, but we regulars were retained. I had made lieutenant (jg) aboard the *Montana,* and was detached from her and ordered to report aboard the U.S.S. *Prairie,* a destroyer tender.

As it turned out, my tour aboard the *Prairie* was far from onerous. We went first to Guantanamo, Cuba, for fleet maneuvers, and then to Trepassey, in southeastern Newfoundland. Our assignment there—my last in the Navy—proved to be both exciting and historic. The *Prairie* served as a tender for the famous N.C. flying boats, assisting in the preparations for the Navy's attempt at the first transatlantic flight. On May 19, 1919, I watched as the three heavily laden aircraft labored aloft against 30-mile-an-hour winds and then circled overhead and winged off to the eastward, against the sun. Two of them were forced down in the ocean short of their goal in the Azores—fortunately, without loss of life—but the third, the N.C. 4, made the crossing to the Azores successfully, and then went on to Plymouth, England.

A month later, I received my discharge. Thanks to Paul, it didn't take me long to settle back into civilian life. He was in the real estate business in Great Neck, Long Island, New York, and lived there. I moved in with him, and helped with the selling end of the business. I was eager to get back into sailing; I felt I had a lot of time and lost experience to make up if I were to reach my goals. Also, I had to make some decisions about the future.

I had been able to save very little from my Navy salary, and the small amount that I had saved was not sufficient to begin housekeeping. So my Larchmont Interclub, *Barbara,* went on the market, and I used the proceeds to buy an engagement ring for Doe. That was one part of the future I wanted settled definitely.

I resumed sailing in the newly formed Victory class with a borrowed boat, *Alert,* and was pleased to find I hadn't lost my touch. If anything, the time away from racing had been beneficial, because I was eager and more aggressive. I was able to capture the Victory class championship in both 1920 and 1921.

By this time, Paul had left the real estate business and was working for the investment firm of Merrill, Lynch. It wasn't long before he became a partner and hired me to sell securities. I wasn't of much use for a while, but as I learned more about the business, I was better able to pull my own oar.

My chief responsibility as a fledgling salesman was to secure new customers. I put together a sales talk that I thought would convince any intelligent listener to turn his money over to us for investment right on the spot. My problem now was to find listeners, intelligent or not.

I had exhausted all of the leads I had been given, both because they were few in number and because I was so eager during the first few weeks. The only thing I could think of was to simply walk in on people cold, like a magazine salesman, and hope that I could convince them. If I had no luck, it would be because I was a poor salesman. At least it would give me a chance to practice my talk on a lot of unsuspecting victims. I could take the rough edges off my salesmanship, tighten up my presentation, find out what questions I'd have to answer, and learn how to deal with people.

I began canvassing the better office buildings from top to bottom, always insisting I had to see the man in charge. Now, it's a difficult job to ring a doorbell and give something away; it's harder still to ring and sell something for a trifle, and it's almost impossible to ring and separate a stranger from a large sum of money. I came to know the buildings that I'd chosen almost as well as their janitors knew them. I was ushered firmly out of some offices, and I had valuable talks with interesting people in others. And, believe it or not, I did a little business. Some accounts were small and some were large, but I was proud of each one, because it showed I could do it. I also got the world's fastest course in human psychology. When I went back to selling from leads, it was fairly easy.

In 1921, Percy Chubb and four British yacht clubs donated a trophy, the British-American Cup, for team races in 6-meter-class yachts. The races were to be held alternately in Great Britain and the U.S. The first year, the series was held in Cowes, England, and the British trounced the Americans by a score of 117 to 88 points. In 1922, the U.S. challenged for another series, to be held at Oyster Bay, New York.

I wanted desperately to be on the American team, for this was my first chance to take part in an international yachting event. I sailed the 6-meter *Viva* as hard as I could in the trials, but in one race she lost her mast because of a defect in the rigging and I was unable to qualify. I had a bad time getting over the disappointment, but I knew there would be other chances. I felt a little better when the Americans won by 111 to 104.

Doe and I were married in New Rochelle on January 21, 1922, and winning the competition against her other suitors was the biggest success I ever had. When we returned home from our honeymoon in Lake Placid, I took stock of my resources. I had returned to work none too soon: I had exactly 25 cents left in my pocket. We moved into a small apartment in New Rochelle and began our life together.

In 1923, Paul decided to go into business for himself, and I went with him. We left Merrill, Lynch, rented an office at 27 Pine Street in downtown New York, and in May the investment firm of Shields & Company began operation.

As with any new business, our greatest need was to find customers, so I continued as a salesman. I had unlimited confidence in our company. I knew that our management would bring in a good profit with a minimum of risk for our clients if they would only trust us. With this belief always with me, I went out and burned shoe leather.

That summer, I sailed Joseph Dunbaugh's beautiful New York 30, *Countess,* and was able to win a class championship for the fourth time. Apart from that, these were lean times for an aspiring sailing champion. I had new responsibilities, a bride, and a new job with a new firm. I had no boat of my own, and I resigned my membership in the Larchmont Yacht Club because I couldn't afford the $100 annual dues. Nevertheless, I had other things to cheer me: I was young, healthy, happy in marriage, and an incurable optimist.

3. The Competitive Spirit

I think that a man who believes he has special talent in a sport should make every effort to meet his competitors, and actively seek opportunities to test his skill against the skills of others. Throughout my racing career, I always sought to meet top skippers in any kind of boat, anywhere, at any time.

Through the 1920's and 1930's, I crowded as much racing as I could into every month. Sometimes, this took careful planning. For example, when I sailed in overnight races aboard the boats of friends, I always arranged to be left off, on Sunday mornings, as close as possible to my home in Larchmont, so I could get back to my International, *Aileen*, for the afternoon's racing. We might have had a strenuous night, but I never missed those Sunday races. I used to be teased about that habit, but it seemed to me as natural as eating or sleeping.

In 1925, a new class of 28 one-design boats, the Sound Interclubs, was founded by John B. Shethar. Joseph Dunbaugh asked me to sail his Interclub, and did Doe and me the great honor of naming her *Aileen*. I sailed her the next summer, too, and in 1927—thanks in part to the fact that Shields & Company was prospering—I was able to buy her. Her hull was white; I had her painted light green, the color I've used on all my boats since. The Interclub class, incidentally, was probably the first major class in which boats were painted a variety of colors. Hulls used to be either white or black, but we had blue, yellow, grey, and red boats among us.

The Interclubs were lively boats, and we had ten years of spirited racing in them, during which I won the class championship a number of times. John Shethar sold his boat and dropped out of the class after the second season, and I was selected as class chairman.

I have always believed strongly that a successful class must attract the best possible skippers. In part, this belief is founded on selfishness—if I were fortunate enough to win a race, I wanted to know I had beaten the best skippers there were. Over the years, I worked hard at persuading top-flight sailors to join the Interclubs. Among the early competitors were Sam Wetherill, Hobey Ford, Ralph Manny, Carroll Alker, Gordon Raymond, Bill Luders, Egbert Moxham, Bill Cox, Arthur Knapp, Lorna Whittlesey, Bus Mosbacher, and my brother Paul. We felt that these men were among the very best racing skippers in the country.

Down through the Interclub fleet, too, there was a high level of ability. This is where the praise belongs for making a racing class really successful. The middle-of-the-fleet skippers, who turn up Saturday after Saturday out of love of the water and racing, keep the rest of the fleet on its toes and make the challenge tougher and tougher every week. Without them, competition—and the fun that goes with it—would die.

As in any class, there were the habitual also-ran's in the Interclubs— boats that never seemed to be well sailed, and that always trailed far back in the fleet. Despite their lack of success, the skippers of these boats still enjoyed themselves, and they often amused the rest of us. I remember especially a boat we'll call the *Frisky*.

The *Frisky* was regularly in last place, and as a result she wasn't the easiest boat in the fleet to get a crew for. One race day a young friend of mine, an ardent sailor named Morgan Valentine, arrived at the dock at the last minute, looking for a boat to crew on—any boat. As the last of the Interclubs were leaving for the starting-line, he hailed them, and one swung past the dock. Morgan leaped aboard, happy to have a chance to sail.

His happiness began to dim, however, shortly after the start. The boat dropped steadily back, until Morgan found himself staring balefully at nearly every transom in the fleet.

This state of affairs rapidly worsened, and as the race was ending, Morgan turned to the skipper and moaned "We're going to be last!" Then he had a happier thought, and brightened. "We can't be last," he said; "not while the *Frisky's* out here. We'll beat the *Frisky*, at least."

The skipper glowered at him. "My boy," he said, "you're *on* the *Frisky*."

The author at the helm of the 6-meter *Dauphin,* out ahead of the pack in her first race in 1924.

During these years, I was also active in larger boats, particularly 6-meter boats. In 1924, I skippered Harold Tobey's *Dauphin,* a member of the team that successfully defended the British-American Cup. In 1930, Paul and I sailed Herman F. Whiton's *Cherokee* in the same series; again, the American team won. In 1928, I was asked aboard William Bell's New York 40, *Mistral,* for the New York Yacht Club Cruises.

This last was both a pleasure and a new adventure for me. Life aboard these boats was luxurious, with professional crews and stewards on hand. I gained further experience in offshore sailing, and had an opportunity to practice my coast-wise navigation. Also, I learned how to deal with problems that we never met in the triangular races.

One day, when we were racing up the coast of Cape Cod to Marblehead, we encountered a strange phenomenon: right in against the beach, stretching off into the distance around the bend of the cape, there was a narrow, dark patch of wind. It extended out only 150 yards; beyond, there was glassy calm. If we could get in close to the beach, we could play that breeze to advantage, and we would also avoid having to buck the head tide running through Pollock Rip Slew.

It was hard to get close to shore because of a sandbar running parallel to it. The chart, however, showed an 8-foot gutter crossing the bar at Monomoy Point. We drew 8 feet, and figured that with the half-tide we could just get through.

Our bearings proved to be correct, and we got safely over the bar and into the breeze. Then, all the way around the cape, we hugged the shore, making over a hundred tacks. Occasionally, in the surge of the swell, we touched bottom and had to push off with the spinnaker pole.

The breeze held for us, and we avoided the head tide; the result was that we beat our nearest competitor to Marblehead by four hours—and there were some big boats in the fleet that day. For me, that narrow strip of breeze was a true marvel, one of the most unusual sights I've ever seen.

The year I began racing aboard *Mistral*—1928—I also sailed the 6-meter *Lea*, and earned the privilege of representing the country in the Gold Cup series against boats from England, Italy, Holland, Norway, and Sweden. During this series, one of our opponents, Sven Salen, from Sweden, used a genoa jib. It was the first time the sail had been tried in competition on this side of the Atlantic, and at first the American sailors tended to take it lightly. (For my own part, I completely failed to recognize the sail: The first time I saw it in use, I thought Salen was going to windward with a ballooner.) Salen soon showed us how effective the sail could be, and the Swedish boat won the cup handily.

At this time, I became active in the annual competition with the Royal Bermuda Yacht Club, which had been instituted by John Shethar the previous year with the famous Trimingham brothers, Eldon and Kenneth. We sailed our Interclubs—which were shipped down on the *Queen of Bermuda*—against their RBYC one-designs. The two classes, although materially different in design, were very evenly matched, and the racing was spirited and hard-fought. This series has established a relationship that has meant a good deal to me. I have a great affection for my Bermuda friends.

I remember one incident that occurred during these races in Bermuda. Gordon Raymond, a friend of mine, was sailing his Interclub with a pickup crew made up of 6-meter skippers who had completed their own series the week before. Gordon was a large, powerful man, and a very competent skipper. He was also excitable, and used to let off steam by setting his hat down on the deck and crashing his fist down on it. You could hear the thump half a mile off.

During this particular race, one of the other men in the boat succeeded somehow in winding one of Gordon's fingers in under the wire on a winch. Ignoring what must have been enormous pain, Gordon made a remark that has become a part of Bermuda sailing folklore: "Four skippers in the boat and not a sailor in the crowd—*get my finger out of this winch!*"

This misadventure ended happily, but there are others that do not.

Accidents are bound to happen aboard even the best-sailed boats. I've had my share of misfortunes, and I've done my best to learn from them. It's a natural reaction for a skipper to want to blame a crew member in these cases, and that, I believe, is a mistake. In most cases, the ultimate responsibility is the skipper's. If he has a proper regard for his own role, he'll be tolerant of shortcomings and will not get excited or rattled. A skipper's assumption of ultimate responsibility is what makes a boat sail smoothly, and divisions of authority and recriminations only make difficult situations worse. Above all, a skipper must make the final decisions, must retain his authority. If he loses it, trouble is bound to develop.

By 1929, Shields & Company was six years old. The firm had been blessed with real prosperity, particularly in 1928, and was continuing to expand. I was especially eager to open a stock brokerage business to supplement our underwriting and distributing operations. Paul agreed this was a good idea, but felt it could wait until we had taken on experienced personnel to manage the division.

In January 1929, we underwrote a large stock issue, and were surprised to find that the stock acted poorly in the after-market: demand for it wasn't as great as we'd anticipated. We couldn't understand the reason for this. We felt that perhaps there was some economic unrest we couldn't see—or that we might be losing our touch. We decided it was time to take a careful look at the firm's position and our own abilities, and we set about getting our house in order, reducing inventory and selling the equities we'd gained through underwriting.

This period of lessened pressure and self-appraisal seemed like a good time to set up the stock brokerage business, so we hired the personnel we needed and bought a seat on the New York Stock Exchange. By sheerest coincidence, we announced our membership in the Exchange on October 24—Black Thursday. As I've indicated, at the time almost all of the firm's assets were in cash. During the next weeks and months, we picked up many customers from other firms unable to accommodate them. Within the next two years, we took over the businesses of eight distressed firms—some of them sizable operations. Through the entire depression, we had losses in only two years, and they were small.

I don't want to make us sound wiser than we were. By no means did we foresee the full size of the storm that was moving down on the American economy—rather, we experienced a small puff and reacted to it in the most natural manner, by shortening sail. There was, of course, a great amount of luck involved; I'm well aware that Shields & Company has much to be grateful for.

An innovation came to yachting in 1931 that has had far-reaching unexpected consequences. This was the birth of "frostbiting," the flourishing winter sport which has transformed competitive sailing from a seasonal affair into a year-round activity. In my opinion, frostbiting is one of the greatest single developments in yacht racing in this century. I've sailed in hundreds of frostbite races, and they're among my fondest memories. To my regret, I wasn't present at the actual birth of the sport, but no account of racing would be complete without a mention of it.

One December afternoon in 1931, a group of sailors got together informally at the Manhasset Bay Yacht Club. (I wasn't there, but heard about the gathering later, the same day.) They started talking about how they hated to be inactive during the winter. Finally, the late Bill Taylor—who was then the sailing editor for *The New York Herald Tribune* and later became a Pulitzer Prize winner—suggested that there wasn't really any good reason why they shouldn't race. All they had to do, he said, was get some boats together, bundle themselves up in warm clothes, and go to it. Why not the following Saturday, January 2, at Port Washington?

The idea caught on immediately, and plans were made to get the boats together. They were a mixed lot, brought in from all over the sound: a flat-bottomed boat, a lap-streak 14-footer, a scow, etc. Drake Sparkman lent me a little Ratsey pram he owned. The idea of the competition appealed to me enormously—an America's Cup race wouldn't have excited me more. I set to work getting Drake's pram ready for the big event, and planned how I would keep warm. The greatest problem, I thought, would be with my hands, and I decided to take along two cans of Sterno, which I would burn inside a bucket to keep them from rolling around on the floorboards.

The day before the race, I learned that I would have to go up to Boston on urgent business and would miss the fun. I don't think I've ever been more disappointed. I sent the other sailors—they included Porter Buck, Gordon Curry, Arthur Knapp, Robert Fraser, Bill Dyer and Colin Ratsey—my best wishes, and unhappily took the train.

The racing was thoroughly successful. I have always treasured Bill Taylor's account of it in the *Herald Tribune,* which read, in part:

The first annual regatta or maybe it was just the first regatta, of the Frostbite Yacht Club was a howling success and was won by several people because of the fact that there were several races. Colin Ratsey and Eugene Kelly, sailing the good ship *Spinnaker*, took the grand prize, but the boats that finished first in the three races were *Dorade*, sailed by Porter Buck and Bob Garland, in the first race, and *Nippy*, sailed by Gordon Curry and Charley Henderson, in the other two.

The racing had everything that a good Frostbite regatta ought to have. It rained during the first race, rained and hailed during the second, and snowed during the third. There was wind and there were several shipwrecks, though none of the shipwrecks happened during the race.

The idea of Frostbite regattas, of course, is to prove that some people are crazier than others and those who are craziest sail races in eleven-foot open boats in the middle of snowstorms—and enjoy it. When daylight gradually dawned this morning—and it dawned very gradually—the wind was blowing the better part of a gale out of the northeast and it was raining cats, dogs, pitchforks, and all the other traditional things, only colder. The breaking waves dashed high on a stern and ice-bound coast and one by one sailors with chilly blue noses looked out and shook their heads. . .

The week after the first Port Washington race, we raced at New Rochelle, the weekend after at Stamford, etc. These times, thank the Lord, I was able to take part. Enthusiasm for dinghy-racing mounted quickly, and more and more skippers joined us, eager to get out of doors and to be doing what they loved best. We soon found that except for really poisonous days such as the day of that first race, we could keep comfortably warm in relatively light clothing. We were always busy and active, and no more felt the cold than a skier in competition does. I never had to use the Sterno.

As frostbiting really took hold, those of us dedicated to it found ourselves going to extreme lengths to get competition. I thought nothing of putting my dinghy on a trailer and driving up to Mystic, Connecticut, or Boston, or Marblehead, for a day's racing. This often meant leaving home at 3:30 in the morning and driving back after the races, sometimes through snow and ice. Like dyed-in-the-wool hunters and fishermen, sailors will put up with amazing discomforts for the sake of sport.

While frostbiting was in its infancy, Bill Taylor continued to support it with his wonderful enthusiasm and energy, attracting new people to it and focusing valuable attention on it. Bill made many contributions to yachting, but to my mind the greatest was his origination and fostering of frostbiting. He was the true "father" of the sport, and sailors everywhere will forever be indebted to him.

As I said, the first frostbite races were sailed in boats of widely varied classes, ranging in length from 10 to 14 feet. There was no standardization as to sail area, displacement, etc. This sort of arrangement has obvious drawbacks. I believe that the most meaningful racing is done in a strictly controlled one-design class, with boats as nearly identical as possible. Under these conditions, the skill of the skipper and his crew is what brings

A frostbite dinghy race start on Long Island Sound. Corny Shields, Jr., gets a nice clear start in the extremely dangerous "coffin corner."

a boat home first, and not some characteristic drawn into the boat by the designer.

In the case of frostbiting, the need for a one-design boat was obvious soon after the sport had caught on. The frostbite skippers, however, disagreed as to what kind of boat they wanted. To resolve the differences of opinion between the various groups, I suggested that an independent selection committee be formed, to which designers would submit drawings. The committee would look over the entries and pick out the boat it liked best, and we would then build ourselves a one-design fleet. The primary restrictions on designs were that the boats would have to measure 11 feet, 6 inches overall and have 72 square feet of sail.

William Crosby, the editor of *Rudder,* announced the contest in his magazine, and soon designs were pouring in from all over the world— South America, South Africa, New Zealand, Australia, England, and, of course, the United States. The selection committee, of which I was a member, checked all the entries and chose one by Nicholas Potter of Providence, Rhode Island. The boats, which were sturdy, lapstreak craft, were built at the Herreshoff yards in Bristol, Rhode Island, and at George Lauder's yard in Greenwich, Connecticut. We named the class the B.O.'s, for B-One Design; they gave us many pleasant years of racing.

The nature of the boats makes dinghy sailing especially educational. Things happen a lot faster in dinghies than in larger boats, and this difference can teach even the most seasoned veteran a great deal. Dinghies are delicate, and they react rapidly to poor handling, whereas a bigger boat, with its greater momentum, gives the skipper a margin for error; if he fluffs, the boat keeps going.

Dinghy sailing teaches the indefinable quality of "feel," and the importance of proper trim. There's also a lot of fun and instruction in the maintenance of the little boats—in scraping, painting, and varnishing them, and in keeping the rigging and fittings in order. All in all, they are invaluable training tools, as well as constant sources of excitement and satisfaction.

Of all the competitions I entered in the 1930's, the one I remember most vividly is the 1935 defense of the Seawanhaka Cup, or Seawanhaka International Challenge Cup for Small Yachts, to give its full title. It was among the most eagerly coveted international small-boat trophies in the world of sailing, and from 1895 to the mid-1950's was raced for by champions from the U.S., Canada, Great Britain, Sweden, Norway, and Finland. The competition always had a special appeal for Paul and me, for in our boyhood in Sydney, Nova Scotia, we had watched Seawanhaka Cup challengers—one of which later became a winner—sailing in the harbor.

In 1934, Paul decided to enter the trials that would produce a defender to race against the Norwegian challenger for the Seawanhaka Cup, and he commissioned A. E. Luders, Jr., to build a 6-meter, *Challenge,* for him. With two additional crew members aboard, we campaigned her through that summer, and sailed her as part of the American team, which successfully defended the British-American Cup. Then, after a rugged series of trials during the summer of 1935, we were selected to meet *Norna IV,* owned by Crown Prince Olav of Norway and sailed by a near-legendary figure in international yachting, Magnus Konow. The series was scheduled for mid-September, and the cup would go to the winner of three races out of a possible five.

I had never met Konow, but I'd heard a great deal about him. A tall, slender, powerful man, he was rated as Europe's finest helmsman, and

Cornelius and Paul Shields aboard *Challenge* during the 1935 trials in preparation for their defense of the Seawanhaka Cup.

he had sailed with particular brilliance in the Olympics. On our way out to the starting line on the first day of competition—the wind was easterly, I recall, and there was a large spectator fleet out—I sailed *Challenge* in close to *Norna* so I could take a good look at Konow. When I gazed across the water at him, I found that he and his three-man crew were all staring at us out of *Norna*'s cockpit, giving us exactly the same cold-eyed sizing-up we were giving them. I still have a mental image of Konow and his crew at that moment; whenever I think of it, I'm reminded of the stares prizefighters exchange just before the bell.

The first two races were back-and-forth battles—and we lost them both, by margins of 45 and 8 seconds respectively. *Norna* outsailed us going to windward, and although we managed to regain lost ground downwind, our recovery wasn't sufficient.

At this point, with Konow only a race away from victory, many of the spectators abandoned hope for us. Word was even cabled abroad that it was only a matter of sailing one more race, and then it would all be over.

My brother and I didn't agree. That may sound over-confident, but we felt that *Challenge* was a good boat, and that we could, and would, make her go. The observers might be discouraged, but we couldn't be.

As we were sailing into the harbor after that second defeat, a large lapstreak motorboat pulled alongside us, and one of the founders of the present Pitney-Bowes company, Walter Bowes was there in the cockpit. Bowes was a highly entertaining, lighthearted fellow, whom Paul and I had been running into here and there for years. He hailed us and said he wanted to see us when we got ashore.

There was a somber note in the air as Paul and I walked up the dock toward the Seawanhaka clubhouse. Bowes met us by the flagpole. He looked serious, which was unusual for him.

He announced that he was taking over as our "manager." "Now I don't want you to get discouraged," he said. "This thing is going to turn out all right. You're going to win."

This was the sort of talk I wanted to hear at that moment. I asked Bowes if he realized we needed to take three straight races to win. He nodded. "It's going to be all right," he repeated. "All you have to do is listen to my advice, and you'll win."

I asked him what his advice might be.

"Well," he said, keeping his voice firm, low, and sincere, "the first thing we'll do is bring ashore that genoa jib you've been using, and lay it out by the flagpole here, and then burn it, just to make sure it doesn't appear again." He went on, still talking like a doctor making a diagnosis. After we had burned the genoa, he was going to visit Konow and his crew, and get to work on their morale. While he was at it, he would extend some of his famous hospitality, and see if he couldn't perhaps keep them up half the night in the bar. That was the sum and substance of Bowes program, and he was sure it would be effective. Within three days, he said, we'd be steaming back to Larchmont with the Seawanhaka Cup safely stowed in the lazaret of his motorboat.

I don't need to tell you that we didn't burn the genoa. The rest of Bowes' strategy, however, *was* put into execution. He stood the Norwegians to drinks in the evenings and played what he called "gypsy music" for them on the piano until the small hours of the morning. He also took Konow aside and told him he hadn't won the cup by a long shot. "You don't know what you're up against," he told him. "These fellows are good —really good. You'll see."

We finally got *Challenge* going in the third race. What made the difference was a larger genoa and our new Wilson mainsail. We had refrained from using the mainsail before because the conditions never seemed quite right. While we were maneuvering for the start, however, we passed close by the powerboat from which Bill Luders was watching. He hailed us and asked why we didn't try the sail. I replied that I didn't want to experiment with it because the weather seemed uncertain.

He shot a question back at me: "What are you saving it for?"— obviously implying that if we didn't use the sail in this race, we might never get to use it against Konow.

We had to hustle to set the mainsail before the start, but we were soon glad we had—in the words of a *New York Times* reporter, *Challenge* went "like a winged witch." We led all the way, and beat *Norna* by 40 seconds.

In the fourth race, we got a good start, crossing the line with the gun. Again, we used the new sails, and this time our margin of victory was large —four minutes and six seconds.

We sailed the fifth and final race in a moderate southwest wind, going twice around a windward-leeward course. As she had before, *Norna* outdid us going to windward, and we overtook her on both of the runs. The summary shows how excitingly the lead changed hands: *Norna* ahead at the first windward mark by 34 seconds; *Challenge* ahead at the first leeward mark by 10 seconds; *Norna* ahead at the second windward mark by 18 seconds; . . . then, in the run for the finish, we clinched it. *Challenge* gave us everything she had, and we won handily, with a lead of 2 minutes and 47 seconds.

Paul and I were, of course, pleased by the outcome, and Bowes was delighted that his "managership" had turned the trick. It's possible that, in a way, he had really helped us. I'm not saying that his hospitality and "gypsy music" were what tipped the balance—Konow and his crew were as dedicated as we were ourselves; but Bowes' confidence in us, his certainty that we couldn't lose, somehow supplemented our own confidence, and honed our competitive edge a bit finer.

The greatest part of success in yacht racing—as in anything else—is belief in yourself.

4. A Racing Life

By 1935, the Sound Interclub class, of which I had been chairman since 1927, was ten years old, and our boats had reached what might be called "early middle age." Although they still had many good years of racing left in them, it was plain to me that within a relatively short time the Interclub skippers would want to switch to bigger, faster boats. I thought it would be wonderful to anticipate this—to form a new class while we were still sailing the Interclubs, and then to move all of the skippers over to the new boats without disturbing the splendid condition of racing we had established. This would not be simple to accomplish; it would take work and planning. The first step, of course, was to find the right boat.

In the spring of 1936, Paul and I went down to Bermuda to race *Challenge* against sailors from the Royal Bermuda Yacht Club. The day I arrived, I went to inspect a new 6-meter boat that had just been built for Eldon and Kenneth Trimmingham in Norway by Bjarne Aas, one of the finest designer-builders in Europe. Her name was *Saga*.

The minute I saw *Saga*, I fell in love with her. I thought she was the most beautiful boat I'd ever seen. I loved her shape, her sheer, her dainty transom, and her long, straight counter. The sheer, although a penalty under the 6-meter rule (which encourages high freeboard), gave her great grace and beauty.

When I got back from Bermuda, I couldn't get *Saga* out of my mind. She seemed very close to what I was looking for, and I felt it would be worthwhile to ask Aas to do some drawings of a boat with her beautiful lines. I knew that a one-design class could be built very economically in Norway. With proper care, I could be certain the class was truly one-design, with the boats as nearly identical as possible. This requirement was extremely important to me, for as I've said, it's only in a one-design class that a skipper's real abilities can be measured.

These were good reasons for exploring the idea, and there was still another. I hoped to bring new life into international racing, which had become rather prohibitive in cost. Because of the expense involved, 6-meter boats were sailed only in years when there was a match like the Seawanhaka Cup or the British-American Cup. In off years, there was almost no competition in 6-meter boats. The founding of a new one-design class would give 6-meter skippers a chance to compete more economically and also every year.

I spoke to Magnus Konow about my idea (he and I were still competing against each other, in boats and on the golf course), and he agreed to get in touch with Aas for me. I asked Aas to send me designs for a semi-displacement boat about 33 feet overall, with a 6-foot, 9-inch beam and a small cabin.

When the initial designs came, I knew we had something good. There were some minor changes I wanted, and I thought them through during all-night sessions in my library at home. The cabin seemed too large to me, and I suggested that Aas shorten it by one frame—approximately 12 inches. Also, I wanted a loftier rig and shorter boom, which would suit the boat better for the relatively light airs of Long Island Sound, and which would also, I felt, improve her appearance. With the loftier rig, I suggested we add more weight to the keel. Aas decided that 100 pounds was sufficient. He also agreed to the other changes.

When I'd made reasonable progress, I discussed my idea with Paul and four friends—Egbert Moxham, Magnus Konow, Henry Maxwell, and Frederic Spedden. The plan excited them, and between us we formed a syndicate to underwrite the construction of 25 boats. It was Paul who named the class—the International one-design class.

In my dealings with Aas, I continued to emphasize the great importance of uniformity. The boats had to be identical. During the actual construc-

The beautiful 6-meter *Saga*, "godmother" of the International one-design class. She was designed and built by Bjarne Aas and owned by the famed Bermudian yachtsmen Eldon and Kenneth Trimingham.

tion, we employed Veritass, a firm of Norwegian maritime surveyors similar to Lloyd's, to supervise operations, and stressed the need for uniformity to them, too. These efforts produced gratifying results. For example, when the lead keels were being cast, we had Veritass send each boat-owner a certificate giving the exact weight of the keel. The original specifications called for keels of 4,100 pounds. The certificates showed that the greatest variance from that figure was 25 pounds, a negligible difference.

We announced the formation of the class in the summer of 1935, in a brochure mailed to Interclub owners and other likely prospects. The response was overwhelmingly enthusiastic: the newspapers featured the idea, welcoming the new class; skippers phoned to reserve boats and down payments came in by return mail.

As we'd expected, the cost of the first 25 boats was moderate. Incredible as it may seem with fiberglass Internationals costing $12,000 today, the price-tag for our boats—fully rigged, fully insured, and including sails, a shipping cradle, and the cost of shipping—was only $2670.

It was my idea to have as many Interclub skippers as possible buy Internationals, and this presented a problem. If we sold our Interclubs all at once the bottom would drop out of the market. To avert this, the Interclub owners agreed that none of them would sell for less than $2000. Eventually, all of the Interclubs were sold, and that basic price was not broken in a single case. So you could say that in way, we got our Internationals for $670.

My boat was one of the first four to be delivered. I had decided to name her *Aileen*. (My Interclub was sold to a man who lived on Lake George, but I preserved the name.) She arrived in early December, and I went to Brooklyn to see her lowered in her cradle from the freighter to the dock. If anything, she was even prettier than I'd hoped—especially her under-body: she had a beautiful entrance, midship section, and run. Like all my boats, she was painted light green.

From Brooklyn, *Aileen* was towed to City Island. For the next few weeks, I stopped off at the yacht yard to see her every chance I got, breaking my trips to and from the city. Naturally, I was impatient to take her out.

I finally arranged to sail her the week after Christmas. It was the first time anyone had sailed an International—not even Aas had done so. I don't think I've ever had a more joyous day on the water. As crew, I had Ducky Endt and another friend. The wind was from the northeast, light in the morning and then stronger at mid-day, so we had a chance to try her out under a variety of conditions. In early afternoon, we put into Larchmont harbor and tied up at the Yacht Club dock so family and friends could look at her. They came aboard in groups of four, all brimming over with the same pleasure I was feeling.

The trip back was as satisfying as the morning's sail, despite the fact that the wind softened. The boat was a delight to handle, and balanced perfectly. I felt great satisfaction at this—the planning and hope and care hadn't been in vain.

We started racing our Internationals the following summer, 1937, keeping our group of skippers together and preserving the high standards of competition that had existed in the Interclubs. Other sailors were soon attracted by the boats and ordered them from Aas, and there has been a steady growth of the class through the years. There are now sizable fleets in Marblehead, Bermuda, San Francisco, and Long Island Sound. The Western Sound fleet, developed under the able chairmanship of the late William E. John, continues to thrive with over twenty boats and an active program under the direction of Joseph Weed. They are still built to the original specifications and under the same controlled conditions. I like to think that wherever they are, they have brought many happy hours of sport to the people who sail them.

International yacht racing, soon to be curtailed by the war, continued through the late 1930's. In 1937, Gerard Lambert invited me to sail aboard his J-Boat, *Yankee,* in the America's Cup trials. *Yankee* was no match for the new *Ranger,* owned by Harold Vanderbilt, but I enjoyed working out the starts, in the majority of which we more than held our own. (I had also sailed with Gerard Lambert in 1934, when, in a somewhat parallel situation, his *Vanitie* sailed in practice trials against Vanderbilt's *Enterprise.* I've always admired Lambert's good sportsmanship in entering these competitions even though he knew his chances were slim.)

The same year I was aboard *Yankee,* the Royal Norwegian Yacht Club issued a challenge for the Seawanhaka Cup, and Paul entered his new 6-meter *Rebel* in the hard-fought trials and earned the right to defend the cup. This we again did successfully, winning three straight against *Buri,* owned by O. Ditlev-Simonsen, Jr. The following summer, *Rebel* earned a position on the four-boat team for the British-American Cup; the American team came out the winner by four races to one.

Gerard Lambert's *Yankee*, with her double-clewed jib, originated and constructed by the famous sailmaker Prescott Wilson.

The war, of course, brought great changes to yachting. Those of us who could continued to race our dinghies and Internationals, and there was considerable activity in the western end of the Sound. Almost singlehandedly, Alex Gest, the chairman of the Larchmont Yacht Club race committee, kept competition going during the war years, not only at Larchmont but at other yacht clubs.

As in World War I, yachtsmen made great contributions to the war effort. They distinguished themselves in all theaters, aboard ships of every description. Many of my yachting friends served, and they often told me they'd made the same discovery I had nearly three decades before: that the knowledge they'd acquired through sailing was invaluable to them. The yachting world was able to make a second direct contribution, too, in the tangible form of boats. Many large pleasure craft on both coasts were converted for the rugged and necessary task of antisubmarine patrol.

When sailing had resumed its peacetime pace, the frostbite skippers on the Sound found themselves in a situation similar to the one that had existed in the larger Interclubs ten years before. Our B.O. dinghies were eleven years old and had to be replaced—but to preserve the competition in the class, it was essential to move all the skippers into new boats in a body.

I asked Olin Stephens to design a boat with more stability than the B.O.'s, which had always been a bit tender. The new boats were also to be 11 feet, 6 inches overall. I suggested that Olin might use as a guide his lapstreak 10-footers that had served as dinghies aboard his New York 32's.

In Olin's first drawings, the boat—we later named the class the Interclub Dinghies—had a flat sheer aft. I felt she would be prettier, and perhaps drier, with a spring to the sheer in this area. Olin very obligingly swept it up, giving the boat a pleasant, sassy appearance. To my mind, these are the prettiest dinghies ever designed.

The reason for naming them the Interclubs was, ironically enough, to attract the dinghy skippers from the Manhasset Bay Yacht Club into the class. I took a scale model to the Manhasset winter meeting in 1945, and though I talked as convincingly as I could about the merits of the new dinghies, I failed to persuade the skippers to make the switch from B.O.'s. I've always thought they missed a good thing: We got our dinghies for only $425, which I consider a bargain. Eighty-five were built the first year, and now there must be approximately 500 in all. Every year, the dinghies are being raced and enjoyed more and more.

Prior to the 1940's, I had been pretty much a small-boat man. Most of the larger boats I had sailed on—the J-Boats, *Vanitie* and *Yankee,* for example—had been pure racing craft, rather than cruiser-racers. In 1945, however, I decided to explore some new territory, to try my hand in competition in the middle-distance, overnight races which were sailed in cruiser-racers in the Sound and up the coast as far as Cape Cod. Through Drake Sparkman, I arranged a summer's charter of *Persephone,* a lovely-looking yawl designed by J. Francis Herreshoff and belonging to the late Philip Roosevelt.

Persephone was a wonderful boat to sail, and the summer proved to be an arduous one, full of surprising, educational experiences. By the time it was over, I had developed a strong, new appetite.

Three races come back to me with special vividness. The first was from Huntington, Long Island, to Stratford Shoals, and return. Some 35 or 40 boats were entered. We had expected the usual gentle summer night, but found instead that it breezed up steadily throughout the first leg, to the point where finally it was blowing 25 or 30 knots. This wind, against the strong flood tide, built up very sizable seas as we rounded Stratford Shoal light.

In my inexperience, I had chosen not to shorten sail, and had kept both the genoa and the mizzen set. Shortly after we rounded Stratford Shoals, the genoa ripped. I sent some of the crew forward to take in the remains of the sail, which they managed to do despite the short, heavy seas that threatened to wash them off the foredeck. In the midst of this operation, the mizzen blew off, leaving us with only the mainsail.

As if these worries weren't enough, I had two additional concerns: Corny, who was then 12 or 13, was miserably seasick; and *Aileen,* I was sure, was in great danger from the storm. I had taken her to Greenwich before going out on *Persephone,* planning to race her on Sunday afternoon, as was my custom, and had not left her on a mooring, but had her anchored with her 35-pound anchor.

The wind—which, according to Coast Guard reports, reached 50 knots in the gusts—continued all night. It was at its height the next morning, when we crossed the finish line in first place. We learned later that only four boats had gone the whole distance.

We set about tidying up *Persephone,* and discovered that the starboard shroud turnbuckle had developed a deep crack. With only a bit more strain it would have given way, and we would have been dismasted. I swallowed this bit of information and then hastened to Greenwich to check on *Aileen.* She had dragged anchor during the blow, as I had feared, but a few yards from the rocks the anchor had caught on a cable of some sort, and she had safely ridden out the worst of it.

56

The night had brought two close calls, which were more than enough as far as I was concerned.

The second memorable experience on *Persephone* was the Vineyard Race. Again, it blew hard, and after we rounded the Vineyard lightship the mainmast was put under such a strain that I feared we'd lose it. (I knew that there was real cause for concern: in previous years, *Persephone* had lost two masts.) We dropped the mainsail and continued with the jib and mizzen set. About 2:00 A.M., off Watch Hill, Rhode Island, one member of the crew was hit on the head by the flogging clew of the jib, and at the last instant was saved from going overboard by two other crewmen. I still have nightmares about what might have happened if he hadn't been caught. How would we have found him under those strenuous conditions—and in the dark?

This time, too, *Persephone* was one of a handful of boats that finished. Although we hadn't done well in the final standing, to finish at all was something of an accomplishment.

Then there was the "Case of the Wandering Blinker," as neat a lesson in the foolishness of complacency as you could find. This occurred on a lovely October night, during a second race from City Island to Stratford Shoals and return. We were beating home in close competition with *Gesture,* Howard Fuller's 47-foot cutter. Conditions were ideal: good visibility, a 10-knot breeze, the air mild. The crew had all gone below to sleep. At one point, the professional hand came on deck, and I asked him to get out the chart and confirm my position for me. He started to do this, but then I recalled that he wasn't particularly adept at navigation, and told him not to bother—I knew where I was. (After all, I told myself, I'd been sailing these waters for years. Besides, I felt I didn't need navigational guidance on such a clear night.)

An hour or so went by, when ahead of us appeared what I was sure was the blinker off Eaton's Neck. I knew that out here we had plenty of water—roughly a hundred and fifty feet of it. The shore would be several miles to leeward.

I glanced in that direction, not expecting to see anything in particular —and there, before my eyes, were what looked like islands. I told myself that my vision was playing tricks on me because I was overtired—there couldn't be islands out here. I was seeing things, that was all.

At this juncture, we hit a rock—and we hit it hard, for we were traveling at a good 6 or 7 knots. The boat staggered, then bumped on for a while, her keel bouncing and scraping. Down below, I heard shouts and the banging of loose gear.

I couldn't have been more astounded. The shock was as great as if a stranger had suddenly struck me in the face for no reason. *My God,* I asked myself, *what have I hit? There can't be a rock in the middle of Long Island Sound!*

The hatches started popping open and the crew came boiling up from below, wild-eyed and yelling. They piled back into the cockpit. We bumped once or twice more, and then, to my vast relief, we were off and under way again. In a minute or two, everyone had calmed down, and we continued our race with *Gesture,* but failed to catch her. *Persephone,* fortunately, was not damaged; only her keel had hit.

With the aid of a chart and by picking out landmarks, I soon figured out what had happened. We had been headed. The wind had hauled slightly to the west, altering our course without my realizing it. Instead of continuing in mid-Sound, we had veered gradually closer to the Connecticut shore. The light I'd picked up hadn't been the Eaton's Neck blinker, but the blinker on the eastern end of the Norwalk Islands. We had fetched up on one of the reefs that dot that section of the coast.

I learned my lesson that night, and from then on never sailed without making constant navigational checks, even in familiar waters.

The year after chartering *Persephone,* I sailed in my first Bermuda Race. Again, an interesting new area of competition was opened up to me. Until then, I thought there must be something a bit crazy about men who got pleasure out of the very demanding and uncomfortable business of long-distance ocean racing. The only way I ever wanted to travel to Bermuda, I said, was in ease, aboard a stable, substantial liner like the *Queen of Bermuda.* However, when Drake Sparkman told me he could arrange for me to skipper the yawl *Good News,* I was excited at having a chance to try a new form of competition and I decided to do it.

We made a respectable showing, placing second. The winner was my old rival *Gesture;* she caught us in the last 5 or 6 miles, sailing around us in a squall while we, a mile or two away, were becalmed. During this and other long distance races, I formed some opinions of how a boat should be raced offshore; I'll discuss them later.

By 1947, I was intensely interested in sailing large boats, while at the same time I continued to race in Internationals and dinghies. That summer I was aboard Arthur Tickle's *Steel Sylph* in the Annapolis race; the following year, I went to Bermuda as a watch captain on *Stormy Weather,* owned by Fred Temple. The summer after that, it was Annapolis again, aboard Bill Moore's *Argyle.* Then, in 1950, the magnificent 72-foot yawl *Bolero* was launched, and her owner, my good friend John Nicholas Brown, invited me to race aboard her with him.

To my mind, *Bolero* is structurally one of the finest yachts of her type ever built. Olin Stephens put strength and solidity into every foot of her, without sacrificing speed and fine handling qualities. I sailed many races on her, and she always performed outstandingly.

I will never forget the last time I sailed aboard *Bolero,* on the final day of the 1955 New York Yacht Club cruise. Our course took us from Marion, Massachusetts, down Buzzard's Bay to Hen and Chickens lightship, and from there to a finish off Padanarum, Massachusetts. The wind blew a full 25 knots, and many other large ocean-going racers chose not to come out at all. (Some of the boats that did come out fared badly, particularly several 12-meter boats, which were over-powered and dropped out.) *Bolero* beat all competitors handily on that rigorous day, and proved conclusively what a powerhouse she was.

My daughter, Aileen, won the Adams Trophy in 1948. This made me extremely proud, of course—but watching her sail for the title was a difficult, uncomfortable business.

Aileen was 24 that summer, and was living at home. The championship finals, ten races in all, were to be sailed at the American Yacht Club, in Rye, New York, in early July. I planned to attend, despite the fact that watching my children compete has always been something of a trial for me. This is difficult to explain. I want to be there, of course, to see them race—in fact, as will be plain in a moment, I can't stay away—but at the same time I honestly suffer when they're racing. I'm sure parents who've sat in the stands while their children played football or field hockey—or whatever—will understand my feelings. You want them to do well so badly that watching them is actually painful.

In my case, there's the added factor of my own sailing experience. I coach Aileen and Corny from a distance. I sail the race for them, so to speak, silently urging them to tack one minute, to slack the main sheet a trifle the next minute. These emotions come over me every time the children race—but I watch them nevertheless.

In the case of the 1948 women's championship, there was an added complication: Aileen didn't *want* me to be a spectator. Shortly before the start of the series, she told Doe that having me there would make her too nervous and jittery. She preferred to have me go to the office as usual while the racing was on.

Doe naturally passed this along to me. I sympathized with Aileen—but I *had* to watch; my pride in her was such that I simply couldn't stay away. So I hit on a compromise—one which, to be frank, involved a bit of deception.

I told Doe to say to Aileen that since she felt the way she did, I'd heed her wishes. Then I went ahead and made arrangements to watch the races from a friend's power boat.

This worked out satisfactorily, in the sense that Aileen didn't realize, during the races, that I was present. However, it had its drawbacks: whenever the boat I was on got too close to the competitors, I had to go below and watch through a porthole so Aileen wouldn't see me. Also, at dinner in the evenings, I had to pretend that I'd been in the city all day.

Aileen did splendidly, beating the finest women sailors in the country, and after her victory we had a celebration dinner at the American Yacht Club. I told her then about what I'd done, and she forgave me. Now that she has children of her own, I'm sure she understands.

The victory that meant the most to me in all my years of sailing came in 1952, when I won the Mallory Cup in the North American Sailing Championship series. As I've said, every race has been important to me, whether a 600-yard dinghy race or the long haul to Bermuda, but for me this series will always stir a special warmth.

Prior to 1952 there had never been a North American Sailing Championship for men. The first one was organized that year, and Mrs. Clifford Mallory put up a very handsome trophy in memory of her husband, a fine sailor who had made many important contributions to yachting—among them the founding of the North American Yacht Racing Union. The trophy had a most interesting history: it was a large Georgian soup tureen which was presented by the Sultan of Selim to Lord Nelson in gratitude for fighting the Barbary pirates; embossed on it, among other things, were replicas of the transom of *Victory*, Nelson's flagship, and the Nelson family crest. The champion would keep the trophy for a year; the next year, it would be competed for again. In addition, each year's winner would receive a bowl marking his victory.

To select the eight finalists for the championship and the Mallory Cup, the North American continent was split into eight divisions. In each, local selection committees were set up, to which sailors submitted their names. The committees screened the applicants, generally choosing men who had won championships. In my district—Western Long Island Sound —there were, as I recall, 24 skippers on the list after the screening.

Then the actual racing began. We were paired off, taking turns in the various types of boat sailed in the area. I found myself sailing in yachts of every description. Alternate races were sailed in my own class, the Internationals. For example, I had to race a Victory class champion in Victories, after which he had to race me in Internationals; I had to race a 210 champion in 210's, after which he had to race me in Internationals; the same for Stars, Atlantics, and so on. All of this was intensely interesting to me—and demanding as well.

I won against the 23 other skippers, which not only qualified me for the semi-finals, but also earned me the Long Island Men's Championship and the Hipkins Trophy. (Corny, I'm proud to say, won this same trophy in both 1960 and 1961.) In the semi-finals, I raced against the two champions from the eastern Sound and Great South Bay. The competition was spirited and keen; when it was over, I had earned a place among the eight finalists. (It was later estimated, that between 500 and 600 different races were sailed all across the country to pick the eight finalists.)

The finals took place in Mystic, Connecticut, in early September. We raced QA's—Quincy Adams 17's, a class of one-design 26-footers—and we changed boats after every race, so each skipper and crew raced in all eight boats. As crew, I had Corny and Bill "Boots" Le Boutillier, my very able first mate from *Aileen*. This was the first time Corny had been a full member of my crew—although, of course, he'd sailed with me ever since infancy—and he couldn't have been more helpful. I'm convinced I would never have won without his able assistance.

The competition in the elimination races was keen, but in the eight championship races, the competition was the toughest I've ever encountered. We sailed in both light and heavy weather, in the very strong, 2- to 3-knot tides of Fishers Island Sound. No single skipper ever "took charge." Through the first seven races, I finished third, first, sixth, fourth, fifth, second, and fourth. The result was that going into the eighth and final race, I held a very slim two-point lead over the runner-up, Charles Ill of the Barnegat Bay Yacht Racing Association. To win the series, I had to either beat Ill or finish right behind him; if he put a boat between us, we would be tied on points. I learned after the race that such a point tie would have made him the winner. We each had the same number of firsts and seconds, and we had each beaten the other the same number of times, but he had two thirds, while I had only one.

We had a strong northeaster, 18 to 20 knots, for the eighth race. A good-sized spectator fleet was on hand, with brightly colored burgees and signal flags snapping in the clear air. I was too conservative at the start, and got away in the middle of the fleet. By the time we reached the first windward mark (we were to go twice around a windward-leeward-windward course), I was in fifth place, with Ill ahead of me in fourth.

During the rest of the race, Ill succeeded in moving up into second place, then dropped back into third. In the meantime, I held my fifth position the first time around, and then, on the second downwind run, managed to overtake one boat; when we rounded the downwind mark the second time and started for the finish line, Ill was in third place, and I was in fourth.

That last windward leg to the finish is one that I will never forget. As the four front-running boats closed in on the finish line, it was plain that Ill was steadily gaining on the second boat—and if he succeeded in passing him, of course, he and I would be tied in points. Ill and the second-place boat approached the finish on different tacks: Ill on port tack, the other man on starboard. With a hundred yards to go, it was evident that although Ill couldn't quite cross the other's bow, he nevertheless had room to cross the line to leeward of him. Ill waited until he could pass the buoy close aboard on the port tack, then went about. A moment later, with the other boat coming in fast on the starboard tack, he shot the line.

In fourth place, we sailed on for several anxious seconds, heading for the line. From our boat, it had been impossible to tell whether or not Ill had caught his man. Finally there were only a few yards to sail, then none —and as we crossed, two guns sounded in the customary salute to the winner of a series. I was still uncertain of the outcome, however, and sailed over to the committee boat for confirmation. They told me Ill had finished third: I was North American Sailing Champion.

At the presentation of prizes, I learned that the margin between Ill's boat and the second-runner was less than the width of a mast.

My racing career came to a virtual end on April 26, 1956. It was a beautiful, warm day, with a brisk southerly blowing, and I was sailing

B.O. dinghies in the overall Long Island Frostbite Championship, held that year at the Manhasset Bay Yacht Club. We sailed four races in the morning, and I felt fine and did well, alternating for the lead in the series with Arthur Knapp, who, in my book, was the man to beat.

At lunch, I sat between a stranger and Glen MacNary, one of the other skippers. The newcomer, with whom I had a most pleasant conversation, told me his name was Dr. Cortez Enloe. At one point during the meal, Glen said he was surprised I was having only a glass of water. He asked if that was my habit on race days, and I told him it was.

He looked me up and down, smiled, and said: "No wonder you're in good shape." I remember those words vividly, for no more than 45 minutes later my good health cracked wide open.

The fifth race of the day—there were to be eight in all—started right after lunch. A minute or two after I had crossed the line I felt a deep, stabbing pain in the left side of my chest. I knew instantly that this was far more serious than indigestion or a muscular twinge. I had never had heart trouble before (in fact, I had been examined only two weeks before at a well-known clinic and told that I was in excellent condition), but it was plain what had hit me. I remember thinking that I was really in for it now—and in the same instant I decided that I would go on with the race. That decision, I know now, was foolish and dangerous. It came to me instinctively, however; there was no arguing with it.

Through the next two races, the tautness and throbbing continued deep in my chest. Then the fourth race of the afternoon got underway, and at the weather mark I met a competitor. He was on port tack; I was on starboard, and therefore, of course, had the right of way. We converged on the mark simultaneously, and I purposely sailed past it a boat length or two, to force him about. He didn't tack, however, and I hit him. There was a scramble as we hastened to recover and continue, and then the pain came surging back, sharper and deeper this time, and I could feel a gushing in my chest and a warm tingling down my left arm. I knew now that I was in real difficulty.

I finished the remaining two reaches and then sailed for the committee boat. Harry Powell, the commodore of the Manhasset Bay Yacht Club, was in the cockpit. I drew up alongside, and told him I had a problem. It was necessary for me to drop out. Could I come aboard the committee boat?

They helped me up over the rail and led me forward, and I lay down on the deck.

The rest of that afternoon is a blur of impressions, some of them distinct, others shadowy. A Coast Guard launch soon appeared, and I was given a shot of morphine by Dr. Enloe. I remember asking him how serious the thing was. He told me not to worry, but I knew he was jollying me along. Another memory is of a discussion between two Coast Guardsmen: They were supposed to be giving me oxygen, but didn't know how to work the equipment, and got into a lively, confused argument, ignoring me while they figured things out. Strange as it may seem, I thought their conversation was very funny.

For the most part, my own thoughts concerned the changes this business was going to bring about. I never doubted for a moment that I was going to get well, but I had a suspicion that my racing days were over, and that was agonizing. I kept saying to myself, "You're not going to race any more, it's all over, they're going to restrict you now."

Everyone was wonderful to me. From the yacht club in Manhasset—while I lay on a sofa in the ladies' lounge—Dr. Enloe called my close friend and guardian angel, Dr. Harold Lovell. Harold in turn made arrangements for me to be admitted to the Doctors' Hospital in New York, and got in touch with Dr. Milton Raisbeck, a heart specialist who had been giving me routine checkups for ten years. When the ambulance arrived, Clinton Bell, a Larchmont friend, very kindly insisted on riding into town with me. We were held up for an hour on the parkway by a flat tire (the ambulance had no spare, and the driver had to send for one), but for some reason the delay didn't bother me: I recall thinking that the worst of it was that we were keeping Dr. Raisbeck waiting.

Finally, I was tucked away in bed. Just before I dropped off into a drugged sleep, that same persistent, painful thought returned: "You're not going to get any more of it." The thought hurt a great deal worse than the thing in my chest.

I had had a coronary occlusion. It was soon evident to my doctors that with reasonable luck and a sharply curtailed regimen, I was going to be all right. I would have to take it easier around the office, and, as I'd feared, racing was *out*.

During my convalescence, both Dr. Lovell and Doe came to see me every day, and Aileen and Corny kept my spirits up with frequent telephone calls. I'll never forget my first conversation with Corny, who was then going to business school in Boston. After I'd reassured him about my health, he brought up a subject that he had obviously been dying to discuss: the collision with the other boat. He wanted to know if I had registered a protest with the race committee. I told him I had.

"How did it come out?" he asked.

I replied that the matter was forgotten: there couldn't be a race committee hearing because I was in the hospital.

This didn't satisfy him. "You should have gotten it cleared up right there and then," he said. "I'm sure the ambulance driver would have waited for you while you went to the hearing."

I found I enjoyed the hospital routine and the rest I was getting, so much so that I arranged to stay a seventh week, one beyond the normal time, just to make sure the job of convalescence was thoroughly done. Even there, I managed to keep in touch with boats. My room overlooked the East River. Doe brought me my binoculars, and I watched the occasional yachts and the pretty little tugboats coming and going. One day John Nicholas Brown came up the river in his son's boat. He called me on the ship-to-shore phone, and we talked as he went by. Another time, Dr. Enloe and Jim Moore went past in a power boat, towing a fleet of the beautiful, brand-new Resolute sloops, just in from Sweden, up to Manhasset.

I returned home in early spring, and spent the summer lazing around, going out for an occasional relaxed sail, but doing no racing. The inactivity, I discovered, was very trying.

In the fall, I presided at the annual meeting of the International class, and was pleasantly surprised to receive a handsome silver bowl, decorated with the signatures of all of the skippers who had sailed in the class back through the years. The thought behind this was most touching, and I shall always treasure the bowl.

By this time—mid-autumn—I felt thoroughly fit, and decided no harm would come of a race or two. I would do a little frostbiting in the winter, spacing the races and taking care not to get overactive during them, and would race *Aileen* now and then the next season.

When I announced this plan, it met with definite disapproval from everybody—Doe, my doctors, Corny. It was Aileen, however, who really made me understand how foolish the idea was. "Don't do it," she told me. "It won't work out the way you think. If you go out there and race and get beaten, you'll only want to do better the next week. And if you win, you'll feel you have to give the people you've beaten a chance to get even. Pretty soon, you'll be back on the old grind. It's got to be all or nothing."

A RACING LIFE

Those were wise words, and I'm glad to say I've had the sense to heed them. With only three exceptions, I have done no competitive sailing since April 1956. Living with this deprivation has been a trial: there isn't a day when I don't long for the excitement, don't wish that I could race the *Aileen* or my dinghy, *Dainty,* again. I am most grateful for all the years of racing I had, but I'd be telling less than the truth if I didn't add that I envy men who can still do it. And I get very upset when I see them pass up a chance to race—to me, that's a crime, to stay on the beach when you could be racing your boat.

I've missed racing immensely and will go on missing it for the rest of my life.

5. The America's Cup

Since 1956, there have been three occasions when I decided to run whatever health risks might be involved in racing. All were special cases, where my desire to participate was irresistible. These were the 1958 and 1962 elimination trials for the America's Cup, and a special "alumni" race for International skippers.

On New Year's Eve in 1957, Corny and I went to a hockey game in Madison Square Garden. We sat right behind my old friend Richard Maxwell, and at one point Richard turned around and said that Corny ought to think about the possibilities of crewing on *Columbia* in the America's Cup trials. This struck both Corny and me as a wonderful idea, and a day or two later I talked it over with Drake Sparkman, who got in touch with Henry Sears, the head of the syndicate that built *Columbia*. Within a few weeks, Corny had been selected.

Columbia was launched in the spring, and I went out on her maiden sail. I thought she looked fine—well designed and fast. Also, her skipper—Briggs Cunningham—and crew seemed highly competent. There were to be three sets of trial races during the summer against the other contending 12-meters—*Vim, Easterner,* and *Weatherly*—and the series against Great Britain's *Sceptre* would be sailed in early September. From the outset, I was convinced that *Columbia* would prove to be the best boat.

The members of Henry Sears' syndicate knew, that because Corny was aboard, I was intensely interested in *Columbia,* and they very kindly asked me to serve as an adviser. I was to observe the shake-down sailing and the trials with the idea that I might be able to offer some advice on how the boat could be sailed most effectively. Although I was more than happy to do this, Doe and my doctors were concerned that I might be subjecting myself to undue strain. I succeeded in convincing them that I would be careful, and by mid-May I was out on the water.

The Sears syndicate had chartered another 12-meter, *Nereus,* as trial horse for *Columbia.* The plan was to take the two boats out in the sound —we would later do the same thing in the waters off Newport, Rhode Island, where the trials and finals were to be held—and sail them against one another, practicing starts and tactics, changing sails between the two boats to see which benefited *Columbia* the most, and so forth. I was asked to skipper *Nereus,* and welcomed the opportunity. I was secretly worried that I might get over tense, but I kept that to myself. If the pressure grew too great, and was affecting my health, I could withdraw.

We learned a great deal from sailing *Columbia* against *Nereus.* The two boats were evenly matched when they were reaching or running— they were, after all, built to conform to the same rule, and not even a man as good as Olin Stephens, *Columbia*'s designer, can produce any really marked difference in performance on these two points of sailing. Going to windward in light airs, they were, again, fairly closely matched. In a breeze to windward, however, *Columbia* showed she was clearly the better boat. I was pleased by that; it confirmed my faith in her.

In those practice races, I sailed *Nereus* as well and as hard as I could, and I always enjoyed the occasions when we were able to beat *Columbia.* However, for the first time in my life, I had mixed feelings about the competition: I wanted to get beaten almost as badly as I wanted to win. I wanted *Columbia* to prove she was the boat I knew she was. This sensation of divided loyalty was brand new to me. Always before, I'd cared only about the boat I was sailing.

These were long, exciting days, and it was delightful for me to be racing again, even if it was only practice. We went out early, and spent the day experimenting, testing, then discussing what we'd learned. We used walkie-talkies to communicate with *Columbia* and Briggs Cunningham's tender. When we wanted to change sails, for example, we'd signal for a conversation, then talk over the change before making it. In the evenings, through dinner and right up until bed time, we discussed the progress we'd made. I felt these informal conferences, attended by members of both crews, were invaluable.

While I was aboard *Nereus* and *Columbia*, everyone was most considerate of my health. If I tried to exert myself, in even the smallest way, a crew member would get ahead of me and do what I'd started to do. Naturally, I was grateful for the treatment, but it made me a bit uncomfortable to be considered an invalid.

I observed the first series of trials, held in late July, from a powerboat. *Columbia* performed creditably, but not spectacularly. To the delight of many onlookers who had a sentimental attachment to an older boat, *Vim*—very ably sailed by Bus Mosbacher—came through especially well.

Watching from the powerboat was extremely difficult and trying. I was taut all the time, and could feel pain and pressure in my chest. I didn't tell anyone about this; I didn't want others to know as I also knew that if I discussed my difficulties, I'd soon be back ashore.

When the second series of trials started, it was suggested that I get aboard *Columbia*—that way, if I had anything to contribute, I could communicate it immediately. As on *Nereus*, I was given the most friendly, considerate attention, and wasn't allowed to do anything physically demanding. I found that although I still experienced tension in my chest, the situation was considerably easier than it had been in the first series. Though I still felt the strain to a degree, on the whole I was more relaxed and comfortable.

In the second series, *Columbia* again proved she was well designed and fast, but as before, she failed to make a truly impressive showing—one that would prove conclusively that she was the best boat. The other boats, notably *Vim,* were still pressing her hard.

The third and last series of trials began in late August. This time, it was suggested that I start *Columbia* and sail her on the windward leg. By now, I was having a hard time getting to sleep at night, and had lost 10 more pounds—making a total of 35 lost since my attack. I hoped that when I actually got a chance to take the helm, I'd feel even less tense than during the second series, but all the same I was a bit concerned that something might happen to me while we were racing. From my experience in 1956, I knew that if it did, the first thing I'd need would be morphine. I decided it was best to be prepared for any eventuality, however remote, and phoned Harold Lovell, my doctor, in New York.

69

During our talk, I commented that I wasn't getting enough sleep, and asked for some sleeping pills.

Harold's reply was that if that was the case, I was in trouble and should quit and go home.

We talked that over for a while, and he finally agreed to send me the pills. Then I told him I wanted some morphine, a hypodermic, and instructions on how to use them. (Morphine is the first treatment for a heart attack.)

Harold practically jumped through the phone. His first response was a flat "no." He said this proved I positively had to come home.

We exchanged a good many more words, and in the end I got the morphine and the needle. I rechecked the rules, and found that I was correct in my belief that a boat wouldn't be penalized if a man were taken off for health reasons. So I had solved everything except the question of how to get the injection if I needed it.

This called for careful planning, for if worse came to worse, I wouldn't be in any shape to do the job myself. I remembered that *Columbia's* professional captain, Fred Lawton, had been a destroyer escort captain in the Pacific during the war—he had probably had experience with morphine.

I didn't want Fred to know I'd brought the drug aboard, but at the same time I had to be sure he would know what to do with it in an emergency. One evening, I drew him into a conversation about the war. I said I presumed that as a ship's captain he had performed many different jobs. I asked if he had ever given medical aid to members of his crew, and he said he had, many times.

Had he ever given morphine injections?

"Often."

That was all I needed to know. For good measure, I pasted Harold Lovell's instructions on the package, and then hid it in my footlocker down below, under some extra clothes.

Fortunately, Fred never guessed the reason for my questions. If he had, and had told the other men on the boat, I would almost certainly have been beached.

In the third series, when I was actually at the helm, the tension in my chest lessened considerably, as I hoped it would. The series started on Labor Day, September 1. We beat *Weatherly* that day, and on September

2 we beat *Easterner*. Then, on September 3, we beat *Weatherly* once more. *Vim* was also the victor in her three races on those days, and as a result the selection committee eliminated *Easterner* and *Weatherly*.

Those two boats provided strong competition, and made the trials an absorbing spectacle for people around the world. To my mind, the handling and organization aboard *Weatherly* were superior to those aboard *Easterner*. *Weatherly's* skipper was Arthur Knapp, Jr., a wonderful competitor in any boat, who is especially talented in light airs and downwind sailing. Unfortunately, *Weatherly* in 1958 lacked power in strong breezes—and it was expected that the cup defense would be sailed in those conditions. (A great many changes, incidentally, were made in *Weatherly* prior to the 1962 America's Cup trials. Among other things, she was lightened considerably, her rig was changed, and she was given a new, reshaped keel. I've always felt that Bill Luders deserved great credit for the success of those modifications. To my mind, Bill is the unsung hero of the 1962 cup defense.)

Getting back to 1958: we now faced the final trials against *Vim*, and I was still confident that *Columbia* was the better boat. Her sails were not, in my opinion, as good as *Vim's*, but she was faster to windward in moderate-to-fresh breezes, and decidedly more powerful in the big southwest seas.

In our match racing with *Vim*, I ran into distressing difficulties. I'd never sailed in competition where tailing was involved. (Tailing is a complicated series of pre-start maneuvers designed to keep your opponent from starting ahead of you.) The result was that I was occasionally boxed at the start. This upset me badly—so much so, in fact, that every single evening since I've gone to bed thinking about the mistakes I made in those particular starts, analyzing them, "replaying" them. That may sound extreme, but it's true. Just as some golfers are haunted by the memories of missed chip shots or putts, so I'm plagued to this day by the lickings I took in those starts.

Vim fought us hard, right down to the wire. On September 4, we won handily over a windward-leeward course. The next day, however, we were beaten by ten seconds; this was one of the times Bus Mosbacher out-maneuvered me at the start, and, in addition, our spinnaker sheet let go in the jibe at the second mark. There was no race on September 6 because of fog, but we went out anyway and practiced. Henry Sears, managing owner of *Columbia* and her navigator, greatly appreciated this weather as it permitted him to practice. He certainly did not need the latter. His accuracy was remarkable.

On September 7, *Columbia* got the heavy breeze she relished, and we crossed the finish line with a lead of a quarter of a mile. But the following day, *Vim* came right back, and after beating us at the start she led all the way. (In this race, *Vim* stayed clamped on our wind, and I tacked *Columbia* 36 times in 42 minutes, trying to shake her loose.) On September 9, it blew hard, and we won decisively, by three minutes.

After the fifth race, it was becoming plain that *Columbia* was the faster boat. Many kind comments appeared in the press to the effect that I'd been responsible for the change—including one by Carleton Mitchell in *Sports Illustrated* which called me a competitor "risking his life . . . for the thing he loves best." *Columbia,* the writers said, was showing more enterprise and life, and was obtaining better results. They also pointed out something I agreed with heartily: that Briggs Cunningham was sailing and racing the boat beautifully.

By this time, the strain on me was severe, and I decided I'd have to get off the boat. Olin Stephens, who had stepped down when I came aboard, resumed his role as relief helmsman.

The last race of the trials was sailed on September 11. The selection committee very kindly invited me to watch it from Harold Vanderbilt's *Versatile.* In a strong breeze, *Columbia* again showed her power, and won the close contest by nineteen seconds.

The selection committee retired for a conference, and when they had made their decision they very generously called me into the main saloon, where the chairman, William A. W. Stewart, informed me that *Columbia* was to be the America's Cup defender; the committee said they wanted me to be the first to know. You can imagine how much that verdict did for my spirits.

The trials had been enormously exciting for everyone involved; unfortunately, what followed—the actual racing for the cup—was, to put it mildly, less gripping. *Columbia* made very short work of *Sceptre,* roundly trouncing her in four straight races. The 1958 America's Cup competition will go down as one of the greatest anticlimaxes in yachting history.

I bring up the subject of *Columbia*'s lopsided victory because it's such a conspicuous example of what can happen when yacht racing becomes a contest between designers and sailmakers, rather than between sailors. *Sceptre,* to be blunt about it, was nowhere near the boat *Columbia* was.

Paul Shields, Cornelius Shields, and Cornelius Shields, Jr., on *Columbia,* in an early spring sail, 1961.

The result was that when the two met, there was an overnight collapse of interest in the racing.

To me, that's sad. I hate to see an event as important as the America's Cup racing turn into a fiasco.

What follows may strike many readers as pure, unadulterated heresy.

I'd like to see the America's Cup races become a competition purely between sailors. To accomplish this, the races should be sailed in truly one-design boats, and the skippers and crews should switch boats after each race. If the cup races were sailed this way, a debacle such as that of 1958 would be avoided—the possible differences between sailors are not nearly as great as the possible differences between boats.

There are those who say that the point of the America's Cup competition has always been to allow designers and sailmakers to compete against one another. This is simply putting the emphasis in the wrong place, and I want to see it put where I believe it belongs: on the sailors. Other people contend that racing in one-design boats would rob the competition of some of its glamour. I maintain that the boats can be as glamorous—as beautiful and as big—as the two countries involved care to make them. As long as they're identical, I—and, I believe, a lot of sailors, too—would be happy.

Probably the sort of competition I suggest will never come to pass. If it should, however, we'd have truly fair and interesting racing.

It's the only way to find out who the real champions are.

I repeat: let's put the emphasis where it belongs—on the sailors.

The International one-design class was 25 years old in 1961. During the spring, the class committee, headed by William E. John, originated an exciting idea: they would hold a race for class ex-champions—"alumni." It would be sailed after the close of the regular season, in October. The boats would be provided by Herman Whiton's Small Boat Training Facility and the skippers would draw lots for them at 10:00 A.M. the day of the race.

All through the summer, I thought about that race. I knew it would be unwise for me to sail in it. I also knew that if I mentioned the possibility, Doe and my doctors would come down hard on me, raise a fuss, and try to make me promise not to enter.

On top of all this, I knew I *was going* to sail in that race. That much was certain. Somehow, I would figure out a way to enter without anyone at home finding out—except Corny, who would be part of my crew. This one afternoon would bring together all the men against whom I'd competed in the past with such pleasure. I just couldn't miss it—it was as simple as that.

Since it had been six years since I'd raced an International, I was afraid I might have lost my touch because of inactivity. I knew that as a warm-up, I should sail in at least one practice race. The problem, of course, was to arrange this without tipping my hand. If my doctors learned my intentions, that would be the end of the alumni race for me.

I chose the "lay-up" race, the last regular competition of the season, for my first warm-up. This was sailed on Columbus Day, October 12. After a good deal of thought, I finally hit on a way to keep word of my sailing from getting back to Doe and my doctors. I went to the race committee and asked them not to list me as skipper. Corny, I said, was going to skipper—I was merely going along as crew. I suspect the committee members guessed what I was up to, but they agreed to cooperate.

The day was sparkling and beautiful, with a steady 10 to 12 knot breeze blowing from the northeast—always my favorite. As we sailed out of the harbor, I was delighted to find that I was feeling none of the tautness or pressure in the chest that had bothered me aboard *Columbia*. On the contrary, I was as composed and relaxed as could be.

There were sixteen other boats out. We got a good start, and going for the windward mark I stayed offshore, as I always had in the past when the wind was easterly. We led most of the way, and beat the second boat by at least 300 yards.

The experience was thoroughly exhilarating and satisfying. Everything fell naturally into place, and it was as though only a week—not six years—had elapsed since I'd last raced an International. A large part of the pleasure was having Corny in the boat; he was a most helpful, ideal first mate.

I sailed another trial race the next Saturday, in heavy rain and a 15 to 18 knot wind. This time I was beaten by eight seconds—and didn't mind at all, for the skipper of the winning boat was Corny. Again, there was no comment at home or from my doctors.

I don't think I'll ever forget waking up the morning of the alumni race. All through the previous week, as the day grew closer and closer, I hoped more and more that it would really blow. I wanted one of those perfect northeasters I'd always enjoyed so in the past. That morning, I woke early and went to the window—and there were the conditions I'd been praying for: 25 to 30 knots of wind, right out of the northeast. The weather couldn't have been better if I'd created it myself.

There were six other skippers entered: Arthur Knapp, Bus Mosbacher, George Hinman, Bill Cox, Arthur Davis, and Bob Bavier. (Bill Luders was ill, and couldn't take part.) We drew lots for the boats at 10:00 A.M., and I spent the next few hours tuning mine up. By race time, she seemed to me to be completely right.

As crew, along with Corny, I had Dick Ronan and Jack Webb, all very able sailors who had crewed on *Columbia*. Once again, sailing out of the harbor, I felt very much at ease, free of nerves and tautness.

Just before our spinnaker blew out in the International Alumni Race.

The line favored the leeward end. My start was good, on the gun and at the leeward end, and we were first going toward the Westchester shore. I'd learned in special Larchmont 6-meter races in the 1930's that in this rare weather condition it was disadvantageous to go too close to shore, so I tacked early, which turned out to be the proper move. Thanks in large part to Corny's fine work with the sheets—so important in working the boat through the seas and very hard puffs—we had a substantial lead over the second boat when we rounded the windward mark. (People in the spectator fleet later estimated it at 300 yards.) The wind was now blowing a good deal harder, and it had started to rain. None of this bothered my crew. As we rounded the weather mark, I glanced quickly astern, to see that we were safely clear, and when I looked back, mere seconds later, the crew already had the spinnaker set and pulling beautifully.

I felt secure now. The boat was sailing at maximum hull speed for this strength of wind, there was no one close enough to overtake me. . . .

At this point, when we had gone 100 or 150 yards past the buoy, the spinnaker halyard slipped off the cleat, and the spinnaker went flying out before the boat, flapping wildly in mid-air for a moment and then dropping onto the water. Before anyone could move, it had filled with water—and was torn.

My crew got it up again, but it lasted only a second or two. One instant it was there, pulling the boat along at a terrific rate, and the next it had vanished, the wind widening the tear into a split and then tattering the two halves to ribbons, until all that was left were the two naked luff lines.

I knew then that it was only a matter of time before one of the other boats, all of which had their spinnakers set now, would pass us. We sailed on, doing our best with jib and mainsail, and then, sure enough, when we had covered 40 percent of the 4-mile leeward leg, first George Hinman and then Bob Bavier went by. The other competitors were too far back to catch us, however; we rounded the leeward mark and beat up to the finish, crossing in third place 30 seconds behind Bavier, the second boat.

I was disappointed, of course—and at the same time I was pleased with the way I'd taken the lead and had beaten the other boats to windward. I felt—pardonably, I think—that there was a kind of victory in that, a proof that my absence from racing hadn't hurt my ability. As for losing the spinnaker: I had forgotten my usual reminder to double-cleat the halyard , so the fault was really mine.

All in all, it was a spendid afternoon, and I'll treasure the memory of it for the rest of my life. I'll also remember the ironic postscript: I soon learned that none of my pretense had been necessary. Doe and my doctors knew all along what I was up to. They decided, however, to look the other way and let me have my fun.

In 1960, Paul bought *Columbia* from the Sears' syndicate, with the intention of entering her in the 1962 America's Cup trials. The plan was that Corny would skipper the boat, and I'd offer whatever help I could in the form of comments and suggestions. The decision to buy *Columbia* was Paul's alone. I wasn't entirely in favor of the idea of taking on such a demanding expensive campaign, but I reminded myself that I'd had similar reservations about *Challenge* and *Rebel,* Paul's 6-meter boats. In the end, both of these boats had been highly successful, and Paul's judgment had been vindicated.

We made some changes in *Columbia,* notably on the keel: the second year we had her—1962—we had the lead V'd at the bottom, and had the removed lead placed in blocks in the deadwood. The changes seemed to me to make the boat decidedly faster before the wind, but it was hard to say whether she was improved going to windward—for the simple reason that the other 12's, including *Weatherly,* were also changed materially, so there was no standard of comparison.

We campaigned *Columbia* through the summer of 1961, and when the 1962 season opened we felt our chances of success were good. This seemed confirmed in the early-season sailing, before the observation trials: *Columbia* outperformed both *Weatherly* and *Easterner,* and won the City of Newport Cup.

In the observation trials, with the new Boston boat *Nefertiti* rounding out the fleet, Corny did remarkably well in *Columbia,* I thought. He particularly distinguished himself in his starts, getting the jump on the other skippers time and time again. This was, in part, a result of my sad experience in the 1958 trials. We had both seen how vital it was to concentrate on match race starting and the tailing procedure, and during the summers of 1961 and 1962 we devoted a great deal of time, thought, and hard work to mastering it. At least once a week, sometimes more often, we'd go out off Larchmont, Corny in one International and I in another, and practice tailing for hour after hour. As I said, the study paid of handsomely. (Later in the book I have set down some of my thoughts concerning tailing.)

Columbia came out of the observation trials with a record of four victories and six defeats. In the final trials, which began August 15, I went aboard as I had in 1958—to advise. My health was good, and I felt only a bit of the tension that had bothered me four years before.

We won the first two races, lost the second two, and won the fifth. Then, on August 21, the selection committee eliminated us and *Easterner.*

To be frank, I felt the committee's decision was premature. *Columbia* deserved more of a chance to show what she could do. The committee wasn't pressed for time—they had until September 8 to make their final selection. Several more races could have been held before cutting the field to two boats; to my mind, these races should have been held.

I say this because I'm concerned about the possibility that hasty decisions such as the one that eliminated *Columbia* may discourage future yachtsmen from entering cup trials. A great deal of time, effort, and money go into the building and upkeep of a contender, and every contender deserves a really thorough testing before she's eliminated. It's already very difficult to get people to make the effort and enter a boat; hasty judgments will make it even harder, for potential owners will feel reluctant if they fear their boat will be written off after only five or six races.

This is not intended as a reflection on *Weatherly,* the boat that was finally selected and which, as we all know, did such a splendid job of

The winning America's Cup team: Bus Mosbacher, skipper, and Olin Stephens, designer.

defending against *Gretel,* the Australian challenger. *Weatherly* was definitely the right boat, and she was very ably sailed by Bus Mosbacher, an extremely smart, cool-headed skipper.

As for *Gretel:* I personally didn't believe she was as good as many others did. I felt, in particular, that she was extremely weak in light weather. She was an amazing 23 minutes behind *Weatherly* at the end of the first round of the third light-weather race. She won only one race, of course, and in my opinion she passed *Weatherly* because *Weatherly*'s crew was too conservative in setting their spinnaker; by the time it was drawing, *Gretel* was on top of *Weatherly* and blanketed her. After *Gretel* passed *Weatherly, Weatherly*'s spinnaker pole broke, giving *Gretel* more of a lead. When the pole was replaced, however, *Weatherly* closed the gap between them by 150 yards. In wind of 18 to 20 knots, with the boats almost at hull speed, it's difficult to reconcile how so much distance could be gained. To me, this is additional proof that *Weatherly* was the faster boat.

After the tremendous worldwide interest in 12-meters during an America's Cup year, it is a sad sight to see them laid up and out of commission thereafter. How nice it would be if the series could be held in boats built to the requirements of the International Offshore Rule. They would provide years of enjoyment and good racing, as well as being candidates for future America's Cups. Such a step might also initiate a circuit of international match races, including the Canada's Cup, and perhaps other series to be sailed in current offshore racing boats. This would encourage design and rig advancements in boats that have a more direct relationship to the rest of the racing world.

6. *Patience*

Not a day goes by when I don't remind myself how lucky I am that I have other interests to occupy me. This is the most important single factor in making a success of these later years. It doesn't matter what the interest is. It could be collecting furniture, or painting, or gardening, or golf—anything will do, as long as you really care about it and do it as well as you know how. I pity a man who hasn't got this sort of resource to fall back on.

While on vacation one winter, I was playing in a golf tournament at The Breakers in Palm Beach when the New York office called to say that the Chris-Craft Corporation might be for sale. I was asked to make an appointment with Harsen Smith, chairman of the company, whose office was in Pompano Beach, not far down the Florida east coast.

Chris-Craft was (and is) the leading producer of pleasure boats in America. The company was founded in 1922 by Christopher Columbus Smith, a marine mechanic and small-boat designer. Three of Smith's sons and his grandson Harsen Smith were the company's trustees, and Harsen Smith was its chief executive officer.

For several years we had heard rumors that Chris-Craft was planning to sell out, but nothing had ever come of them, so I was neither optimistic about our chances nor enthusiastic about withdrawing from the golf tournament. But I went down to see Harsen Smith in Pompano Beach the next day.

He was rather quiet and reserved, and as we began talking I thought to myself how difficult it would be to make a living trying to sell securities to men like him. Time was short, because I had been told that several other companies and banking firms were sitting on Smith's doorstep, notably the Brunswick Corporation. It was the plan of Shields & Company to have the NAFI Corporation, a diversified industrial company that we controlled, make the offer to acquire Chris-Craft.

I soon surmised that Harsen Smith himself didn't want to sell Chris-Craft, but that he might be outvoted by the other trustees. During that first meeting we spent a good deal of time discussing power boats and yacht racing. After a while, Smith said, "We should be able to do business, because we have a common love—the water." He also mentioned that we were both members of the same "club"; he was referring to our both having been *Time* magazine cover subjects.

Encouraged by the freeing up of his attitude, I felt at least I was making progress. We talked further about the company and I told him I would very much like to see the company's figures—balance sheet, income statements, etc., to guide us in our bid for the company.

Harsen Smith opened the top drawer of his desk, but made no move to bring out the sheets that I knew must be inside. Instead he spoke of the company his family had built and of its tradition of fine workmanship. If they sold it, it must be to people who would preserve the excellent condition, spirit, and happiness that prevailed in the organization.

I assured Smith that we wanted to keep Chris-Craft intact and that it was our desire to preserve the present management in its entirety; that the company would be run by them, not us, and that it would not become a division of a giant corporation. This obviously impressed him. Nevertheless he continued to open the drawer partially and close it without producing the figures. I sensed his growing enthusiasm for my presentation and at last he produced the balance sheet and income account. I tore off the top part, which contained the company's letterhead, so if by chance the sheets went astray, no one could relate the figures to Chris-Craft.

I knew we had to work fast. Theodore Crockett, our research partner, flew down to Florida that night to study the balance sheet. My brother Paul and two of our senior partners, H. Virgil Sherrill and Macrae Sykes, conferred with Chris-Craft's lawyers in Detroit. After several days of negotiation in Michigan, Florida, and New York, we finally settled on a price of $40 million for Chris-Craft. It was a great accomplishment for us, since we were competing with many firms that were much larger both in the banking and industrial fields.

Obviously I knew that Brunswick was eager to acquire a boat manufacturer to add to its varied line of leisure-activity products. As a director of Owens Yacht Company, second only to Chris-Craft in the industry, I thought I might persuade the four Owens brothers to sell their company. I told Paul after our second meeting at Pompano that if we were successful in closing the Chris-Craft deal, I was going to try to sell Owens to Brunswick.

Several days later, on a bleak, snowy Sunday after Virgil Sherrill had been successful in his final Chicago negotiations and I had returned to New York, I suddenly decided I could not wait until Monday to contact Brunswick—when someone else might approach them with the same idea. I did not know the name of the Brunswick president, but I finally got in touch with a member of the White Plains office of our organization and asked him to open the office for me so I could obtain Brunswick's financial manuals.

I called all over Chicago that afternoon and finally tracked down Edward Bensinger, the president of Brunswick, at his club. He knew only too well who I was, as he had just learned of our purchase of Chris-Craft the day before.

Before calling him I had telephoned the Owens brothers and obtained their authority to deal with Brunswick. When I told Bensinger of this possibility he was casual, but I knew he was seriously interested. A few days later he came to Baltimore with his associates to meet the Owens brothers, whose father had founded the company in a Chesapeake Bay backwater. The negotiations were completed in less than a week, and Brunswick acquired Owens for $16,000,000.

We had made a real double play. My Sunday efforts were most timely; on Monday, a St. Louis firm tried to obtain an option from the Owens brothers, stating that they were confident they could quickly sell the company. I learned later that their prospective buyer was Brunswick. This fortunate Sunday urge once again bore out what I have experienced so many times: if you are blessed with an idea, capitalize on it immediately; otherwise there will be a dozen reasons for delay. Enthusiasm may then evaporate or some enterprising competitor will make your deal.

Our relationship with Chris-Craft was an extremely pleasant one. Because boats were involved, it was all the more enjoyable for me. I was

Start of one of the 1973 Shields Class National Championship races on Long Island Sound. Arthur Knapp, Jr., sail number 197, won the series.

delighted that I could persuade the company to enter the sailboat field with a 35-foot fiberglass motor sailer, which seemed a logical first sailboat for a powerboat manufacturer. We engaged Sparkman & Stephens to design her, and she was an immediate success. A keel centerboard 30-foot cutter, also designed by Sparkman & Stephens, followed next in a line that ultimately included five different sailing craft. The most successful of these was the Shields one-design, currently being produced by Cape Cod Shipbuilding.

I was pleased that Arthur Knapp won the 1973 Shields Nationals. Naturally, I wanted my son to win (he finished second), but Arthur's victory was well-deserved. He sailed a fine series, averaging well, which is a good way to win any series, especially a long one. I remember a skipper in one of the early Mallory Cup series who won five races out of eight and only finished third in the final standings.

Arthur has always been a great friend of sailing, and the contribution of his great book, *Race Your Boat Right* (now available in a new 1973 edition), would be impossible to measure.

Arthur Knapp represents a group of skippers who sailed Interclubs in the late 1920's and early 1930's. This group also raced together in the International class from 1937 on. It included, Bob Bavier, Sr. and Jr.; Bill, John, and George Hinman; Phil Howard; Bill Luders; Bus Mosbacher; Gordon Raymond; Lorna Hibbard; Egbert Moxham and his sons Bud and Jim; and myself. Arthur's 1973 Shields class win was a victory for us all.

Youngsters all have dreams of heroic achievement. I vividly recall many of mine. I would, in some magical way, make a great deal of money and buy my mother a beautiful automobile. I wanted a sailboat that I could race. Another, of less importance of course, was when I made my first slingshot: One Sunday during a long sermon I imagined myself shooting down every bit of bric-a-brac in the church—I never missed. When I grew older and learned to play football, tackling intrigued me more than any other part of the game; again in church I became the hero who made beautiful flying tackles and brought down a group of robbers who were attempting to escape up the aisle after stealing the proceeds of the collection plates.

Fanciful dreams carry over, and grown-ups, too, express their wishes through this wonderful mysterious medium where everything we desire materializes. Sometimes they really come true; one of mine did.

For many years I have observed the great problem involved when series are conducted and it is necessary to borrow one-design boats for the contestants to race in. The committee must persuade owners of class boats to loan their boats, and owners are reluctant to do so for obvious reasons. Then contestants are unhappy because seldom are the boats evenly matched. Of greatest importance, sails are not equal on all boats. Some boats are generally run down. In other words, important series have had to be conducted on lop-sided bases. It was forcefully brought home to me in all our series for the North American Sailing Championship and the Mallory Cup.

I have gone somewhat astray in reciting the foregoing, but it does have some relationship to my dreams. What a wonderful thing it would be, I thought, if a class of completely one-design boats were presented to the Yacht Racing Association (YRA) to be used for the various important series that are run on Long Island Sound. The Hipkins Trophy and its qualifying series; the Mallory series when it came to the Sound; the SYCE

Cup for the Women's Championship on the Sound; the Adams Trophy for the National Women's Championship when it came to the Sound, and the Sears Cup for the National Junior Championship. Well, this was a sizable dream because of the cost of the type of boat that would be appropriate for these important events. People just can't make gifts of this magnitude, and I couldn't see how it could be done.

Then, in 1961, we were being blessed with a wonderful year in our business, which placed me in the position of being able to make a gift. But the YRA didn't qualify as a tax-free recipient. Why couldn't I make a gift to a university or a school and ask them to consider building a fleet of one-design boats, and when they were not using them in the summer to loan or charter them to the YRA? I approached a number of institutions and obtained disappointing reactions. Time was running out by late November, as I had to make my gift before the year's end. I went in other directions with no promising results. I will always remember a call I made on the subject (it was getting to the point where there wasn't time to wait for replies to my letters) to a professional member of the Olympic Committee. He was actually rather annoyed and said he would call back when he found time to give further consideration to the proposed gift. I never heard from him.

I was really becoming discouraged. I have always taken pride in being able to sell my ideas, whether it was the sale of securities, industrial companies, etc., and here I was unable to convince an institution that it should accept a considerable gift. In a talk with Drake Sparkman about my problem, he asked if I had considered the U.S. Merchant Marine Academy at Kings Point, Long Island, and the New York State Maritime College at Fort Schuyler. Here were two logical candidates right in our front yard. It was exactly the same reaction I used to have in the firm when we were trying to sell a difficult deal and I unexpectedly found two possible purchasers.

I couldn't wait to formally write them; I telephoned Captain Tyson at Kings Point and Admiral Moore at Fort Schuyler. They exploded with enthusiasm. In fact they couldn't believe it was true. I think I was even more excited than they after some of the receptions I had received. The idea of the boats being made available to the YRA was entirely agreeable to them, as the cadets were away a big part of the summer on cruises and vacations. The final arrangements with each academy were completed a week or ten days before New Year's, so it was indeed a happy ending for us all. One of the nicest parts came some months later when I met the cadets. Their enthusiasm and appreciation was most inspiring to me. They immediately named the boats the Shields class and suggested the sail insignia be a shield with the letter "S" on it.

"My dream" pictured a boat of about 30 feet overall, with a nice, long, straight, countered stern and a dainty little transom, and the bow would have a saucy, straight raked stem. I had always loved sheer, so, of course, this was embodied in my fanciful boat. As a token of appreciation for Drake Sparkman's many favors to me, I wanted Sparkman & Stephens to do the designing. Olin Stephens made her come true in beautiful fashion. He shaped an underbody whose sections are ideal. She is extremely lively in light weather, and very stiff and able in a hard breeze— an unusual combination indeed.

The winter of 1963 was a very sad one for me as that was the year my brother Paul died. His loss was a frightful shock to me and continues to be difficult to actually accept. He had always looked out for me, and wanted me at his side in everything he did. He introduced me to sailing, which has dominated my life; and to golf, which has provided me with so much pleasure. He was most interested in my plans to give ten of the Shields boats to the New York State Maritime College and the U.S. Merchant Marine Academy. I know he would be very pleased that the Paul V. Shields Foundation, which he created, contributed five of these boats to the U.S. Naval Academy and two to the Naval War College at Newport, and more pleased that I have continued this program and given 85 Shields class boats in his memory to colleges, universities, schools and maritime academies.

I also ordered a boat for myself and have enjoyed it immensely.

As with any new boat, there is the fun of rearranging small details, and perhaps the most fun of all: the enjoyment of thinking of her; and obviously the delight of sailing her. This sounds like the beginning of senility, but if so I must say it is a pleasant state. I recommend it. Only another boat lover can understand, and I know I can count on his sympathy and wholehearted support. Golfers, who normally would not go down the block to buy a newspaper, delight in walking five miles every time they play eighteen holes. Horsemen enjoy the smell of a stable. Hunters risk being shot at by their friends in the woods, duck hunters lie in cold wet blinds in freezing weather—and so on in all sports. But isn't it wonderful to have an interest to lean on that permits us to forget the troubles that come to everyone?

Whatever other boats I may sail on nowadays, there's one in particular I return to with special pleasure. Her name is *Patience*. She's a sponge boat, 12 feet long. I've owned her since 1932.

To tell the story of *Patience*, I have to backtrack a bit. I first saw her the year frostbiting began—1932. At the time, she belonged to a wonderful fellow named Slade Dale, who owned a large yacht yard in New Jersey. Slade had purchased her in Tarpon Springs, Florida, from some Greek sponge fishermen. She was a workboat on one of the schooners. She's a heavy little boat, 400 or 450 pounds, with carvel planking and unique, saucy lines: a lovely sheer, a graceful stern and beautiful bow, and the prettiest forefoot I've ever seen on a boat.

I was completely taken by *Patience* the first time I laid eyes on her. Every weekend, during the frostbite races, I used to admire her while talking to Slade Dale. One day he said to me: "You know, you love this boat so much, I'd like you to have her."

I told him I'd welcome a chance to buy the boat. His reply was typically generous. He said I didn't need to buy her—when the Frostbiting was over, he would lend her to me, and I could rerig her and fix her up any way I liked, and sail her during the summer.

We lived on the water at that time, between Larchmont and New Rochelle; there was an anchorage right off the beach where I later kept *Aileen*. I took *Patience* home, and I had a centerboard put in her. She had a lateen sail and gunter rig; I replaced this with a pole spar and a dinghy mainsail—the same rig she has today. She was painted white with yellow and black trim—I understand many boats built by Greeks have that combination—and I repainted her my favorite shade of light green. At the end of that summer, Slade did me a second great kindness and again showed his generosity: he sold *Patience* to me for exactly what she had cost him, $85.

I love *Patience* more every year. To see her jumping at her mooring, exposing that lovely forefoot, is an endless source of delight. Corny and I do most of the maintenance work on her, with an assist from Toby Brekne, the captain at the Larchmont Yacht Club. She's nailed, which is unfortunate, for the nails have a tendency to rust. Whenever Corny or

Toby or I find a nail that has rusted, Toby pulls it out and replaces it with a brass screw. Apply Austin's boatyard in Connecticut has also attended *Patience* each winter with a great deal of tender loving care.

Sailing *Patience* is sheer joy. She has the most wonderful motion in a sea you can imagine. She's dry and doesn't throw any water. She has great personality—more than any boat I've ever known—and she's a little tender, so you have to watch her. I take her out on race days, or any other day, and sail around, going out alone on the Sound, sometimes sailing to another harbor to see what's going on there. *Patience* has countless admirers: Wherever I go, people hail me and tell me how pretty she is.

Every morning, before setting off for the city or wherever else, I drop down to the harbor to take a look at *Patience* and the other boats and to see and smell the water. If, for any reason, I'm feeling a bit down, I get great solace and comfort from these visits. If I'm cheerful—as I generally am—the half-hour at the harbor makes me even more so. The pleasure I get from looking at the boats and feeling the breeze is great no matter what the weather is—but it's greatest on a clear day when the wind is from the northeast, producing that wonderful air, while the sun gives the water that special sparkle.

People have asked me why I don't get something bigger—a motor sailer, for example, for cruising. I just don't think I'd get as much fun out of an elaborate, demanding boat as I get out of *Patience*. She offers the kind of sailing that suits me best nowadays. It may seem strange: perhaps it's odd to enjoy that simple little boat as much as I do. All I can say is that the facts are the facts: I don't want a bigger boat; I love every minute aboard *Patience;* and I always regret the sail being over.

Part Two

I greatly appreciate the honor of having my ten friends join me in this section of the book. Their generous response is truly a compliment. I am sure that you, the reader, will enjoy and learn a great deal from their fine work. Dealing with so many busy and successful men, whose time is always at a premium, took so much of my time that, as the deadline approached, it was my opening chapter that was behind schedule! After chiding the others, I was the most remiss of all.

7. Choosing a Racing Boat

I envy the man who is about to buy his first racing boat. It is an experience that can happen only once in a lifetime, and no matter how many boats he buys after that, it is never quite the same.

All boats, of course, are beautiful, but they can be beautiful in different ways. A boat can be beautiful in her lines, in the way she carries out her function, in her speed, or she can be beautiful in your eyes because of the attachment you have for her. Don't let the beauty of one aspect or another blind you to the complete picture; when buying a boat, as in getting married, it pays to make your choice carefully. Don't judge a boat hastily. As with many people their nicest virtues and characteristics are not always immediately disclosed.

First, you must consider the purpose for which she will be used. If your family does not plan to participate in your boating activities—and I certainly hope that this is not the case—then your choice will depend only on your own preferences. You can pick any design that appeals to you. Be sure, however, that there are other boats of the same design available to race against. The best way to do this is to spend time around the yacht clubs in your area. Make inquiries to find out just what classes are popular in local waters. Make an informal survey to find out how many boats are in the various fleets, and if there is a proper feeling of spirited competition. The larger the fleet, the more skippers you will have to match skills against. In any event, a good class organization is vital. If the fleet is small, you will soon lose interest after beating, or being beaten, by the same competitors over and over again. Armed with a sound knowledge of the local racing picture, you will be in a good position to choose the right class and boat.

Merits of the Dinghy

For the beginner, an unlimited amount of sailing know-how can be acquired from the small centerboard one-design dinghy. In these tender, fast little craft, you can learn all the complications of sailboat racing with a minimum of expenditure and a maximum of fun in competition. Everything happens at a tremendously accelerated pace, whether it's rules, tactics, or the sailing demands of the boat itself.

A larger, heavier boat has considerable momentum to keep her moving even if occasionally poorly sailed. But in a poorly sailed dinghy, mistakes are magnified. If you have not trimmed her properly, or if you are sailing her too high, it will be immediately reflected in her speed. Her reaction in this regard will be much quicker than that of a boat of larger displacement, which will carry her way longer and help to overcome your errors. Conversely, everything that you do to improve the trim and handling of a dinghy will pay off in an increase of speed that you can feel immediately.

Another thing to consider is that on a single day of dinghy competition, you can have as many as eight races with 24 triangular course marks to round, as against one race and only three marks in the bigger boats. In other words, you will sail 21 more courses and meet many more tactical situations in a day of dinghy sailing than in a day of big-boat racing. In terms of a season's competition, the gain in intensive experience is obvious. With this kind of practice and racing drill, both you and your boat cannot help but improve.

I began sailing in my brother Paul's 27 footer; there were no dinghy classes in those years. Since then, I have regularly raced dinghies, and I have gained more racing knowledge from dinghies than from any other class of boat I've ever sailed. I learned an enormous amount about tactics, construction, racing rules, helmsmanship, sails, and boat handling from these exciting little craft.

There is another advantage to beginning in dinghies; the learning can be naturally transferred to a bigger boat. Anyone who can sail a small boat well can step up to a larger one, whereas it is seldom that the man who learned in a bigger boat can take over a small one and get the most out of it. Many of the fine 12-meter sailors who have defended the America's Cup were men who had been first trained in dinghies.

Since the price of a racing dinghy is well within the reach of persons of moderate income, there are a lot of these dinghies. This makes for good competition. There will always be someone with less skill whom you can beat, and there will be first-rate skippers you can strive against. If you live in northern climates where the larger boats are hauled for the winter, you can take advantage of frostbiting. The catchy label is actually a misnomer, for—as I said earlier—you don't feel cold while sailing a dinghy, however low the thermometer. Even a mid-January capsize isn't as harrowing as you might imagine, and I speak from three such experiences. But the possibility of capsize will keep you on the alert and you will think faster, develop split-second reflexes, and therefore become a better skipper.

If the idea of winter sailing does not appeal to you, then wait for summer, but start racing in a dinghy anyway. You will have the pleasure of keen competition and you will receive a basic training in sailboat racing that will be of priceless value for the rest of your life, no matter what boat you sail. Incidentally, one of the greatest pleasures of cruising is to take along a sailing dinghy to enjoy sailing in waters away from home port. Don't miss this opportunity.

WHAT TO LOOK FOR IN A DINGHY

I would like to be able to recommend a particular class of dinghy, but there are many of them that are excellent. There are, however, certain qualities that I would look for in any class. Liveliness under sail is always the first thing that interests me. A boat that plows along sluggishly—pushing a wall of water before her, a boat that refuses to tack smartly, or is cranky and trialsome, will soon dampen the joy of sailing. Look for a smart sailer that handles excitingly and has pretty lines. Remember a boat is to be looked at and admired as well as sailed—an aesthetic bonus granted the sailor.

The dinghy you choose should be in reasonably good condition, requiring only minor painting and refurbishing to put her into racing shape. The novice who hopes to buy a boat cheaply, in advanced stages of deterioration, and fix her up, more often than not is deluding himself. As with an old home or automobile, too often the "bargain" turns out to be an expensive one requiring more investment of time and money than had been anticipated. Extensive rebuilding can be a giant headache even for the experienced, well-equipped boatyards. Better to start with a craft in good condition and keep her that way.

In some classes, there are considerable individual differences from boat to boat. For over 50 years I have maintained a vehement conviction that for proper racing, boats must be truly one-design in nature. Therefore, pick a class that has a reputation for rigidly maintaining class standards—you will enjoy better racing and become a better skipper.

Racing and Family Fun

If racing will be only a part of your sailing activity, and you plan to take your family afloat when there are no races scheduled, a boat a little larger than a dinghy is called for. Something that will accommodate about three passengers besides the skipper will generally do very well. It's possible to select a good, fast, seaworthy racing one-design and still have a good family boat.

In a family boat, look for good stability and ease of handling. The cockpit should be large enough to seat passengers comfortably, but this is usually no problem in a racing boat, since the cockpits of these boats are generally designed to accommodate racing crews.

There should be some kind of small cabin or shelter cuddy so your wife and children can get in out of the rain, and so youngsters, when tired, can nap out of the sun and wind. A good one-design racing boat has nothing in her nature that prevents her from being a seaworthy pleasure boat for family use as well. Planing boats, mentioned below, naturally

Advanced Racers

Olympic one-design planing sailboats also provide the thrill of fast sailing. The hulls of this type of boat skim across the top of the water with a minimum of wetted surface. Unlike displacement hulls, the live ballast of the crew provides the only stability to prevent capsizing. To facilitate proper balancing, the more sophisticated of these craft are equipped with extension tillers, trapezes that hang from the rigging, and hiking straps, so the crew can get as far outboard as possible in stiff breezes.

Although they are wonderful fun to sail, these boats represent a very specialized type of sailing craft, and because of their tenderness and large sail area in proportion to their size, they require experienced skippers to sail them.

The advantage of these high-speed planing hulls lies in the large number of boats in the fleets. Competition is extremely keen, and sailing skills develop rapidly. Because of constant international competition, these craft are carefully kept to rigid one-design standards, which is the prime requisite for the best racing.

The Ocean Racer-Cruiser

My feeling is that even if a man is buying his boat for cruising purposes, there's no reason why he shouldn't have a boat that is pleasant and lively to sail—therefore, a fast boat. All true sailors, after all, love nothing better than fast and able runs. A man will get a lot more enjoyment out of a lively boat than one that is sluggish, dull, uninteresting to sail, and won't move at all except in a hard breeze. It is just as easy to get comfort, stoutness, and everything that you could need for family cruising with a boat that is fast, as with one that will not get out of her own way. I think it's safe to say that there would be more permanency in an able boat than in one whose sailing is on the drab side, because interest is bound to dwindle in sailing a poor performer.

It might be argued that the big, heavy, beamy ketch is a safer, stauncher boat. I don't agree. Certainly such a boat is no safer than a well-designed modern ocean racer, which will out-perform the heavy ketch a hundred to one in sailing. You can get just as much seakindliness in a good performer as in a poor performer, you can get places quicker, and you can get out of trouble faster.

If the rig must be divided, I favor the yawl. It is very tiring to get anywhere to windward in a ketch. By nature of her design, she will not go to windward with the speed of a yawl and certainly not with the speed of a cutter. This holds true for the schooner rig also. If a boat doesn't sail up to expectations, I might tire of getting anywhere with her, and she would become more of a floating home than anything else. I believe that a boat ought to be a joy to sail as well as to live on.

Then there is the matter of scantlings in the modern ocean racer. Massive timbers alone do not guarantee strength in a boat's hull. Undoubtedly there are some poor boats built today, but I think that a well-designed ocean racer is undoubtedly a more staunchly built boat. Most designers today comply with rules for the building of yachts laid down by Lloyds. You have only to read through these rules to realize that ideal standards for the modern yacht are extremely rigid with a more-

(A) (B)

(C)

(D)

(E)

A few of the popular One-Design advanced racers in use today. The 5-0-5 (A), the Tornado (B), the Finn (C), a group of Fireballs (D), the 470 (E).

than-adequate built-in safety factor. There will always be unscrupulous builders who will cut corners, but these individuals are soon discovered by serious yachtsmen, and they do not remain in business long. By hiring the services of a skilled yacht surveyor before buying, you can protect yourself from this kind of profiteering.

I don't think there's ever been a yacht built as staunchly and as thoroughly strong as John Nicholas Brown's *Bolero*, and I don't care what the scantlings are on the other boats. I think that if you were to thoroughly study the old-fashioned, gaff-rigged cruising boats that some people believe to be about the most rugged boats, you would find that these boats fail to measure up to the overall ruggedness of *Bolero* because of weakness in the rigs of these older designs.

The modern masthead rig is a marvel of engineering, with each element working toward the efficiency of the whole. It has evolved through many decades of trial and error, plus imaginative, creative thinking by designers and yachtsmen alike. If the object is maximum drive for a given weight-to-strength ratio, the permanent-backstay rig is unsurpassed. I love the traditional "character" boats as much as the next man, but I love racing more.

8. *Design Makes the Difference*

BY OLIN STEPHENS II

Olin Stephens must be called the world's most outstanding yacht designer. His innovative ideas and the consistently better performance of the many different types and sizes of boats he designed make his position in sailing unique.

I remember the first time I ever saw Olin. He was making notes and photographing the new English 6-meter *Zenith* at the old Nevins' yard. He looked a great deal like he does today, wearing a white shirt and bow tie as he took pictures of the boat's run, beam on, forward sections, and profile; making careful notes in his handbook of all the details. That same attention to detail and new ideas has marked Olin as the single outstanding force in yacht racing in this century. From his great 6-meter *Cherokee* in 1930 through the legendary *Dorade* and *Stormy Weather*, the J-Boat *Ranger*, many 12-meters, the Lightning and Blue Jay one-designs and *Saudade*, winner of the Admiral's Cup in 1973, he has been in the forefront. Excellence and the Stephens' name have become synonymous.

A curious thing about Olin is that he is an excellent helmsman, but doesn't sail very much. Too bad, since he would undoubtedly be tops in this field too. He often escapes from the sea to his New England farm to spend his leisure time.

DESIGN MAKES THE DIFFERENCE

In 1920, when I was 12 years old, I had my first sail and the quiet, easy motion of the boat made an impression which has influenced my whole career.

My father, mother, younger brother, Rod, and my sister, Marite, had taken a small cottage on Sandy Neck, a point on the inner shore of Cape Cod which forms Barnstable Bay. It was a very quiet spot where Captain Shirley Lovall, a local fisherman, rented a few cottages.

Barnstable Bay was a good place to learn to sail. Boats were already a part of our life. We had spent our previous summers at Lake George, where my grandparents had a summer place. We had learned to swim, row, paddle a canoe, and handle a small motorboat. Something about drawing boats had always appealed to me, and my first recollections of putting boats on paper have to do with motorboats. Crude as these early drawings were, I think they were prompted by the Gold Cup races which were run on Lake George in 1913. Both Rod and I were excited spectators but the excitement did not have the personal, intense quality of sailing. After that first summer on Cape Cod though, sailing and drawing boats became a powerful commitment.

Rod and I were close in age and had similar feelings about sailing, although we applied ourselves differently. I don't know whether it was because I was older, or because Rod was quicker, but during the early years when we sailed together I was usually the helmsman while he took care of sail handling. I was more interested in drawing and general design while he gave his thoughts to structural and mechanical details.

I sometimes have reflected on an example of this which occurred about the time of the America's Cup races in 1920. We both had made drawings of the competing boats, and I recall one of our arguments about the correct location for the keel. I had drawn my keel rather far aft where I claimed it had to be to have the boat trim correctly and balance well under sail. Rod's keel was further forward where he felt that it should be to carry the heeling forces exerted by the sail plan. Even today, our ideas follow similar lines. I look after general design with a special interest in performance, while Rod is always thinking about the structure and the mechanics of handling.

Our first boat was named *Corker* and was a centerboard knockabout of uncertain age built by the Crosbys in Osterville on lines not unlike those of the Cape Cod Cats. She had a slightly overhanging bow and her mast was stepped just far enough aft to permit setting a small working jib. She was a good beginner's boat, and Barnstable Bay was a safe place to learn a lot about sailing. One of the most important things we learned was to respect the tide.

I haven't been back to Barnstable Bay for a good many years, but I suppose it is still the same. Then it was a wide expanse of flats and eel grass at low water with narrow channels coming in to Barnstable and Yarmouthport, while at high water, well-protected, inviting, and wide open. After a few afternoons of pushing across the flats, with the water dropping fast, we learned how to anticipate low and high tide.

I suppose we were a typical family in our eagerness to progress, and gradually we became more sophisticated in our ideas of sailing. We spent two summers at Barnstable Bay and then two more at Edgartown on Martha's Vineyard. There I spent my days sailing around the harbor in the little Charlie Mower designed centerboarder in a class known as the Flapper. Rod furnished the family with more reliable transportation, being somewhat of an expert with an Elco outboard motor. The high point of our second Edgartown summer was when John Alden came into the harbor with *Malabar IV*, his Bermuda Race winner of that year.

We were avid readers of yachting magazines and interested in all phases of sailing. In the spring of 1925, my father bought a tiny centerboard yawl, which was the first boat we owned with a fully enclosed cabin and self-bailing cockpit. We picked up *Trad*, as she was called, from her designer, builder, and owner, Edward Merrill, of Riverton, New Jersey. In the early summer, we brought her over through the old Delaware and Raritan Canal across New York Harbor to Larchmont and later on to Edgartown. Though I can't recall any great adventures that summer, *Trad* must have sold us on cruising since the next year we had a larger, huskier and roomier boat designed by William Atkin and known as *Sou'wester*. She was a sister ship to *Harpoon*, the successor to W. W. Nutting's *Typhoon*, and owning her made us feel very close to a real hero of that period.

This heavy ketch, *Sou'wester*, influenced my career as a yacht designer. I say this because of the enthusiasm with which we acquired *Sou'wester* and the greater enthusiasm with which we let her go. It wasn't that she was a bad boat of her type, but in less than a summer's sailing, the Stephens family, and in particular the younger members, reached the conclusion that this was not the boat for them. We had acquired a strong feeling for the fun of handling a fast and lively boat, and just could not get *Sou'wester* to go to windward the way we thought she should. I know that Rod and I felt we would be happier with something much simpler and smaller as long as it was lively and fast. During the next few summers, the direction of our sailing turned toward racing, and my thoughts on yacht design have ever since been concerned with making boats sail fast.

About 1926, there was a good racing fleet on Long Island Sound, and most of the classes were the one-designs. Our interest centered on 6-meters as the most active open class and the object of much competition among the designers. In the New York area, most of these boats were built at City Island and the great majority at the yard of Henry B. Nevins. Frequent Sunday visits to City Island during the winter and spring encouraged my interest in yacht design and construction. I became acquainted with the people who designed and sailed 6's. Clinton Crane, an amateur with earlier professional experience, was the most successful designer. Sherman Hoyt, who had also designed some good boats, was considered the outstanding helmsman. My first sail in a 6-meter came in the spring after we had sold *Sou'wester*. Rod and I had a small one-design-type boat from Nova Scotia with a very small enclosed cabin and galley. We had sailed over to Cold Spring Harbor with a friend on an early season weekend. For reasons which are not too clear now, except that it was a miserably cold weekend, we headed back for Larchmont early Sunday morning. We arrived about lunch time and were just getting into dry clothes when we were invited to go out again on the recently launched 6-meters, *Red Head* and *Lanai*. We made a quick change back to sailing clothes and went out into the cold wet weather with very different feelings. The way these heavily ballasted boats with their efficient rigs could go to windward was something quite new to me. I was thoroughly bitten by the 6-meter bug that day, but had to wait one more summer before Rod and I were able to persuade our father to buy a 6.

When a boat is built for racing and is relatively unsuccessful she can be bought reasonably. The Stephens family thus became owners of a 6-meter known as *Natka*, which had been designed by Frederick M. Hoyt for Henry Plant. She had been considered a good boat to windward but not a good enough all-around boat to get into the racing for the British-American Cup, the important small-boat series at that time. Since we didn't expect too much, we found *Natka* an ideal boat. Whenever, with effort and luck, we placed against the newer and faster boats, we felt well rewarded. The extra effort required to win gave us more experience than we could possibly have gained from a boat that could have won more easily. I am sure that this quest to get the most out of a boat which may not be quite as fast as her sisters was a very important lesson for a budding yacht designer.

Sailing and racing a number of different boats fed my interest in yacht design. My family encouraged me but naturally felt that I should be as well-trained as possible. They arranged for me to enter M.I.T. I was interested primarily in yachts and anxious to start designing. I felt that courses in other subjects would only be a waste of time. I entered M.I.T. in the class of 1930 but dropped out, officially because of health, before completing my freshman year. I mention this to warn others tempted to follow my example. Considering yacht design as practiced today, I was very lucky rather than wise. I would strongly urge anyone planning to enter this field to get the best possible engineering education. This does not even have to be in the immediate field of naval architecture, which can be learned by anyone with aptitude. A thorough knowledge of hydrodynamics and structural engineering should be mastered by the yacht designer. Other highly technical areas of design can be better learned in college than anywhere else.

My own knowledge of the subject is the result of many varied experiences. I have also been very fortunate in my associates, particularly my brother, Rod, whose knowledge of structures, deck arrangements, and rigs has been so valuable. My long-time associate, Gil Wyland, our firm's chief engineer for many years, received his excellent training at the Webb Institute. During recent years, we have been able to support a large enough staff to justify the presence of a number of very well-trained younger men with a fine knowledge of up-to-date fluid dynamics and the use of the computer.

If any one activity of my own has compensated for the lack of a college education, it was my close association with Professor Kenneth S. M. Davidson, founder of the towing tank at the Stevens Institute in Hoboken, New Jersey. He helped me with many of the problems of theoretical yacht design while I was testing early models in the tank he founded. He had a way of sticking to fundamentals which simplified what others might have complicated. I remember working out what he called the "potato problem." We represented the various air and water forces acting on a sailing yacht by sticking toothpicks in a potato. It was a very simple, graphic, and effective method.

I left college in the spring of 1927 and worked at home on the design of a 6-meter while looking for a job. I had interviews with John Alden, Starling Burgess, and B. B. Crowninshield, who designed the Sound schooner *Alicia,* which Rod and I had sailed the preceding summer. During the summer of 1927, we raced *Natka.* In the fall, with the help of Sherman Hoyt, I obtained a job at Henry J. Gielow, Inc. The firm was very active in large diesel yachts, and Sherman was their sailboat man.

Despite my consuming interest in design, I was naïve and inexperienced as a draftsman. All of my own drawings had been lines and sail plans. I had watched boats being constructed but had never considered the conventions of drafting as applied to a construction plan. At Gielow's, I was given the menial job of making reduced scale arrangement plans primarily for the Yacht Brokerage Department. This was good experience and the job was a most welcome one, but I was ambitious and anxious to get on with the kind of work I liked. After a few months, I found a job as a hull draftsman with Philip Rhodes. He overlooked my inexperience and taught me many details I should have known about the actual drawing of a wooden yacht.

These autobiographical details may suggest an attitude toward yacht design which contains a good deal of the amateur's approach. I have always been enthusiastic about what I have been doing, and very anxious to do it right even if I have not always known quite how. My idea of the "how" has been to stay very close to fundamentals. I think my approach turns a little from the amateur to the professional in a certain skepticism I have toward extremes, so frequently discussed and suggested, which might be tempting to adopt. Many talk about relative performance, something which is not self-evident. If something has not happened repeatedly, I prefer to assume it has never happened at all. On the other hand, something you really know had happened once is certainly going to happen again. Yacht design entails much sifting of evidence to retain the good and drop the lesser characteristics.

I have always been interested in cruising and racing, but I think offshore racing is the best part of the sport of sailing. I was fortunate in the early days to have had successful designs in both. In the spring of 1928, after working a short time for Phil Rhodes, I was approached by Drake Sparkman to discuss a joint venture into yacht designing. Sparkman, a young and active yacht broker, had design arrangements with Roger Haddock which were being terminated by Mr. Haddock's retirement. I was most anxious for such a partnership so we proceeded with the arrangements. During the first year, Drake found two commissions for me. One was the design of a small-class boat for the Junior YRA of Long Island Sound. These boats were successful and some of them are still sailing as the Manhasset Bay One-Design Class. It is possible that the aging wooden hulls will be replaced with fiberglass and I am ambivalent about this. I think they could certainly be improved today, but I am happy that the owners of the boats like them the way they are.

The other commission was a 30-foot overall cruising boat called *Kalmia*. She was built by the Minneford Yard at City Island, later builders of my 12-meter *Constellation* and *Intrepid*. Though I would not design a boat of her shape today, there was nothing radically wrong with *Kalmia*. Her owner, Arthur P. Hatch, of Stamford, was good enough to let the Stephens family take her in the Gibson Island Race in 1929, and we won the smallest class.

Drake was also able to arrange with Henry Nevins of City Island for me to work in his drafting room and help with his drawings to gain knowledge and experience. Here I received good practice and a great deal of helpful training from both Charles Mower and George Crouch. Later, I became busier and moved into an office on the other side of City Island Avenue. I was always very much at home in Nevins Yard, and could not have had a better example or source of advice for yacht construction.

I am grateful to a number of older people who helped me in those days, but to none more than Mr. Clinton Crane. Mr. Crane was educated at the University of Glasgow as a yacht designer. After some very successful professional work in that field, he went into the St. Joseph Lead Company, of which he eventually became president. He designed and built a number of 6-meters, and the 12-meter *Gleam* for his own use as well as a number for friends. When we became acquainted, he steered several prospective clients to me, and I believe he was just as happy as I when these boats turned out well.

The first 6 of my design was built during the summer of 1929 and was launched in September of that year after the racing season was over. She evidently made a favorable impression during certain tryouts, but she was not a fast boat except maybe in very light weather. Evidently, Mr. Crane was pleased since it was largely through him that four more clients came to me for 6-meters to be built for the next season. I also received one commission for an 8. This happened during the autumn of the stock market crash of 1929, but before the depth of the depression.

107

There was a good deal of money around but not too many of the older yacht designers had been very successful in the design of international rule boats. Frank Payne of Boston had had considerable success, but in New York, Mr. Crane was the most successful professional, which gave me an almost open field. Two of my 6-meters and the 8-meter went to the Great Lakes. The better of the two that raced in Long Island Sound was a boat called *Cherokee,* designed and built for Herman Whiton. She won the Long Island Sound Championship and was sailed even more successfully by Corny Shields and his brother Paul. It was through *Cherokee* that Corny and I became well acquainted.

The goal of the season's racing in the 6-meter class was the British-American Cup. This was a series of races between four boat teams representing the two countries. It opened up very exciting possibilities for me, but in the fall of 1929, I heard that the series scheduled for 1930 was about to be called off. This was disastrous news, since I had already been commissioned to design several boats. I immediately went to see Mr. Johnston de Forest, chairman of the committee to organize the series. He explained that the series was being cancelled due to the poor economic situation. He also pointed out that there was an America's Cup series scheduled for 1930, which he felt would siphon away a great deal of enthusiasm for the 6's. I argued for the series as persuasively as I could, emphasizing that several boats were already ordered and that English interest in the Cup race would bring business to this country.

A few weeks later, I was overjoyed to hear that the 6-meter match had been reinstated and confirmed. I don't know if my own views influenced this decision, but it confirms my belief that strongly held points of view should be expressed no matter what the odds. The youngest and least of us may have an unexpected influence in changing the direction of seemingly set events.

The 1930 British-American Cup series was important to me for another reason. Although *Cherokee* had had an excellent record racing on the Sound, she slipped very badly during the Cup trials. *Emerald,* one of the older and presumably slower boats sailed by Corny and Paul Shields, went so well that she was selected over *Cherokee.* I was aboard their powerboat serving as a tender to *Emerald* on the final day of the trials. There was a fresh breeze perfect for a big boat like *Cherokee.* I stood on the pilothouse watching the puffs of a fresh northerly breeze swing first to the north and then to the west. I saw how Corny played these shifts to perfection, getting *Emerald* upwind ahead of newer and faster boats. It was heartbreaking to see this happening to the boat I had counted on to make the team. After *Emerald* was chosen, Corny and Paul discussed the make-up of the team with the selection committee. With the consent of *Cherokee*'s owner, the Shields with their crew decided to switch to the newer boat. This move resulted in *Cherokee*'s becoming the high point scorer on the American team, and helped establish me as a successful 6-meter boat designer. I hope Corny knows how much I appreciate this contribution to my later success in the 12-meter class.

In addition to my involvement with the 6-meter class and the success of *Cherokee,* I also had a good opportunity offshore. In the fall of 1929, things were going well enough to persuade my father that we could build our own ocean racer. At this time, my brother, Rod, was working at the Nevins Yard, and I had a small office across the street on City Island Avenue. Nevins had taken on too much work to build the boat we planned. We made arrangements with the Minneford Yard where we had already had successful experience and received wholehearted cooperation. Rod was given as much time as he needed to follow the construction of the boat. We christened her *Dorade,* and she was launched early in 1930. Our first race was the Bermuda Race. We finished second to the small schooner *Malay.* This was a great disappointment to us. Others were enthusiastic that a boat of relatively radical design performed so successfully.

Dorade was heavily ballasted and in certain respects was much like a 6-meter although her ends were much finer and sharper. In my opinion, her shape owed something to Dr. Claude Worth, a well-known English cruising yachtsman and author of a book called *Yacht Cruising,* which had almost become a bible to me. I never met Dr. Worth, but he was one of my real heroes. I doubt whether he would have felt complimented at being told that *Dorade*'s rather extreme design was based on his views.

While *Dorade* was obviously a fast boat and made a good name in her first season, our experiences in sailing her suggested that she was considerably over-rigged for an offshore boat. We decided to cut down on her sail area during the following winter as a step toward entering her in the Transatlantic Race of 1931. The 6- and 8-meter designs provided a pattern for this alteration. With the shorter rig she became a very fine offshore racer during her second and succeeding years. She won both the Transatlantic and Fastnet Races of 1931.

Design Makes the Difference

Looking back at this period, it is interesting to recall the chain of events. The ketch *Sou'wester,* which we owned in 1925, was the sister ship of a boat designed for Bill Nutting. I absorbed Nutting's book, *The Track of the Typhoon,* which was where I first saw the name Casey Baldwin, and incidentally, also Uffa Fox. A little later Phil Rhodes, for whom I was working at the time, was doing hydrafoil designs for Casey Baldwin. We became close friends. In the winter of 1930 and 1931, my father and Rod and I had decided to sail in the Transatlantic Race. As the time for the start approached, there was a lot of thinking and a good deal of talk about the course to be sailed. There were articles printed which pointed out the favorable effect of the Gulf Stream and the success of certain boats in the 1928 Transatlantic Race which had gotten good boosts from the easterly current.

While reading these, I could not get Nutting's book out of my mind, remembering that it recorded a very fast run across the Atlantic from Baddeck, Nova Scotia. Casey Baldwin had been a member of Nutting's crew and now lived in Baddeck. I wrote asking him whether he thought the conditions found by *Typhoon* were normal, and if the fishermen from the Nova Scotia ports found wind in the foggy weather which prevailed there. Casey did not consider the condition of *Typhoon's* passage unusual, and thought there was usually a reasonable amount of wind in the fog. Based on these answers, we decided to sail *Dorade* as close to a great circle course as we could go. The results were better than we could possibly have hoped for, and we arrived in Plymouth, England, two days before the larger boats which had sailed further south.

Being young, and I am afraid not very tactful, we took *Dorade* out to meet *Landfall* and *Highland Light* as they came in to finish. These two large yachts had been built more or less to take part in this particular race, and their owners were hoping to finish first, if not to win on corrected time. In spite of the fact that *Dorade* seemed to be splashing salt on their failure, the skippers of these two boats have been our good friends to this day. Paul Hammond, the owner of *Landfall,* has gone out of his way many times to be kind and helpful to me.

In recalling these early days, I feel I am being very immodest recording so much success. Things always look rosier in retrospect. We had our share of failures during those years. The world of sailing has become more sophisticated every year. Rating and tuning are causing more design problems than ever before. Getting the most out of a boat today requires a great deal of effort. Even *Dorade* had a radical change in her rig before her second year. *Cherokee,* though much less radically altered, had her stern chopped off to eliminate an adjustment in ballast that would otherwise have been needed to keep her in the class. The process of design and redesign never ceases.

Dorade floated considerably deep of her designer's waterline, which I now call the datum waterline to reduce the emphasis on flotation as opposed to ballast. A certain amount of ballast seems to be an absolute necessity for a boat that is going to perform well. Accurate weight estimates are undoubtedly a very important part of yacht design, but I think it is altogether fair to say that the builder can make the designer's calculations very weak. Though some boats are undoubtedly sensitive to the weight they are asked to carry, most of our designs need adequate ballast so a little extra hull weight on an offshore boat seldom does any harm. In a strict racing boat, especially the international rule type which has to float to certain marks, an exact control of weights is much more important. It is also a good deal easier because of the absence of interior accommodations and varying equipment.

The season of 1931, completed by our Fastnet win, was followed by another visit to England the following summer as skipper of the 6-meter *Nancy* in a British-American Cup team series. As well as being enjoyable, these visits to England and Europe brought much welcome design work.

EDLU's Bermuda Race win in 1934 and *Stormy Weather*'s transatlantic victory of 1935, with Rod as skipper, led to orders from abroad and in '36, '37, and '38, we did three designs for three Dutch clients. In 1939, my brother, Rod, went abroad with Harold Vanderbilt in his 12-meter *Vim,* and had a very successful season. This followed our first experience with the America's Cup in which Clinton Crane was more than ready to help a young colleague.

I have always been particularly grateful to Mr. Crane for inviting me aboard *Weetamoe,* the J-Boat he designed. She was owned and raced by Frederick Prince during the America's Cup trials in 1934. We did not go particularly well in *Weetamoe,* but it was a wonderful opportunity for me to become acquainted with the practical aspects of sailing a big boat. That year, the trials were won by *Rainbow,* and she successfully won a very close match against the first *Endeavour.* In the summer of 1936, when a Cup challenge made it necessary to think about building another J-Boat, and the whole situation seemed rather critical because of the near success of *Endeavour,* Harold Vanderbilt invited our firm to collaborate with Starling Burgess in the design of a new J-Boat. This was *Ranger.*

I want to conclude by mentioning particularly two people who were friends before I even knew them: Drake Sparkman, my late partner, and Corny Shields, the author of this book. Drake not only had confidence in what I could do but backed that confidence with everything he had, bringing commissions and support from the most able people in the world of sailing. Corny was outstanding among these. Since Drake passed on, I have had to do many jobs that he once did for me and while our firm has remained fortunate, somehow the effort seems to have multiplied. I wish Drake could know how much his loss has been felt.

As time has passed, sailing activity has grown in a way that I could not have imagined 40 years ago. The big factor has been the growth of standardized boats, which seems like very big business to a yacht designer. I believe that the early days in which I was so closely involved personally with everything that came into or went out of our office have been of incalculable help as the scope of yacht-design work has expanded. Special knowledge is useful, but there is no substitute for a close acquaintance with the fundamentals.

9. The Well-Found Boat

The racing boat must be "well found"—that is, it must have everything necessary for safe and efficient operation according to the best practices. To this end, I think it is foolish to leave the main anchor ashore to save a few pounds of weight, and it is foolish to load down a day sailer with fifty pounds of lunch, a beer cooler, and other unnecessary gear. When you are in competition, you are out there to sail a taut race: you should have the tools of the trade—good ones—and nothing more.

It is important not to load the racing sailboat with superfluous gear, for weight slows a boat, especially the light-displacement type. A great deal of thought and effort is expended in shaving ounces from the fittings of boats even as large as the 12-meters. And yet racing men often let unnecessary and seldom-used gear accumulate in their boats over the season until hundreds of extra pounds are added to their weights.

BINOCULARS

One of the tools you will need is a good pair of binoculars. They are most handy, and you will have occasion to use them many times in the course of a race. You will use them to find the mark when visibility is poor or the range is greater than the range of the naked eye, you will use them to spot the numbers on the sails of competitors and to read committee-boat signals, and you will use them to look for the little cat's paws in the distance—the first indications of a breeze.

I suggest you buy a good pair, for they will last you all your life, provided they are well cared for. I use a wonderful pair of 7 x 50's; they are precision made, very rugged, and have a marvelous light-gathering power. Even at night under the most abominable lighting conditions, you can pick up objects clearly.

Do not purchase yachting binoculars any larger than 7 x 50's; they will be unsatisfactory for your purposes. Glasses that magnify more than seven times are too powerful for use on a boat; it is difficult to keep a target centered when you use them. Everything will appear to jiggle, making it impossible to define sharp outlines. On the other hand, glasses with less than seven-times magnification are not powerful enough to reach out and pull in horizontal navigation markers with the precision a sailor must have.

If you hang binoculars around your neck by the strap while you are racing, you won't have them long. Sooner or later they will smash, or snag on something and go hurtling overboard. Build a small wooden box to fit, and glue a lining of chamois on the inside to protect the glasses when you slide them in and out. Fasten the box to a bulkhead with wingnuts or other stout-but-removable fasteners: the glasses will always be handy, protected, and where they belong.

Although one shouldn't carry binoculars around the neck while racing, to guard against loss of an expensive favorite pair of binoculars, make it a rule aboard your boat that *for the time they are in use* the strap must always be placed around the neck. People are more butter-fingered than we think.

YACHT TIMERS

The accuracy of your starts will depend, to a large extent, on the accuracy of your yacht timers or stopwatches. An instrument that does not keep track of the time steadily, with a constant rate of gain, will find you early or late at gunfire. I am a fanatic about my watches for this reason. I run three of them on every start.

I keep one timer with a two-inch dial in a wonderful little watertight case at the forward end of the cockpit. Another, also with a two-inch dial, is visible in a sheltered spot under the port deck. I use the customary pocket-watch-sized timer for practice runs. All of these timers are regularly serviced and rated; I treat them carefully like the precious instruments they are.

The use and placement of watches is largely an individual matter. Some racing skippers hang the timer on a lanyard around the neck. I never cared for this idea because, again, it requires looking down occasionally. During a close start I don't like to lower my glance for even an instant; too much can happen in that fraction of a second in a close start. That is why I prefer a large-dialed, readable watch placed next to the compass at the forward end of the cockpit. Both instruments are in the natural line of forward vision and you needn't take your eye from the race to check them.

ANCHORS

Many skippers make the mistake of leaving shore with only one small anchor aboard. I think that two anchors, a light drifting anchor for racing and a large main anchor, are an obsolute minimum. A good· anchor, preferably of the Northill, Danforth or plough design, with five or six feet of chain, should be stowed where it is readily accessible and rigged for immediate use in an emergency. Even in day of racing, so many unexpected things can happen that it is foolishness to neglect this precaution merely to save a few pounds of weight.

If a particularly vile blow makes up, or if you are dismasted, that anchor can keep your boat from going ashore or drifting into a foul area that might hole the bottom. I'm afraid that most skippers are not prepared in this manner, and either carry no storm anchors or else bury them under mounds of gear in the remote ends of their boats where it takes forever to extricate them. Also, have anchor drill occasionally so your crew becomes accustomed to the procedure. I would like to see even the little racing dinghies carry at least a small anchor on a light nylon line, for you never know when the anchor will be needed.

You cannot win a sailboat race by going backwards in a head tide. For this reason I carry a light "drifting" anchor with about 15 fathoms of very light nylon rope; it is kept with the line carefully made up to run quickly without fouling.

When the breeze becomes very light, and the tide is a head one, I have the anchor silently passed out, lowered over the side, and secured to the shroud on the side where it cannot be seen by competitors. I make no noise to give away the secret. The cabin of a small boat acts as a sounding board; the slightest clink or jingle resounds over the still water, so you must be very careful about this.

The maneuver has proved very profitable for me. Sometimes you appear to be sailing ahead while the other boats are going backwards. It is frequently possible to gain many lengths before the rest of the fleet realizes that the reason you are not losing distance is *because you are anchored*. All of which brings to mind a cardinal principle of racing—always try to conceal your next move from your competitors.

CLOTHING

Be sure that you and the other crew members wear proper clothing for racing, because it is hard to be efficient if you are uncomfortable. Even in the springtime it can become chilly on the water after the sun goes down, so be sure there is a sweater or woolen Navy shirt aboard for each crew member—as well as oilskins. In the winter, you will not need as many layers of clothing while racing as you think. The excitement and constant movement keep you quite warm.

Winter dinghy sailors have found that clothing need not be bulky or heavy to provide adequate warmth for frostbiting. Knitted thermal underwear insulates natural body heat so that only a light quilted nylon-dacron outer jacket is needed.

It is always a problem to keep the feet warm and dry in winter sailing. The best solution I have found is to wear soleless rubber slippers under heavy pullover socks.

BOSUN'S STORES

Even the smallest boat can keep a good supply of bosun's stores aboard. One need only select carefully and stow everything in a small waterproof plastic bag. The medium-sized racer can and should carry spares adequate for most emergencies.

Some things that come in handy are: plenty of marline and small-stuff for seizings; a sailmaker's palm, waxed thread, and different sized needles for whippings and emergency sewing; extra shackles and turnbuckles in graduated sizes, and jars of extra cotter pins and turnbuckle pins. A 6- to 10-inch length of quarter-inch chain, and wire rope clamps to fit the standing rigging, should be included. If a shroud or stay lets go, the broken end can be run through the chain, doubled back upon the standing part, and secured with the wire clamps. The short piece of chain will lengthen the shroud enough to reach the turnbuckle, which is then tightened. This jury rig is easily made and stout enough to allow you to finish the race and sail home, thereby saving at least part of your over-all fleet standing. Without the foresight to carry this simple emergency gear, a withdrawal is the only alternative.

The bosun's locker should also contain plenty of chafing gear, for chafe is the major cause of wear and failure aboard a sailboat. Wide sailmaker's adhesive tape is unsurpassed for quickly mending tears in spinnakers and other sails. A strip applied to either side of the sail over the rent will hold the wind and prevent further ripping. "Chafe-Guard" tape, sold at most chandler's and marine supply stores, is excellent for wrapping around shrouds, turnbuckles, and anchor rope where it bears on the bow chock. A spool of soft copper wire and one of annealed stainless steel wire will come in handy for safetying shackles and anchor keys and will have countless other uses aboard the boat.

For making repairs you will want to carry an assortment of wood screws and various sized bolts. Try to standardize on three or four sizes to save space. The best way to stow them is in a compartmented plastic box. Another good idea is to attach the lids of small mason jars underneath a seat or locker. When the jars are screwed into the lids, their contents are visible, and the jars are easy to get to, secured against breakage, and watertight.

For Safety's Sake

What to carry aboard your boat and how to stow it is mostly a matter of common sense and experience. You will pick up many hints by visiting the other boats in your fleet.

Whether or not you have a motor or a cooking stove aboard, you should have a fire extinguisher. If you will never need it yourself, you might some day render aid to another yachtsman. The same holds true for a first-aid kit: you should have one aboard and know how to use it. Thanks to the boom in pleasure boating, one unpleasantness has been removed from first-aid kits—many companies now make the kits of plastic so they do not rust away to nothing after one season. Especially, be sure a resuscitube is packed with the kit, and learn the most efficient methods of giving artificial respiration.

The Coast Guard regulation requiring an approved life preserver for every person aboard the boat applies to racing yachts as well as other boats. Do not neglect this rule of the sea. Carry one or two children's life preservers, because the adult size is useless for little fellows. Make certain you *always* have light-weight life preservers readily accessible for immediate use.

10. On the Future of Yachting— An Architect's View

BY BRITTON CHANCE, JR.

I first met Britt Chance during his foredeck stint aboard *Columbia* in 1961. My son Corny felt Britt showed great promise and had recruited him for *Columbia*'s crew. Corny couldn't have been more correct. Some of his other crew selections were also rather prophetic. Bob Derecktor, now a top helmsman, designer, and builder, John Marshall, an excellent sailor in both small boats and offshore yachts as well as an accomplished sailmaker, and Charlie Morgan, now a very successful designer and builder, were also a part of *Columbia*'s team.

Britton Chance designs have won many championships in the 5.5-meter class and a Chance modification of the Stephens-designed *Intrepid* won the 1970 America's Cup. In offshore boats, Britt's 68-foot, ketch-rigged *Equation* has set records in the Annapolis-Newport and other major races. At the present time, he is turning out his original 12-meter for the Mariner syndicate's 1974 America's Cup drive. In this venture, Britt is blessed with an excellent administrative officer in George Hinman. This relieves him of the burden of shoreside responsibility which so many skippers must assume. Hinman has proven his value in this department and also has great ability to sail the trial boat.

When Britt was sailing aboard *Columbia,* he often stayed in a room that we kept at the Larchmont Yacht Club for many years. One morning, I was up in the room, where much of my sailing gear was stored, and I noticed a thick book on yacht design standing open on the dresser. Britt had been reading into the early hours of the morning and sailing all day, proving the devotion that it takes to achieve greatness in any field. His efforts toward the light displacement 12-meter with short ends, a short keel, and a double rudder system were startling innovations, but seem to have been accepted by many as the new direction in design.

The architect's function is to design a seaworthy yacht, incorporating, as far as possible, the requirements and desires of the client. Examination of the restraints imposed by these objectives is interesting, perhaps even prophetically revealing.

Seaworthiness offshore implies survival without injury to the crew, and normally the ability to continue the passage or race unaided. Let us explore the implications of achieving this kind of seaworthiness.

Survival offshore demands adequate buoyancy to remain afloat, and therefore sufficient structural strength to maintain that buoyancy and to protect the crew. To achieve this in a heavily ballasted yacht, substantial watertight integrity is necessary; in an unballasted boat, the structure may suffice.

The ability to survive under adverse conditions requires that the hull and partial rig remain intact and that the vessel be self-righting. To be self-righting generally requires heavy ballasting, and therefore imposes more severe buoyancy requirements which, in turn, increase the probability of loss due to foundering.

This places us on the horns of the following dilemma in actual offshore sailing. Is it better to risk foundering in order to be able to continue unaided (providing the condition of the rig permits), or is it preferable to most likely be unable to continue, but without the risk of foundering?

Pride as well as practicality must be considered when attempting to answer this question. Certainly, the offshore passage unaided is an ideal to be emulated, but not at the unnecessary risk of life—although we must recall that yacht racing is a sport, subject to the sufferance of commerce.

The choice, in the beginnings of offshore yachting, seemed clear; now less so. Then, survival required the voyage unaided. Lack of speed, traffic, and communications made help improbable. Today help is probable, and if we are going to go on the sea, we should do so in such a way as to minimize danger to life, consistent with legislative survival of the sport.

We may conclude that close examination and development of unballasted types is now called for, and this has the certain benefit of dramatic increases in average speed, and opens the way for substantial improvement and simplification of rigs.

What of seaworthiness alongshore, where requirements are more severe, being dependent on sailing ability as well as structural integrity? In both offshore and coastal yachts, structural problems, as well as a capsize, are likely to lead to the loss of the vessel. The better sailing ability of the unballasted vessel should permit her to sail out of danger faster; her greater inherent susceptibility to structural problems and capsize might not permit her to do so. Alongshore, then, there is not a clear choice, but when offshore sailing is considered, the unballasted boat deserves strong consideration.

Consider the yacht from the viewpoint of the owner. His requirements are largely determined by precedent, with strong leanings toward increased speed, good aesthetics, comfort requirements, and cost.

The major factor determining precedent, other than seaworthiness, has been, and will be, rule requirements. It probably is fair to say that all rules attempt, with varying accuracy, to assess the effect of major variables on speed. It follows that, as knowledge of the mechanics of sailing yachts improves, rules should improve, to the point where vessels of all types may race together equitably and, thus, the choice of type of yacht will not be rule-determined.

In particular, multi-hulls are now not permitted to compete against mono-hulls, nor are lightly ballasted boats. This is a major failure of rules, and has had strong detrimental effects on the development of yachting. Prediction of yacht performance, as it relates to rule making, therefore, should, and is beginning to, receive strong emphasis. A most important side effect of such a rule will be increased racing life of yachts and the consequent lower rate of depreciation.

Implicit in the above is determination of resistance characteristics from leading dimensions of the vessel, involving extensive use of the computer. Application of slender body and lifting surface theories, coupled with regression analysis on data from existing mono-hull tests, promises to lead to reasonably accurate speed predictions in the short term. Sail characteristics can be determined through lifting surface and biplane theories for windward work and through wind-tunnel testing offwind. Multi-hull performance is more tractable, as wave making is less dominant. Let us rid yachting of bad precedent and rule-related depreciation once and for all.

Interestingly, architects must increasingly consider the inverse of rule making—yacht performance—as a means of conducting a rule search, so as to be able to analyze the effect of rule changes. It appears probable that, for a time, his tools will be better than the rule makers', and a period of rule instability will result.

Speed has also been measured relative to the rule for too long, rather than absolutely. The fast boat now is that which wins under the rule, and which may be slower or less desirable than her elder sister.

This is not to say that there have not been improvements; rather I am saying that there can be far more achieved through the application of basic principles to the design of yachts without the fetters of rules. Those improvements that have been attained are substantial, however. The modern ocean racer has routinely made passages at about twice the speed/length ratio of the record clipper passages. This has been achieved, however, through the total loss of cargo-carrying ability, and largely by use of the fore and aft rig, which permits considerably improved windward performance.

Recently, average performance has been meaningfully improved in light winds through increased attention to the problems of separation, means of carrying greater sail while close reaching, and substantial reductions in wetted surface. Little gain has been achieved in heavy winds due to the dominance of wave making, and we must look to the multi-hull for improvement in this area.

Even aesthetics are largely rule-determined, and we are, therefore, far from an objective judgment of them, if this is ever possible. Seaworthiness does dictate freeboard, and to some extent the sheer, but a rule-free study of the requirements could well lead to radically different—and more efficient and beautiful—forms.

Comfort requires volume, proper adaptation to the physical characteristics of man, and a variable speed vessel. Normally, the slowest vessel is the most comfortable, unless in a hurry to get home, so it is only fair to

Jack Potter's 68-foot ketch, *Equation,* looks like a high-performance planing racer as she drives on a reach. Designed by Britton Chance in 1971, *Equation* only draws 5 feet 4 inches and carries a 10,000-pound swing keel. In this picture, the art aspect of yachting is rather obvious.

judge types at the same speed. In the smaller multi-hulls, volume is a problem; in the large mono-hulls, transverse subdivision of space is probably turning the balance to the multi, where good use can be made of the bridgedeck.

Costs cannot be expected to decrease, nor can disposable income be expected to increase. Durability and longevity of the yacht assumes even more importance, and the effects of rules again become the dominant factor in determining the size and number of yachts.

What lies in the future? Freer form in design through improved knowledge of hull resistance and rig capabilities, and, hopefully, extensive improvements in rules permitting the fair, unified racing of all types, which will result in free development of types based on owners' preferences.

The transition will be a period of challenge as exciting to today's architect as the applications of statics, dynamics and strength of materials was to the architect of the 1880's, when the modern ballasted yacht was substantially developed.

The face of yacht design will change. Cut and try will be replaced by computer-aided design requiring thorough grounding in physics, mathematics, and programming. Engineering will assume renewed importance in the application of new materials and analysis of complex structures.

It is comforting to think that the economics of yachting are such that design and building groups will likely remain small, and the satisfaction of creation will remain for the architect, the builder, and the client.

Finally, does yachting need justification? For those who pursue it actively, the question is rhetorical, but it must be considered from the view of others less interested, or even uninterested. Justification is required, and perhaps it is found in art, in artfulness. I submit that sailing yachts are one of the highest art forms, set on a moving canvas, and if art has justification, yachting does.

11. One Hundred Construction Faults

BY RODERICK STEPHENS, JR.

An interesting aspect of the Sparkman & Stephens success story is the wonderful relationship between Olin and his brother Rod. The two of them are most complementary. They make a perfect team, combining Olin's design talent and Rod's unceasing attention to the details of hull construction, rigging, and rigs. Working aboard *Columbia* in 1958, Rod was tireless in his devotion to duty. As soon as we were finished with a day's racing he was aloft, to the masthead, inspecting every, and I do mean each-and-every, bit of hardware and rig. Rod is perhaps the most energetic and devoted worker I have ever seen around boats. He will be on a job at 7:00 A.M. and work through until 9:00 P.M. without seeming to need a rest.

A revealing and humorous illustration of the Rod and Olin team in action occurred during the 1958 *Columbia* effort. It shows Rod's desire to reach perfection and Olin's sound basic attitudes. Rod was the deck officer and had been working for weeks to develop a new spinnaker jibing system. It involved a great deal of complicated equipment spread over the foredeck and connected with a complex network of lines. One day, as we practiced jibing with the new system, Olin observed the activity from the cockpit. Finally, he went forward to where Rod was directing the operation, up to his knees in lines. Olin said, "Rod, you know I can't help but feel that this is a rather complicated procedure. I think that you have too much gear to make it practical, because if we ever did get into a tight situation and one thing went wrong, it could cause a complication that we might not get out of for many minutes."

I can see Rod's face now as he turned around and said, with a calm and pleasant expression, "Well, you feel that way, do you?" And Olin replied, "Yes, I do, Rod, and with much emphasis I would say that it may be hazardous to proceed with your system. I know you have worked on it for weeks and of your interest in it. I know that on paper it looks fine, but what I am worried about is the practicality of it."

Then Rod said, again with calm affection, "Well, Olin, I think you are right." He turned forward and casually ordered the foredeck crew to put the gear away and switch back to the regular spinnaker set-up. There are never arguments between these brothers, merely discussions.

In 1973 I purchased a 40-foot stock fiberglass sailboat. The hull was number seventy, the design is well recognized and this type boat has won many races. I know that many of the problems we had are due to the fact that much of the interior work is subcontracted and the boat is assembled by people who have never sailed nor even received the proper feedback on previous errors.

Here are some of the aggravating faults that we encountered during our first months of ownership. The engine was mounted too close to the bulkhead so that it was impossible to get to the dipstick to check the oil level. The engine was also poorly aligned and loosely bolted. Many of the control lines burned through because they had been left lying against the manifold.

The expensive instruments such as the speedometer and log were poorly calibrated and installed so that the through hull sensors were not set properly. They were not deep enough in the water to give accurate readings.

The propeller was the wrong size and pitch and the engine controls had to be put in the reverse position to make the boat go forward. There was constant vibration due to a short propeller shaft. This shaft was so short that the blades almost hit the bottom of the boat, which could have caused great damage.

The companionway ladder was merely screwed in place and collapsed under the weight of a crewman the first time we had the boat out in heavy weather. Thank God no serious injury resulted.

The galley sinks emptied through a hull fitting so poorly placed that it was all but impossible to close. Whenever we heeled in heavy weather the sinks filled with salt water.

A new monomatic anti-pollution head was installed but not bolted down. During our first heavy weather beat to windward the head came loose and rolled around the cabin banging into everything.

The blocks and sheaves at the masthead did not have proper spaces between them and the mast. As a result the sheaves were frozen and after hoisting the main four or five times the sheaves were nearly severed and the main halyard was so bent and creaked it had to be replaced.

The rudder was poorly placed and did not have full freedom for turning. There were leaks in the deck around fittings and even around the chainplates due to poor installation. Due to the false ceiling in the cabin, water, which leaked in from the deck, ruined much of the electrical wiring before we cut access holes for airing and drying.

The batteries were poorly located in the lower part of the hull near the bilges. A slight heel wetted them, rendering them inoperable.

Drawers in the cabin were installed snugly without allowance for swellage that occurs when at sea.

These are just a few of the constant annoyances that spoiled the first few months aboard our boat. I hope this account helps others to avoid similar experiences when they buy their dream-boat.

You have just read an actual account of the experiences of a dis-illusioned owner of a recently purchased yacht. Similar stories could be told by almost any owner of a new production boat or custom-built one-off. Each will tell you of a great number of individually minute faults which collectively made the difference between a boat that is almost acceptable and one that is really a pleasure to own and sail.

I am going to discuss in some detail one hundred different items which are not directly related to cost, but more to construction and design ex-perience. If these were considered at the proper time, during the production of a boat, a far better end product would be produced for the same amount of effort and expense. It is my opinion that 90 percent of these faults can be found on just about every boat constructed during the past few years. Few of these faults are attributable to the fundamental design or specification, but rather to the builder's lack of know-how and attention to detail.

The following twenty defects we can classify under hull construction:

1. *Stiff steering* is prevalent in at least 97 percent of all the boats that I have ever inspected, tried, or visited. A really free steering system makes any boat easier to sail faster and much more pleasant to operate.

2. *Poor limbers and poor bilge drainage.* I have always felt that a cup of water, poured in at the forepeak, and another cupful just inside the transom should find its way immediately to the lowest part of the bilge, where the pump intakes are located. The capacity of the limbers must be such that water can travel to the pump intakes a little more rapidly than the properly operating bilge pumps can expel it.

3. *Lack of reference marks.* To permit intelligent study of trim for optimum performance and rating, it is desirable to have reference marks on forward and after centerlines, generally one each end on the datum waterline. A second mark should be made 12 inches above the first. By measuring from the surface of the water to these reference marks, it is possible to ascertain, with considerable accuracy, just where the boat is floating. In a glass boat, these points must be marked in the hull mould. In one-off boats, they must be picked up from the mould-off floor and marked on the backbone when the boat is first set up. These marks must be retained throughout construction.

4. *Unguarded sheaves in cable-steering gear.* The sheaves may have a deep score, so that if the cable is properly adjusted it will have little chance of jumping. Unfortunately, the cable is not always properly adjusted, and under great stress, considerable slack can occur. Without effective guards, there is a possibility of the cable jumping, which immediately renders the steering system inoperative.

5. *Poor access to all parts of the steering gear.* With a chain and cable-steering gear, it is a good idea to inspect, remove, and replace chain and cable when there is ample time. Adjustment, lubrication, and replacement are hindered by poor access to parts. When the sailing situation is difficult and quick replacement mandatory, easy access is absolutely essential. Many races could have been won and many disasters avoided if proper access had been provided during construction.

6. *Other cable-steering gear defects.* Too many quadrants have shallow grooves and sharp corners where the cables come around the ends. Even more important, inadequate and improperly cushioned stops are often part of the standard gear.

7. *Omission of lightning grounding.* A high-capacity electrical path must be provided from the spar and rigging to a suitable ground. This means from masthead to a ballast keel bolt, assuming outside ballast, or to an adequate grounding plate below the water, assuming all ballast is internal.

8. *Omission of clear marks on the propeller shaft* to indicate when the propeller is in the optimum position for minimum resistance.

9. *Omission of a simple and effective and safe shaft lock.* For example, a relatively lightweight brass pin can be sheared in an emergency and permits using the engine for generating without damaging anything, or creating the heat which results from driving through a partially released brake.

10. *The presence or absence of sharp corners throughout the boat* pretty well reflects the experience of a builder. Anything sharp is not only potentially dangerous, particularly if it is metal, but it is also hard to maintain, particularly if it is wood.

11. *Dirty bilges* are a common fault. Worse yet is a rough finish which may make it virtually impossible to clean the bilges properly.

12. *Complex cabin liners.* There are too many production glass boats that have complex cabin liners, which prevent access to fastening of the deck fittings, and adequate inspection of the interior of the hull.

13. *Inadequate exhaust systems.* A properly installed exhaust system must take the waste emissions from the engine and discharge them outside of the vessel without admitting water under any and all conditions. It must be properly insulated to prevent unnecessary heating of the cabin. Provision for noise suppression must be made. The outlet should be above the waterline, even at full speed, so that the system is resistant to flooding without any dependence on valves. Adjusting valves can be forgotten, and forgetting leads to trouble whether they are left open when they should be shut or vice versa. Finally, the whole system should be accessible for ease of repair and replacement of parts.

14. *Electric switches in a vulnerable position,* with relation to exposure to salt water, and salt spray. It is much better to have to reach a little further and have the switches work. The proper switch, cleverly located, can last indefinitely without any attention.

15. *Magnetic items near the compass.* There is a great myth in the boating industry that the compass adjuster is omnipotent, but the best results are obtained when an installed compass is not subject to any items creating deviation. This reduces the possibility of any heeling error and is a blessing to the navigator.

16. *Non-tested emergency tiller.* A strong non-magnetic emergency tiller should be conveniently stowed with the necessary tools for installation. It is good to have installation rehearsals from time to time. Rehearsal should be held with the boat peacefully at anchor. The emergency tiller should be installed and a reasonably strong person should treat it very roughly indeed. If there is any tendency to show distortion, it should be adequately reinforced or replaced with an emergency tiller that is adequate.

17. *Chainplates for shrouds, stem fitting, and permanent backstay fittings should all line up precisely with the rigging,* which is attached to them. Any departures from the straight line of the tension weakens the system.

18. *The currently popular destroyer-type steering wheel is nearly useless in cold or wet weather, except where the rim has been covered tightly with Elk Hide; rough side out.* This is the only product that doesn't seem to change in either wet, dry, hot or cold conditions. It provides just the right grip without being hard on the hands of the helmsman.

19. *Steering chains and cables should be adjusted with the rudder straight, so that a spoke is on the centerline.* This spoke should be clearly marked with something that can be felt easily at night and shows up well in the daytime, so that it is possible to observe the position of the wheel from any place on deck. Knowing the rudder position enables you to make the obvious adjustments in sail trim and provide the best possible balance. There should also be a very precise centerline reference mark on the rim of the quadrant to permit proper adjustment of the cables.

20. *Oversize cabin windows.* Large windows look light and airy, especially ashore at a boat show. They are dangerous in rough weather at sea, sometimes fatally so. The designer will probably be aware of this and keep them suitably small. Be sure the builder doesn't "improve" on the design.

The next category relates to the cabin, and contains the following thirteen items:

130

1. *Friction catches, magnetic catches, anything similar on doors, can never be satisfactory,* except possibly in an apartment house in a non-earthquake area. It is bad enough to be uncomfortable in extremely rough weather, but you hardly need the added aggravation of making temporary provision to hold doors shut and picking up gear that has been dumped on the cabin floor.

2. *Floor boards are universally too tight.* Great relief can be provided by a simple expedient of a 10-degree under bevel. The floor boards will still fit reasonably tight but free-up immediately upon lifting. Any floor board that is adjacent to a vertical surface must have a margin piece, or the adjacent surface will be scratched when the floor board is raised.

3. *Bilge access is poor on the majority of fiberglass boats and inadequate floor lifts are frequently used.* A simple keyhole-shaped plate, strongly bolted through the floor, and two T-shaped keys with a good oval handle will permit adequate force to be applied when the floor boards get wet and tighten.

4. *Quarter berth ventilation.* Quarter berths are the best place to sleep, if proper ventilation is supplied. The most effective means of ventilation is the lazarette hatch, which can be opened when the boat is underway. This hatch should not be positioned under the helmsman's usual location. The lazarette hatch can be supplemented by an opening port in the side of the cockpit well. Something that tends to draw the air out, as, for example, a good hood over the main companionway, will add greatly to the effectiveness of the intakes.

5. *Bunk beds are invariably too weak and too low.* A number of people unnecessarily are injured by falling out of bunks in rough weather, due to the inadequacy of the bunk board facilities.

6. *The master fuel valve for the stove should be put in a position where it is easy to see, reach, and operate.* It could be clearly marked so that anyone can observe that it is turned off when the stove is not in use.

7. *Inadequate marking of individual stove burner valves.* In connection with the frequently installed swinging stove, where the tank is not on the stove, a flexible feed line must be installed. This line must never touch the hot body of the stove and should not restrict the stove motion. The swinging stove should be able to move 50 degrees each way from horizontal to provide for any surge in rough weather. There should be enough friction in the pivots to reasonably dampen the stove reaction.

8. *The pumps on alcohol stoves are usually inadequate.* They generally fail to hold pressure and require an excessive amount of pumping.

A pressure gauge which indicates the operating range should be standard. There should be a close-off valve on the pump to eliminate pressure loss back through the pump.

9. *Few boats really have adequate fiddles on tables, dressers, and counters.* Fiddles must be high, strong, and planned to function during considerable periods of excessive port or starboard heel. Adequate counters with proper fiddles are essential in the galley as well.

10. *There must be adequate dresser space in the head so toilet articles can be laid out for use.* Separate storage space should be provided for all necessary articles. Provide a scrap basket to minimize putting trash into the toilet bowl.

11. *The drop sash drawer is a very practical method of retaining drawers.* Too many are installed without adequate clearance, so if the drawer swells, there is no way to open it. The only cure for this is an axe. Frequently, the catch on these drawers is poorly positioned and does not engage unless the drawer raises or lowers with the drawer face perpendicular. This applies particularly to drawers that are not very long front to back.

12. *Any door that is not essential should be eliminated from the design.* Doors, particularly those in transverse bulkheads, must be provided with enough clearance to compensate for the inevitable working of construction material that results from boat use.

13. *Ecologically speaking, a galley will be a disaster area without an extra large refuse container capable of storing waste until it can be discarded in an acceptable manner.*

The next category relates to plumbing and associated fittings:

1. *The scuppers are often dangerously over-restricted* by the use of a plate with a few small round holes, or at the other extreme, totally unprotected. The logical arrangement is to use a lightweight cross. This prevents the scuppers from being blocked by large objects, but offers no resistance to harmless waste material.

2. *Inadequate drainage of cockpit seats can result in carrying undesirable quantities of water inside the lee coaming.* This water is not only a nuisance but particularly dangerous if there are related cockpit seat hatches. Even when the cockpit is at deck level, it is no cure to cut through the coaming, since this merely lets water in from the windward deck. There should be large capacity scuppers, which lead athwartships outboard and drain when the boat is heeled. The seat area should drain

into a T-section of the cockpit well which provides almost unlimited capacity.

3. *A number of boats have a useful and convenient locker in the wide type of coaming associated with the modern glass construction. There is no easy way to provide drainage for such lockers.* You need an internal drain and some floor filling to provide an incline toward this scupper.

4. There are many excellent diaphragm pumps such as the Edson, Henderson, or Whale. These pumps have a pretty good capacity of handling expected impurities, but do not prevent objects from blocking the pump hose and rendering the pump useless. *No matter how invulnerable a pump appears during a boat show demonstration, it is imperative to provide a cross guard or similar screening device which will prevent large objects from getting into the intake piping without reducing the maximum capacity of the pump.*

5. *The layout of bilge pump discharge piping is a critical detail.* There are many boats that leak excessively in heavy weather. In many such cases, some of this water is coming in through the pump system since the pump valves themselves are not completely foolproof. Miscellaneous solids can and do go through the pump system, temporarily holding the pump valves open. The only sure way to cure this is to have the pipe looped up high, close to the deck and as near the centerline as is feasible. If possible, pump discharges should be above the waterline, which will prevent any tendency to siphon in and will permit you to observe how well the pump is operating.

6. *Deck bilge pumps are too often located inside of one of the cockpit seat lockers, which is the poorest place for access when the pump is necessary during heavy weather at sea. Pumps must be so located that they can be used, cleaned and repaired without admitting any water into the boat.* The best location is on the centerline on the lazarette hatch. Ideally pumps should be arranged so they can be pumped through a tight gland in the after end of the cockpit well. One pump should be located so the helmsman can use it in short-handed sailing to keep the bilges dry, without having to go below. The second pump should be located below deck, so that in extremely heavy weather it is possible to pump without going on deck. In an emergency, both pumps can be used at the same time. Ideally, they should be the same type to minimize the requirement for spare parts. In an extreme emergency, if both fail, it may be possible to steal parts from one to make the other work.

7. *Galley sinks and toilet washbasins should be located so they never* *go below the waterline, even under extreme heel.* It is not good enough to hope that somebody will remember to close some particular valve. Even with such valves closed the sink or washbasin could not be used. Years ago a washbasin well off the centerline could be drained into a toilet bowl, but with restrictions on toilet discharges, this is no longer desirable. Sinks and washbasins should be located high near the centerline. If the sink or basin is poorly located, a spring loaded gate valve can be installed as a temporary expedient, which can be held open to permit emptying.

8. *The toilet should be located with the edge of the bowl 4 to 6 inches above the plane of flotation, which will prevent flooding if the intake valve should fail.*

9. *Too often the toilet seawater intake is placed too high so that either it comes out of water in rough weather, or when the boat is heeled in one direction.* If the intake is located too near the outlet, an undesirable amount of recirculation occurs when the boat is stationary. The intake should be down low and reasonably near the centerline. The outlet should be positioned higher up, and further aft.

10. *The toilet discharge line should be looped inboard,* well above the waterline, so it still performs its protective function, even when the boat is heeled.

11. *All tanks, both water and fuel, should have provision for sounding and marked sticks should be furnished.*

12. *There should be provision for cleaning all tanks except the gasoline tanks.*

13. Tank vents seldom get the thought they deserve. *Fresh-water tanks should never be vented on deck since this provides a possibility of salt-water contamination.* The vents should be located reasonably near the centerline, and arranged so they discharge into a sink or washbasin that drains overboard. There should be a separate vent for each tank. To make sure that each tank is completely filled, continue filling until the vent overflows. Fuel tanks should invariably be vented to the deck, and positioned where the normal air flow does not carry vapors back into the cabin.

14. *A well-planned arrangement of all through hull openings will insure a safer and more efficiently operating craft.* For example, toilet intake seacock must be at a point where it will be well below the waterline, under all conditions. This also applies to the engine-cooling water intake. Overboard drainage from sinks and washbasins should be straight to facilitate cleaning. Frequently a toilet *intake* can be tee'd to the same seacock that is used for the basin drain. Cockpit scuppers should be above the waterline, which not only decreases the possibility of leaking, but assures that any fuel vapor in the cockpit will drain away. It has already been mentioned that exhausts should be above the waterline, even when going full speed, and that pump discharges should be above the waterline, where they are visible. Finally, seacocks should be located so they are reasonably easy to service and operate. In all cases, they should be clearly marked in the *full open* and the *full closed* positions.

15. *One of the most universal shortcomings in the fresh-water system is failure to install a high-grade check valve in the lowest part of the supply line leading to galley or sink pumps.* Such a check valve keeps water in the line, and insures satisfactory operation of the pumps, eliminating many unnecessary strokes otherwise required to get air out of the line.

The next category relates primarily to the deck:

1. *A most common fault is leaky cockpit seat hatches which allow a great deal of water to get below.* While it's difficult to build a really tight hatch, reasonable gasketing can help a lot. In addition, large capacity drains should be provided to minimize the time during which the hatch seams are under pressure.

2. *The so-called Dorade vents have been copied in many unfortunate ways.* Boxes must not be too low. The attendant cowl vents must be large enough, and boxes must be correctly scuppered. Scuppers should be in the after face, which is the most sheltered surface of the conventional Dorade box. Further, these vents should never be screened as the use of screens greatly reduces the ventilation provided. Insects do not go through them with or without screens.

3. *Spongy lifelines,* particularly characteristic of fiberglass boats, are largely a by-product of inadequate diagonal bracing on pulpits and gangways. The problem is aggravated by inadequate dimensions of the stanchion socket base and by inadequate pad below deck. The stanchions are often too light and bend in themselves. Another common fault is the almost universal use of closed barrel turnbuckles and/or turnbuckles without toggles.

4. *Gangways in the side liferail are inherently dangerous,* all too frequently having the inadequate diagonal bracing mentioned above. They often have horizontal pelican hooks which if not stretched taut under a lot of tension can be knocked open merely by passing by. The safest scheme and the most economical is to omit side gangways altogether.

5. Since the days of Herreshoff, and later Nevins, there have been relatively few nicely made tillers. *The average tiller is too heavy in the grip area and too weak in the hinge fitting where it takes the greatest load.* The end which one holds in hand should be down to one-inch diameter with a reasonable ball or knob on the extreme end and the sections should increase with more or less straight taper to appropriate size at the hinge fitting.

6. *There are few boats which have adequate winch handle holders* and yet with the present-day boats really designed around winches, it is obvious that well-located and securely stowed winch handles are an absolute necessity.

7. *The correct angling and spacing of cleats* with relation to the winch which they are normally serving can contribute a great deal to the ease and efficiency of handling. A simple rule states flat cleats should be turned 10 degrees counter-clockwise from the oncoming line so that the first turn around the cleat is made clockwise just as the turns are made around the winch. It is desirable to have a minimum of 2 feet between cleat and winch, though frequently this has to be compromised because of insufficient space.

8. *Bow chocks.* Again we have to look back to Herreshoff, and later Nevins, to find boats built with really useful bow chocks. In general, the chocks are too small, too weak, with edges too sharp, many of them designed apparently with the thought that the line will always pull straight out ahead. In reality, it's just about always going downward and may swing in an arc of more or less 180 degrees. European boats suffer from rollers which often have inadequate and sharp cheeks. These work moderately well for a chain if it's leading straight ahead, but the chain can jump the roller if the boat is swung around by the tide as so often occurs. In view of the desirability of using the inherent spring of nylon ropes in preference to chains, it is also important that there be no sharp corners associated with either the chocks or chain rollers which might chafe the nylon.

9. *In spite of many ingenious arrangements, there are relatively few hatches that are in themselves really tight in extremely bad weather.* It is important to get ventilation, and the only way that a hatch can be kept watertight and also offer some ventilation in moderately bad conditions is to be fit with a tent-type cover which is absolutely tight on each side and across the forward edge. A rabbit to retain the edges of this cover, with a continuous inner lip around three sides of the hatch and with the outer lip simply broken at each corner to facilitate installation of the cover, is a very necessary basic provision in connection with all hatches. An exception is the lazarette hatch, where any small leaking can be much better tolerated. Moreover, that hatch is located in a basically protected area.

10. *Genoa sheet tracks should have numbers presumably on every fifth location hole and the sliding members should travel easily without one's having to resort to kicking or the use of a hammer.* Best results can be obtained when the location member (a sliding stop) is divorced from the actual sheet lead member (a sliding block). With this arrangement, the locating unit can be easily released and relocated while the heavily loaded sliding member is temporarily kept just clear of the locating unit.

11. *Compass alignment* should be considered a pretty simple detail, but is seldom right on the mark. Frequently, raising the compass can improve visibility and reduce forces that cause deviation. A higher compass location is far more suitable for taking bearings.

12. *With further regard to the compass, the use of built-in correctors should be avoided.* A properly located compass, in other than a steel hull, can frequently be "dead-beat" with no magnets at all and this is, by all odds, the best arrangement. Built-in correctors often introduce an error of their own. Instruments must be kept somewhat further from the compass than the instrument manufacturers optimistically suggest. This also applies to such things as fire extinguishers, magnetic curtain rods, bows for bridge deck companionway hoods, and many stainless or chrome-plated winches.

13. *Few boats have really effective and tight mast coats,* but the job is basically simple. It requires the use of neoprene as a water barrier and then a protecting coat of dacron to protect the neoprene from the deterioration created by sunlight. The most vulnerable joint is at the upper end of the coat where it fits around the mast itself. An extra long stainless steel hose clamp, protected by the dacron cover and backed up with some good silicone sealer, can make an absolutely tight joint. If the mast must be removed, the joint should be broken around the deck collar without disturbing the seal around the mast.

14. *Spinnaker pole chocks are frequently less than optimum.* The right type has a sort of streamline sheath that fits over the inboard end of the pole. The outboard end is held in place using its own hook. The pole should be placed where it interferes least with the usable deck space. The old-fashioned saddles, each located about a quarter of the way in from the ends of the pole, leave pole ends vulnerable, which not only can cause a bad tack, but may actually tear the spinnaker pole from its chocks. A loose pole can easily be lost overboard.

15. In general, similar provision must be made for a *boat hook* on deck forward, and for a *jockey pole* in an out-of-the-way place. Where possible, it's a good practice to stow the jockey pole below deck, though handy to the forward hatch.

Rigging and Fittings

1. A cotter pin can provide a very safe way of securing many connections in the rig, but because of failure to follow simple rules, the cotter pin is often unfairly disparaged. For good results the pin should be cut so that from just inside the head to the tips, the length will be one and one-half times the diameter of the pin in which it will be installed. Having been cut to length, the ends must be carefully rounded with a smooth flat file so that there are no sharp corners. When cotter pins have been put in place, they should be opened very slightly, each side bent only about 10 degrees, and never bent right back against the pin. By properly controlling the length, the opening, and the sharpness, there is little likelihood of creating damage, but nevertheless all cotter pins should be taped. There will be much less tendency for them to come out through the tape and less tape will be needed to cover them if they are short, smooth, and not excessively bent.

2. The lower end of all standing rigging should have toggles and a toggle should be included in the upper end of the headstay as it may be pulled considerably out of line by the headsails attached to it. Toggles should also be included on life line turnbuckles as turnbuckles are strong in tension, but very vulnerable to bending loads.

3. The commonly used double-plate mast tangs are more often than not improperly beveled. Apparently, the underneath plate is brought out close to the line of its shroud. The upper plate has a double bend in it to make room for the width of the upper eye. All the offset, or most of it, is thus in the outer plate. When such a tang is heavily loaded, the outer plate gives and lengthens more as it tends to straighten out. The underneath plate is already straight, so the pins then are no longer square with the load and considerable basic strength is lost.

4. It is my firm belief that closed barrel turnbuckles should be completely outlawed. I don't feel they're suitable for use anywhere, and the same reasoning applies to compression lock nuts, which necessarily slack up when the turnbuckle is heavily stressed. If the lock nuts don't slacken up, then they must have been so tight they were applying additional undesirable load to the turnbuckle threaded section.

Furthermore, there is no way you can tell by looking at them whether they are doing their job or not. A cotter pin, by contrast, is either in place or not. Another important defect of the closed barrel turnbuckle is that it is difficult to see how much thread is buried. When it is necessary to slack a shroud or stay a little bit to get the correct mast trim, you may be getting dangerously near the end of the threads. If you can't see that, you may have an unnecessary accident.

5. A similar situation prevails in the rod rigging fittings, the majority of which are what could be termed "closed barrel," as opposed to having slots which enable you to observe whether there is sufficient thread in the terminal to be safe. Again, the same comments regarding lock nuts and cotter pins apply.

6. It seems logical to install turnbuckles and terminals on rod riggings so the right-hand thread is downward. If that is done, one tightens with the normal motion used in putting a screw in. When all turnbuckles and terminals have been threaded this way it is very simple to tighten or loosen any piece of rigging with confidence. All too often, however, it is either hit or miss, some one way, some the other, and occasionally all are what I would term as "upside down." After carefully studying the mast, you want to tighten one turn here and slacken half a turn there. You think you've got it, but when you look at the mast again you find it is considerably worse. Then you know that the turnbuckles have been carelessly installed, making the adjustment problem unnecessarily difficult.

7. A great majority of present-day boats are rigged with internal wire

main clew outhauls with various schemes for applying tension. Almost none of them has any scheme for replacing the wire, short of a real ship-yard job. If you have the good luck of the wire's lasting a reasonable length of time, it will be all the more difficult to get the end fittings off the boom to make the necessary replacement. Where roller reefing is in-volved, the screw type of outhaul should last the life of the boat, and where roller reefing is not involved, then the old-fashioned wire tackle, on the outside of the boom, is perfectly acceptable. It is very easy to ob-serve its condition, and when necessary, to make a replacement.

8. It is astonishing how many boats, and particularly those equipped with single lower shrouds near the mast centerline, have a dangerous lack of clearance for mast and boom at the gooseneck when the boom is all the way out. Obviously, with such extreme leverage the gooseneck is going to break and an unnecessary and disabling accident will occur.

9. There are innumerable places where one piece slides on another, as for example the main gooseneck, spinnaker gooseneck, genoa leads, not to mention mast tracks and boom tracks. In all cases, both the track and the sliding member must be well polished and all exposed edges ade-quately beveled so that minor temporary misalignment will not cause a hang-up.

10. Roller reefing is considerably in vogue and frequently combined with a sliding gooseneck, but unless the slide is somewhat longer than standard, one can scarcely expect the slide to operate when the sail is reefed and considerable torque is placed on the slide, through the goose-neck. Again, smooth finish and adequate beveling will help this situation.

11. Where there is a sliding gooseneck it is difficult to have the sail track come right down to the top of the boom when the boom is in its lowest position. It is very desirable to do so, however, and provision must be made in the design of the gooseneck track and the sliding member to accomplish that result. It is the only way the sail can be neatly and safely furled in very heavy weather, particularly when offshore.

12. On any boat that will sail offshore, there should be a gate just above the stacked mainsail to permit setting a storm trysail. With roller reefing, the gate also permits sail slides to be taken off in case very deep reefing is required. Unfortunately, these track gates are seldom properly aligned, nor are their edges sufficiently beveled. Frequently, they are lo-cated so high that they're unnecessarily difficult to operate and occasionally so low that the trysail cannot be bent on without letting a good part of the mainsail come completely adrift. The pins and whatever scheme is used for locking them should be securely retained so there is no chance of losing them, as the gate frequently must be operated in very adverse conditions.

13. The same general comments apply to track switches, which are helpful on large boats to permit a trysail to be set near the deck on a track that is displaced to one side. As it goes up, it can feed back into the mainsail track, thus saving the additional weight of carrying a separate track all the way up the mast for the luff of the storm trysail.

14. Presuming the mast is stepped in the keel and passes through the deck, great importance must be attached to properly securing the mast as it passes through the mast partners. Fore and aft positioning should be very secure, as there is generally a long panel from the deck up to the headstay. As the boat works through a head sea, the great tendency for the mast to jump fore and aft can be minimized by proper wedging. At the same time, fore and after rigidity can be coupled with provision to let the mast move slightly sideways to reduce the inevitable localized bending and fatigue as the mast moves over to take up the stretch in the windward shrouds. Live rubber wedges, each 25 percent of the available space and about 110 percent of the fore and aft clearance, should be installed, one in the fore centerline and one in the aft centerline. The second wedge must be put in after considerable pressure has been applied to the first. This system will be quiet and provides optimum support for the mast and the deck as well.

15. A majority of the larger boats have considerable wiring for lights and instruments in the spars, which is generally pretty vulnerable. Wires tend to be damaged when the mast is either stepped or removed under other than ideal conditions. A good arrangement is a longitudinal hole that permits the wire and all terminals and connectors to be stuffed inside the mast where it is adequately protected from any damage while the mast is being stepped or removed. The wires can be fished out after the mast has been stepped. The necessary connections can preferably be made on the underside of the deck, sufficiently away from the mast partners to be unaffected by leaking.

16. The average boat, particularly the one that is not racing-oriented, generally has the mast heel too far forward with relation to the position of the masthead. Assuming the mast is kept in the center of the partners, the fore and aft adjustment of the heel has profound effect on the fore and aft position of the mid-point of the mast. If the middle of the mast tends to come aft under pressure, moving the mast heel further aft immediately tends to push it forward without any adjustment to fore and aft rigging other than the lower shrouds, if they are double.

17. The rope and wire splice is more often than not very badly accomplished. When done properly, the splice should last just as long as either the rope or the wire that is involved. It requires no external serving. Its overall diameter will be just less than the diameter of the rope plus the diameter of the wire. All too often, it is instead a very bulky and rough job, which starts to come apart the first time the boat is sailed. It is dependent on yards of external serving, which has a very short life, and which starts to come off also before the trial trip has been completed. A poor splice is invariably bulkier than necessary, and usually too wide to go through the sheaves or blocks provided. Finally it is apt to jam up completely when one strand of the wire pokes out and gets on the wrong side of the halyard block or sheave. The right splice takes more skill, but doesn't take any more time or any more material, and is basically not more expensive.

18. The conventional wire splice is probably most durable for jib halyards, but it should be no longer than five tucks, and should be served with multi-strand flexible stainless wire over light taping. The serving should be just long enough to cover the splice. These precautions are planned to permit maximum hoist with minimum chance of damage or failure.

19. The length of the wire in the halyard is very critical. The headsail halyards should have 3½ turns on the winch, when they are 5 percent of the fore-triangle height down from the maximum possible hoist position. The main halyard should be just long enough so the halyard shackle can be attached to the lifeline leaving a bare minimum on the reel winch. Additional wire just makes it more difficult to get the wire neatly started on the reel whenever the halyard is used. In general, headsail halyards have too little wire, and main halyards too much.

20. A lot of effort and money are wasted on running rigging that is either too short or too long. The short rigging is useless and hence wasted. Of course, overly long rigging creates unnecessary expense, and makes it harder to organize, sort out, and coil down.

21. One of the most unnecessary difficulties is for the halyard to come unrove. This can result only because of inadequate bitter end attachment. With internal halyards, a properly tied figure eight knot will do the job; with external halyards, there should be an eye that the end of the halyard can be passed through and the same figure eight knot made in the end. With such treatment, it is easy to take turns out of the halyard when it is being coiled down without fear of the bitter end getting away.

22. A great deal of excellent engineering has gone into many different types of reel winches, but all too few of them have a really shipshape and secure method for bitter end wire attachment. The attachment must at once be secure, yet unobtrusive, and not interfere with the smooth spooling of the wire.

23. As a by-product of the masthead fore-triangle, and with the general acceptance of stretchy luff headsails, the necessity of halyard marking is pretty obvious, but unfortunately, it is all too seldom encountered in the field. Main halyards have been marked for some time, and always should be marked when the headboard is just at the underside of the black band aloft. The use of this mark is pretty well understood. The jib halyard, or halyards, should also be marked, but for a different purpose. Here the marking should indicate when the maximum hoist has been achieved. Any tendency to go beyond the mark does not create a problem of exceeding rating, as would occur on the mainsail; it creates a more immediate problem of causing mechanical damage, and a very real possibility of making it either difficult or impossible to get a headsail down again. The best marking is tightly consecutively hitched waxed synthetic twine, supplemented by paint or nail polish markings above and below. It should be replaced from time to time as necessary.

24. The internal halyard is pretty much accepted; but all too often the exits are arranged with no relation to where the halyards enter the mast aloft. This can create extreme difficulty in replacing internal halyards, as will invariably be necessary from time to time. Halyards that go in the forward part of the mast should come out forward of halyards which go in the after part of the mast. This is a matter of simple logic, and only requires somebody to think it through clearly.

25. Whether the mast be wood, or as more common today, aluminum alloy, it is imperative that the mast track be straight before any steps are taken to rig up or step the mast. If the mast is delivered with a straight track, it is very easy indeed to adjust the rigging, so the mast will stay essentially straight under a wide range of conditions. If there is some misalignment, because of extrusions that are not fair, butts that are not fair, or tapering that is not fair, there is no way in which the defects can be corrected by tuning.

26. The rig of any modern boat pretty well defies very effective climbing aloft and thus puts a lot of importance on the boatswain chair. These tend to have many common faults. The most serious is no boatswain chair at all. The next is rope straps that are too long, so that when the halyard is two blocks, you are still far short of the area that you want to inspect or work on. These straps should be synthetic to eliminate danger of rot if stowed damp, and they should be so short that the chair is pretty tight for the biggest person that may use it. This gets you up good and high. The straps should have a metal ring sufficiently small to be easy to use in connection with almost any type of end fitting on a reasonable halyard. The seat part of the chair should not be varnished, nor should it be made overly rough. The former is too slippery and the latter destroys the pants of the unfortunate individual who has to use it.

27. It is all but impossible to properly sail a boat without access to a reasonable number of small lines, as well as sail stops. All too often, there is nothing but a coil of large and expensive line, which is entirely unsuitable for securing the boat hook, or the lee runner, or for tying up a genoa jib after it has been folded. A small bag marked "small lines" and filled with a reasonable assortment, diameters from $1/8''$ to $3/8''$ and lengths from one fathom to two or three fathoms, will be worth its weight in gold.

28. Adequate lubrication is a very important requisite of the modern rig. The best material for threaded parts, and pins, is Anhydrous Lanolin, a product available in drug stores. If turnbuckle threads are thoroughly coated, prior to initial installation, and the entire turnbuckle including pins and toggles covered with a dacron boot, one good job of lubrication should do literally for four or five years. The same applies to pins which connect the toggles to the chainplates, the upper terminals of the standing rigging, and all parts of the rig where there may be motion, and where without lubrication, there will be unnecessary and considerable wear.

29. Most boats have a pretty good arrangement for genoa sheets, frequently using a sliding lead sheave, which is effective and reliable. On the other hand, for small headsails, too often there is simply a conventional diamond base padeye intended for a snatch block. In the heavy weather, for which the small headsails are planned, it is important to have a sheet scheme that is dependable, and here there should be a block made right in the screw eye which should go into an otherwise flush padeye. This arrangement protrudes above the deck only the thickness of the surface flange. Use of a snatch block will only invite the probability of the block flogging open, usually just when the sheet is badly needed both to keep the boat in control and to save the headsail from flogging itself to pieces.

30. One way that considerable economy can be accomplished along with improvment of the product is to eliminate splicing in running rigging. It is much better to tie in rope halyards, and rope sheets, and guys. This permits end for ending in the event of chafe damage and to equalize wear. In the case of the mainsheet, it is very simple to unreave the sheet by simply taking out the knot and pulling it out the short way. If there is an eye splice, the end first has to be unshackled, and then the entire sheet pulled out through the blocks the long way.

The final category contains a few suggestions relating to sails:

1. Battens are almost invariably too light for the three lower pockets, and too stiff for the top pocket. The best arrangement is a more or less indestructible, considerably tapered fiberglass batten for the top that is very flexible at its inner end. The center battens can be well-tapered wood or glass, and should be a lot stiffer but still have some taper. The lower batten would be generally similar, but should be fiberglass, particularly in conjunction with roller reefing, so that when it is rolled around the boom, it will not suffer damaging distortion.

2. Leech lines generally create an unnecessary requirement for more corrective work. They should be sized in keeping with the job they are intended to do, and the length should be reasonably controlled to save the need of cutting at the time of trial and the attendant need for heating to prevent the line unlaying. No sail, with the exception of spinnakers, should be furnished without leech lines; and these lines should be used to prevent undesirable flogging, which seriously wears the stitching.

3. There is a standard complaint about sail stowage, as it is much easier to sell a boat with more staterooms and berths, but big headsails are still necessary to make the boat go. All of this points up the desirability of learning to fold the sails, generally by the foot, flaking them down, and then rolling them, either from the luff or the leech very tightly indeed. When this is done, the sail occupies less than 25 percent of the volume an unfolded sail requires. With a little practice, it is pretty easy to do, and it is certainly worth it to let you enjoy what space you do have below deck and help you find the sail you may be looking for when you are in a hurry to make a change.

4. All headsails, which are more than 5 percent or 6 percent short of the full hoist on the luff, should be fitted with appropriate head pennants. In the case of a storm jib there is frequently a tack pennant as well. The combined length of the fully stretched luff, plus the head pennant (and tack pennant, if there is one) should be about 5 percent less than the overall length of the headstay. The pennants should be invariably shackled on, but the shackles should be moused, so an over-enthusiastic crew member will not remove them. The reason for urging the shackle is that it is then very simple to have a head pennant either shortened or replaced with a longer one without having to take the whole sail ashore.

5. The final step after any type of sailing will be to furl the mainsail. Adequate sail stops are needed. The best thing is to have them really long and all the same length. They should be synthetic, so they will dry more quickly, and there should be a full set of spares to replace those that blow away or that may be used for other purposes.

In conclusion, it is hoped that a review of the points mentioned will remind all involved of fundamentally easy ways to accomplish really worthwhile improvements. Certainly, there are many more items of a generally similar nature and the best time to think them through is before the work to which they relate has been accomplished. The following checklist might prove beneficial to boat owners, both actual and prospective.

No one will deny that a yacht is a major investment. Experiences like that recounted at the beginning of this chapter should never occur. With greater awareness of the details that are necessary to make a boat a pleasure to own and sail, prospective buyers should demand that builders deliver a better product.

SPARKMAN & STEPHENS SAMPLE CHECKLIST FOR PREPARATION OF SAILING YACHT FOR LAUNCHING AND TRIALS

I. *BEFORE LAUNCHING,* check the following:
A. *Flotation Marks*—One pair on design waterline and a second pair 12″ vertically above. Furnish 12″ marked measuring stick.
B. *Rudder Alignment and Marking*—Tillers must be exactly centered with rudder. Wheel king spokes clearly marked ex-

actly aligned with rudders. All quadrants and/or yokes to have precise matching marks indicating when rudders are exactly straight.

_____ C. *Ease of Rudder Operation*—All parts of steering system must be absolutely free.

_____ D. *Propeller Shaft Marking*—Double matching marks showing fixed or feathered propellers vertical and folding propellers horizontal.

_____ E. *Centerboard Pennant Marking*—Red marks on pennants at full up and full down positions and green marks, one for $\frac{1}{4}$, two for $\frac{2}{4}$, three for $\frac{3}{4}$ down. Centerboards to be proof-tested to operate freely throughout entire range, and pennants easily replaced.

_____ F. *All Below Water Fittings Flush*—No external screens. Fathometer transducers may be partially exposed only to provide specified transverse bevel.

II. *BEFORE STEPPING MAST*, check the following:

_____ A. *Mast Lighting.*

_____ B. *Proper Function of Mast Instruments*—Precise matching marks on aft centerline fixed part of wind guide and marks for 0°, 30° left and right, 90° left and right, 180° on rotating skirt. Adjust indicators as needed.

_____ C. *Mast Wire Exit*—Center 12″ below top of partners appropriate rotational location.

_____ D. *Bury and Heel Bevel*—For masts aligned with head one percent of fore-triangle height forward of sail plan position. Final rake secured by slight curvature after heel is fixed.

_____ E. *Provision for Moving Heel*—2″ each way for 50′ fore-triangle, similar proportions for other sizes.

_____ F. *Longitudinal Dimensions*—Fore-triangle from main deck line and black bands. Add reference line 2′ above main deck line.

_____ G. *Halyards*—Routing and wire length. Reel winch wires so shackle just reaches main deck line. Headsail halyards four full turns of wire with splice 3 percent of fore-triangle height below sheave aloft. Provision for messengers on all standing ends.

_____ H. *Tangs*—Bolts riveted, nuts smooth. Fit of all terminals and pins and clearance between double-shroud upper terminals. All bevels.

_____ I. *Turnbuckles*—Right-hand thread down. No lock nuts. No closed barrels. Terminal fit upper end and toggle fit to chainplates. All pin diameters and hole diameters to match. Handles for backstay turnbuckles, all greased with Anhydrous Lanolin.

_____ J. *Cotter Pins*—Diameter, $\frac{3}{32}$″ pins to $\frac{3}{8}$″, $\frac{1}{8}$″ to $\frac{5}{8}$″, $\frac{5}{32}$″ to 1″. Length, 1.5 times pin diameter. Ends absolutely smooth rounded and spread never more than 20° included angle. For backstay turnbuckles length twice thread diameter—not spread but secured with lanyards.

K. *Mast Partners*—Shall have a parallel opening with a clearance all around the mast of approximately one-tenth of the mast fore-and-aft dimension, although this may be reduced a little with a very small mast.

L. *Tracks*—Track joints shall be checked to assure that all joints are fair and in exact alignment. Adjacent ends at each joint shall be beveled on all sides and edges so that if misalignment should occur, the beveling will reduce possibility of the slides "hanging up." The gooseneck track shall have strong permanent stopper at the lower extremity, with lighter, removable stopper at the upper end. The sail track shall extend to the bottom of the gooseneck track. The spinnaker gooseneck track(s) should have strong, well-faired stoppers at each end. All tracks should be lightly greased, preferably with white Vaseline. (Note that Anhydrous Lanolin referred to above for turnbuckles is too sticky for a good track lubricant.) All sail slides proof-tested for fit. Track gate for bending on the mainsail shall be at a height just above the top slide of the stacked mainsail, which can be determined by counting the mainsail slides and allowing two to three inches extra. The pins which lock the track gate shall be secured with a serviceable lanyard. If a switch is used with an auxiliary track on the larger boats, the lower junction of the movable member of the switch should be right at the upper joint of the track gate. Proof-test switch with luff slides.

M. *Mast Coats*—One-piece neoprene placed in position on mast.

N. *Spreaders*—Spreaders and spares must fit easily and stand on thwartships centerline with designed dihedral angle.

O. *Spinnaker Halyard "U" Fitting*—Single long cotter pin above nuts, spread 5° maximum, must fit swivel eye in spinnaker halyard blocks and must be *easily* removable without tools.

III. *BEFORE TRIALS,* check the following:

A. *The mast*(s) shall be stepped *rake* as described in II—D above.

B. The *standing rigging* shall be set up, the halyards rove off, and all wires thoroughly cleaned with solvent and rags.

C. The *main* halyard shall be clearly *marked* at the top of the winch drum to show its position when the top of the headboard is right at the underside of the black band, with a tension of about 150 lbs. on the halyard or equivalent to a light-air sailing condition.

The *jib halyards* shall be similarly *marked,* with similar tension, at the point beyond which further hoisting would result in damage to the halyard splices and/or mast sheave boxes.

These halyard markings are most effective if a light piece of waxed synthetic twine is put on tightly with consecutive half-hitches with a small color band of nail polish immediately above and below the servings.

It should be noted that there are different purposes for the main and jib halyard markings. The former is normally used, except in very heavy weather or when sailing with a reef in the mainsail, hoisting the mainsail to this point. On the other hand, the jib halyard markings are merely a warning in case of an over-long headsail, or when a temporary tack is added that could create an over-length situation. It should be apparent that *under no circumstances* should either jib halyard be taken up beyond the marked point. Note that the jib halyards and spinnaker halyard should have Flemish eyes in the standing ends, and the spare jib halyard and spinnaker halyard should normally be removed by pulling through a 2mm or 3mm messenger in place of the halyard. Likewise, a spare main halyard with a small wire loop extending beyond the part having the silver solder for securing to the reel winch (if reel winch is used), can be pulled through from the deck, using the messenger running over the extra masthead sheave.

D. *Bitter end eyes* shall be fitted to the mast just above the mast coat. They should be of a diameter large enough to allow passage of each halyard. Halyards should be retained at bitter end eyes by means of a "figure eight" stopper knot.

E. *Winch handle holders* shall be provided adjacent to all winches, and shall be of a type that permits the handle to be readily removed (without the use of springs or catches), but which will safely retain the handle even under extreme conditions. Generally, there should be a handle for each winch, except where several winches on the mast can use the same handle, in which case one handle on each side will be sufficient. In addition, there shall be a handle holder in a position where the roller reefing crank can be placed temporarily during conditions when reefing gear may be employed.

F. *Lifelines* shall be set tight and shall be tested by letting a heavy individual jump on them (conservatively!). It is important that all end attachments have toggles or other arrangements to provide a certain freedom of movement, so that under no conditions will the wire or turnbuckles be subject to bending. Nylon toggles are *not* acceptable.

———— G. *Fresh-water tanks and fuel tanks* shall be filled, and this opportunity shall be taken to mark the measuring sticks. The stick for water shall be marked every five gallons; the stick for fuel shall be marked for every gallon on small tanks and every five gallons on large tanks.

———— H. *All sails and specified equipment* shall be placed on board and in the position that they would normally occupy.

———— I. *A measuring stick* ¾″ square x 1′ long, divided into inches, shall be prepared and utilized to check the flotation of the boat. By holding the 12″ end of the stick at the upper flotation mark and observing the average point where the surface of the water cuts the stick, it can be ascertained what the actual flotation is in relation to the design waterline. The upper set of flotation markings should be used in this measurement as reference points, as it is not expected that the design waterline markings will be visible when the boat is loaded. The initial flotation should be carefully noted, after which sufficient inside ballast should be added to bring the boat parallel to the designed waterline. However, ballast should not be placed forward of Station 2, nor aft of Station 8. Rather, ballast should be added in greater amount between these limiting points (if necessary) to provide correct flotation. For the benefit of all concerned, the architect should be apprised of the exact amount of ballast and its correct location in the boat after final flotation has been determined.

———— J. Prior to bending on the mainsail, all *luff slides should be beveled* on all edges, to assure slides' passing minor obstructions that may occur on the sail track or at the track joints.

———— K. *Gooseneck slides* must be cleaned and edges beveled and tracks lubricated with Anhydrous Lanolin so they will slide as required.

———— L. *Bosun's chair.*

———— M. *Miscellaneous small lines.*

———— N. *Sail stops.*

———— O. *Rigging tape*—four rolls.

———— P. *Waxed twine.*

———— Q. *Shackles*—a good assortment.

———— R. *Pliers, wrenches, screwdrivers,* and *Allen wrench* for attachment of ends to reel winch. Also, *large Allen wrenches* to disassemble winches.

12. Sails, Your Source of Power

Long ago I became convinced that sails are the most important single factor in successful sailboat racing. I think that 75 percent of the success of a racing boat is attributable to the quality of her sails. Racing sails have the same relative importance to a boat as an engine would to a racing car. Their function is the same, to drive you at the greatest speed.

I don't believe that a talented skipper can overcome the handicap of poor sails, for there is no touch on the helm magical enough to surmount this disadvantage. For this reason, you can't have fair and equal racing competition unless all sails are completely one-design. Other things being equal, if the hulls of two boats are identical and the skippers equally matched, the boat with the better sails will win every time.

Early in my racing, I tried to learn everything I could about sails. Few of us can be fortunate enough to have a professional sailmaker in our crew to achieve perfection, but if you educate yourself thoroughly on the subject of sails, you can come close to this ideal. I suggest that the racing skipper get several books on sailmaking, and learn how sails are put together. If at all possible, I would spend time in a professional sailmaking loft, paying close attention to the workmen as they go about the complicated art of building a sail. Talk with the sailmaker and learn the many factors that distinguish a well-setting, efficient sail. If you are familiar with sailmaking, you will be able to talk

Van Allen Clark at the tiller and Bruce Dyson on the trapeze of the *Tempest* that won the 1973 North American Championship. Notice the nice set of the sails and flat sailing attitude of the hull.

intelligently about changes—to know what can and cannot be done. Sailmakers are more than merchants. They are individualistic craftsmen practicing an ancient and skilled art. If you are cooperative and aware of their problems, your relationship can be a warm, personal one, as mine has been.

SYNTHETIC SAILS

In 1953, the Long Island Sound fleet of Internationals decided to adopt one-design sails of dacron: it was probably the first class in the world to do so. We had been using one-design nylon spinnakers with great success since the inception of the class. Since dacron was a relatively new development, we had the firm of Ratsey and Lapthorn construct a suit of test sails. We sailed a dacron-equipped boat against one with Egyptian cotton sails; we changed boats, we changed crews, and no matter what we did, the dacron-equipped boat proved her superiority.

We worked closely with Ratsey until we had achieved what we considered a perfect sail, and then we ordered 22 identical suits. So they would be as nearly alike as human skill could make them, bolt rope was taken from the same coil, and panels were cut from the same run of cloth. The same cutters, sewers, ropers, and sailmakers were used on all the sails. When we received delivery, there was not one-quarter inch of variation in the whole 22 sets.

The adoption of one-design sails was the greatest stimulus conceivable for the already highly-successful Internationals, and the wisdom of the change was evident. Skippers formerly at the tail of the class, because of poor sail equipment, began to improve their standings markedly. The racing was leveled out, and the skill of the crew and skipper became the greatest factor in winning championships.

When we decided on uniform dacron sails, we agreed that for economy, no new ones would be purchased for three years. The dacron sails stood the test of time, and in seven years only two suits were replaced. New skippers were attracted to the class when they realized they would not have to build up expensive inventories, and everyone was relieved of the irksome necessity of deciding which suits of sails to use for different weather conditions.

Synthetic sailcloth, together with fiberglass construction, will, I believe, prove to be one of the greatest technological developments to come to yachting in this century. Synthetic sails unquestionably make a boat go faster. But synthetic sails still require some special attention if they are to be maintained properly.

After each season carefully check your entire wardrobe. Look at all the stitching on every sail, watching for wear, especially around grommets and where the sail might chafe against standing rigging. Also inspect the luff and leech with care, looking for wear at those important points. If repairs are needed, don't wait until the beginning of the next season, but take them to the sailmaker directly so that he has time to repair them properly. The sailmaker can also clean them correctly, or you can do it yourself by scrubbing lightly with lots of plain fresh water and a mild detergent. Be sure to use a soft surface like a lawn to lay the sail out. Rinse with care before hanging the sail in the shade to dry. Be sure to dry thoroughly before storing to avoid surface mildew. Fold the sail for storage and put it loosely in its bag in a cool, dry place.

When sailing, make sure that the sails are not in the direct sunlight any more than necessary. The ultraviolet rays can weaken the fiber. Store the sails below or use a cover in the case of the mainsail.

One of the most important decisions in equipping an offshore boat is the selection of a sail inventory. This is important for one-design sailors as well, but class rules limit the choice to a great degree.

For most offshore boats, a basic racing inventory will look something like this:

Mainsail	Starcut Spinnaker
No. 1 Light (3 oz.)	Radial Head Half-Ounce
No. 1 Heavy (6 oz.)	Radial Head Three-Quarter Ounce
No. 2	Radial Head 1.5-Ounce (Heavy)
No. 3	Tall Staysail
Storm Jib	Genoa Staysail
	Blooper
	Drifter

Many successful One Tonners will carry 16 to 22 bags of sails, and use many of them during a five-race series.

The first thing to do is select a sailmaker or sailmakers to turn out the wardrobe. Make sure that they have at least an idea of what each one is providing. You might also try and have a sailmaker's assistant and an experienced skipper go out with you on your first sails. Take care to ask as many questions as possible, and have a good idea of what you should be looking for in the new sails. After that, it is up to you.

If you have any problems with the sail, be sure that you call or write the sailmaker rather than taking the advice of friendly "experts" who may not really be the best source of information.

The subject of trim for the mainsail and headsails has been well covered in Ted Hood's excellent chapter.

13. On Sails

BY TED HOOD

If Olin Stephens is the greatest yacht designer of this century then Ted Hood is secure in his place as the outstanding influence on sails and sailmaking. He is the only man in the sport who can do all the things that go into a successful boat and campaign. He designs the hulls and rigs, builds spars and sails, makes the sailcloth on his own special looms, and then steps aboard to take the helm, where he is also a real champion. It is not too much to say that Ted Hood, along with his father, the "Professor," revolutionized the sailmaking business with their tightly woven, strong, and lightweight cloth. The slotted headstay and many innovations in rigging are all Hood products.

My favorite story about Ted Hood again goes back to *Columbia* days. We had many Hood sails aboard and Ted would always come along for sea trials and then recutting and further sailing. As he was squatting on the lee rail looking up at a genoa, he would make a search of every pocket for a scrap of paper to jot down notes on the shape and required modifications to a sail. After finding his paper, the search would begin anew for a stub of pencil. Somehow the notes must have been accurate, as the sails always came back in perfect shape; but how humorous it was to see Ted Hood, the world's greatest sailmaker, searching for that tiny scrap of paper and stub of pencil several times a day.

On Sails

Before I begin this discussion of sail trim, among other things, I would like to make one specific note on articles in sailing books. If the authors of the books, and I mean all of them, could remember all of the things they have written while they are out racing, they would all do very well. Racing is always doing the fewest wrong things and most of the right things, rather than doing anything perfectly.

Sailing will continue to be more of an art than a science, no matter how many technical advances are made in sail cloth, hull construction, or rigging. The proper setting and trimming of sails will also be one of the most important aspects of this art.

A mainsail serves two purposes. It provides lift when you are sailing to windward and it provides drag when sailing off the wind.

The main lifts like a kite as you beat to windward. The air passes over the sail to create areas of differing pressure: higher pressure on the windward side and lower pressure on the leeward side of the sail. The lift is transferred to the hull and the boat moves forward. The proper shape of the sail, along with the velocity of the wind and the sea conditions, determines the speed of the boat.

Sailing downwind, the main is no longer important for providing lift as the force that drives the boat is the drag of the sails in the wind. The main stops the flow of the wind and the boat moves forward, so the area of the main is most important downwind. Its shape is far less important, except when reaching off the wind when a full draft is helpful.

One of the most important steps in sail control is attaching the sail to the spars. The main is fastened along the mast and the boom and attached at the tack, clew, and head. The tack should be attached so that the foot of the main lies parallel to the boom. After the sail is hoisted, look for wrinkles radiating from the tack. If you see them, the tack is too tight and must be raised. The clew also should be attached so that the sail is parallel to the boom. If wrinkles appear at the clew after hoisting, raise the clew also, but use strong fittings as the clew is under great strain. The headboard should lie snugly against the mast. It should not fall away from the spar or jam tightly against the track. In either of these cases, wrinkles will reach into the sail much like those from the clew or tack. If the headboard falls away from the mast, add an extra slide near the top of the headboard or to the halyard. If it is too tight, rework the masthead so the halyard has a fair lead. The leech line should be led forward along the boom through several sail slide grommets and tied on itself with a rolling hitch, where it can be adjusted even when the boom is outboard.

The battens also are important as they support the roach and help to shape the sail. Always use a flexible fiberglass batten in the top pocket, since it is the most sensitive. The thin or most flexible end of the batten should always head forward in the pocket.

The mainsheet, vang, outhaul, traveler, Cunningham, and leech lines are all used to control the shape and position of the main. The line should be trimmed so that it presents a smooth, efficient contour without wrinkles or hard, flat spots.

The draft of the main is important for power. The following are a few general guidelines which, while good points to begin with, are not meant as definitive statements on trim for maximum performance under all possible conditions.

In light winds, from 0 to 10 knots, the main should be full and baggy. The draft should be deep and about 50 percent back from the luff. Tighten the leech line a bit and slack the Cunningham and outhaul to obtain the desired draft. Going to windward, the boom should be on the centerline of the boat, with the sheet eased and the traveler to windward. Of course this varies with the rig and aspect position (length of the boom). Off the wind, use the vang only to steady the boom but don't tighten it so much that it flattens the sail and overtrims the top of the main.

In moderate winds, from 10 to 18 knots, the main still should be fairly full with the draft relatively deep and about 45 percent back from the luff going to windward. Put firm tension on the Cunningham and outhaul. Tighten the leech line only enough to stop the flutter between the battens. Zip in or tie in the reef along the foot of the sail if a flatter sail is desired. The boom should be just to leeward of the centerline with the sheet taut; ease the traveler to leeward to ease weather helm or to tighten a sloppy leech.

Heading off the wind, the sail should be bagged out by easing on the outhaul, Cunningham, and leech lines. Let out the foot zipper or flattening reef. Strap the vang down only enough to take the twist out of the leech. Too much tension on the vang only flattens the sail, which is quite undesirable.

Heavy air, over 18 knots, requires several major changes. The main should be flattened and the draft reduced by one-half to three-quarters and adjusted to keep the draft from moving aft. Tighten the Cunningham and outhaul completely. Tighten the leech line only enough to stop the flutter between the batten pockets. The boom may have to be well to leeward with the mainsheet strapped in tightly. The sail may even have to be luffed in puffs to ease the helm. If the wind really builds, the sail may have to be reefed to balance the helm and keep the boat on its feet.

Off the wind in heavy air still requires easing the Cunningham and outhaul, and using only enough vang to keep the extreme twist out of the leech. The reefs, if any, should also be taken out.

There are three basic rules to keep in mind. First, as the wind increases, the draft of the mainsail is pushed aft and your controls must adjust for this. Second, going to windward the main should be flattened and the draft prevented from moving aft as the wind increases. Third, when off the wind the main should be bagged and made as full as possible.

Tension along the luff, foot, and leech of the mainsail controls its shape and draft. Tightening any one of those will have several effects. Cloth from other areas of the sail (the draft) will move toward the tight area. The opposite side of the sail will loosen and the sail will flatten. For example, if the Cunningham is pulled tight, the luff will stretch. The draft of the sail will move forward, toward the luff. The whole sail will be flattened and the leech will be freed.

The boom vang acts as an auxiliary mainsheet to control draft and twist when off the wind, as the mainsheet doesn't have much downward force with the boom end outboard. Without the vang, the sail will twist off at the top, easing the leech and riding the boom up in the air.

The Cunningham allows a main to be built with the maximum luff length and still be tensioned without violating the measurement rules. The sail is hoisted to its limits and then tensioned within those limits. The Cunningham consists of a simple cringle placed 12 to 18 inches above the tack along the luff of the sail. A line is dead-ended at or below the tack and run up through the cringle and back down. To tighten the luff, the line is tightened, bringing the Cunningham cringle down toward the tack.

The mainsheet and the traveler are really a matched pair of controls and should be adjusted together. In partnership, they control the position of the boom athwartship and the tension along the leech which, in turn, controls the twist.

Going to windward, the boom is usually inboard, very close to the centerline of the boat. The mainsheet and the traveler should be adjusted together to maintain this position. The tension of the mainsheet and the position of the traveler can be infinitely adjusted to adapt the mainsail to changes in wind velocity. Mainsheet tension directly affects the leech. The greater the tension, the tighter the leech. This relationship is one that should be the subject of many experimental practice sessions in tuning your boat.

Where most boats will have only one, or perhaps two mainsails and a storm trysail, the same boat might have several varieties of headsails.

The genoa is a headsail that overlaps the mainmast and is used primarily sailing to windward. For ease of description, they are usually numbered, with the largest a No. 1, the next No. 2, and so on. The weights of fabric also are used, as there might be a 6-ounce No. 1 for general use as well as a 3-ounce No. 1 for lighter air.

The reacher is a high-clewed full-cut genoa used for reaching or for light air windward work with or without a staysail double-head rig. The drifter is a genoa made of light cloth to be used in drifting conditions. The windseeker or windfinder is a super-light headsail usually smaller than the drifter, used in flat calm conditions to keep steerage and headway.

The jib is a headsail that doesn't overlap the mainmast. A storm jib is a small jib made of very strong fabric designed for storm conditions.

Most genoas are described by sailmakers and sailors using the IOR dimensions along the luff and the LP. The LP is the luff perpendicular; the distance between the luff of the sail and the clew along a line perpendicular to the luff. The LP is used along with the fore-triangle base (J) or spinnaker pole length (SPL) to derive a percentage overlap for a headsail. A 150-percent genoa might have an LP either one and one-half times the length of the J or of the SPL, whichever is longer.

When measuring headsails, the area is considered to be the luff length times the LP, divided by two. There is no credit for leech hollow or penalty for extra round in the foot.

The headsail, especially the genoa, must be considered both as a single airfoil and as a part of the total sail plan as it relates to the mainsail.

Like the main, the headsail is an airfoil creating areas of higher and lower pressure as the wind flows over it. The difference in pressure again produces lift, as in the main. Because of this airfoil role, the shape of the headsail is very important.

On Sails

There are four primary shape considerations: first, the leading edge; second, the position of maximum draft; third, the shape of the leech; and fourth, the overall uniformity of shape.

The leading edge should present a smooth, flat entrance to the wind. This allows the sail to be sheeted close inboard and increases the pointing ability of the boat. The angle of attack (the angle at which the sail meets the apparent wind) should allow the sail to luff evenly from head to tack. Since the apparent wind is farther aft at the head than at the tack, the sail must be able to compensate for this.

The draft of the sail should be between 33 and 45 percent back from the luff and vary from full to flat fore and aft while remaining nearly uniform from head to foot. The draft also must be adjustable to make up for wind and sea conditions. A light air sail should be fairly full with its greatest draft nearly 40 percent back from the luff, while a heavy air jib should be very flat with its maximum draft about 33 percent back from the luff.

The after portion of the sail should be flat and not hook to windward. The leech also should be about the same distance from the shrouds from the deck to the upper spreaders.

Overall the shape should be smooth and uniform. The draft should be nearly equal throughout with no hard spots or areas where the sail is overly full or flat.

The aerodynamic interaction of the headsail and the mainsail is almost as critical as the shape of the sail itself. The genoa and the mainsail create a slot when they are properly trimmed. The air that is funneled through this slot accelerates and produces a larger area of lower pressure air on the leeward side of the main. This increases the lift of the sailplan and increases the power of the boat.

The shape of the slot is important to get the most from the two sails. If the slot is too wide, the effect is lost. If it is too narrow, the air slams into the leeward side of the main and backwinds the sail excessively, decreasing its effectiveness. Some backwinding is often desirable. A properly trimmed genoa leech should parallel the mainsail's leech, making the slot a uniform width from top to bottom. This requires constant attention and trimming to achieve the potential of the boat's sails and rig and is often the major cause of a boat's speed to windward.

The shape of the headsail is controlled much like the shape of the mainsail. The controls include luff tension, sheet lead position, and sheet tension.

Luff tension affects the position and depth of the draft in the sail, much like the Cunningham on the mainsail. Often maximum-size headsails are built with Cunninghams to adjust draft. Tightening the luff of the headsail moves the draft forward; easing it moves the draft aft.

The correct sheet lead position is as important for the headsail as the mainsheet and traveler adjustments are for the mainsail. The position of the lead controls the tension in the leech and foot as well as the relative angle of attack of the luff. The position can move fore and aft and also athwartship. The lead position athwartship is termed the sheeting angle and is measured from the centerline of the boat, with the tack of the sail as the apex of the angle. The angle should be from 6 to 10 degrees, depending on the velocity of the wind. A good general rule of thumb for the lead position is: inboard in light air and outboard in heavy air. The main thing is to watch the slot and make sure it isn't too narrow, with the lead too far inboard; or too wide, with the lead too far outboard.

The fore and aft position is equally important. If the lead is too far aft, the sheet will pull the foot too tight, making the sail luff aloft much before it luffs near the deck. If the lead is too far forward the opposite will occur, and the sail will luff much sooner down low than aloft as the boat heads up. The entire sail should break into a luff at the same time when the lead is in the proper position fore and aft. Remember that both the fore and aft and the athwartship positions will vary as one or the other is changed, and they also will vary as the luff tension is changed. Trimming the headsail is a full-time job.

Sheet tension is the other method of adjusting shape. The best advice, until you have experimented with your own boat, is to avoid either extreme of trimming too hard or easing too much. Overtrimming stalls the air in the slot and distorts the shape of the headsail. Too much ease will decrease the boat's pointing ability.

Different headsails and conditions require varying trimming techniques for top performance. The best way to accumulate the data you need to make the right decisions is to practice. Here is a suggested routine.

Start on a day with a light to moderate wind, between 5 and 10 knots apparent wind. Hoist the headsail with the minimum tension, just enough to eliminate the wrinkles along the luff. Set the initial sheeting angle at about 7 degrees, and the fore and aft position to put the lead at a point that is a natural extension of the leech. Sheet the sail in close to the shroud and bring the boat up into the wind. Watch the point at which the sail luffs first. If it luffs aloft first, move the lead forward an inch or two; if it luffs down low first, move the lead aft a couple of inches. Keep adjusting until the sail luffs evenly from tack to head.

Now look up the leech from the clew. The sail should be an equal distance from the shrouds from deck to spreaders. If it is farther away at the spreaders than at the deck, move the lead forward. If it is farther away from the shrouds at the deck, move the lead aft.

Move to the transom or the stem (whichever gives you the best view) and look at the slot. With the main trimmed correctly, the leeches of the two sails should be parallel and the slot should be a uniform width from deck to masthead.

If the wind built up to, say, 15 knots, the sail would appear fuller, without any change in trim. The draft would have moved aft, giving the sail a rounder appearance rather than the flat entry and leech that make for a powerful sail. Looking up the leech, the sail will appear to have moved away from the spreaders more than from the chainplates at the deck. To get the sail back to optimum shape, the luff must be tightened, with the halyard or the Cunningham. The sheet may have to be trimmed harder and the lead moved forward slightly to complete the job. The leech should then be back in its proper place.

As the wind continues to build, the sail will reach a point at which the leech cannot be trimmed back into place. That is the time to change to the No. 2 and start the process all over again.

It should be obvious by now that there is an amazing amount of detail to manage aboard a modern racing boat. I think that is one reason why a skipper cannot do it all himself. If he is steering the boat in a tough situation, he needs a right-hand man to assist him by taking care of sail trim, tactical considerations, and all the other things that must be taken care of to eliminate mistakes. All the 12-meter campaigns have taught us the importance of the number two man. He might not be able to order the correct sail change or adjustment, but he will remember it and remind the proper person to make or prepare for a sail evolution adjustment. He will make sure that no one is missing anything. He may not say, "You do this and you do that," but he will say, "Don't forget that," and "Shouldn't we be doing this?" He is like a copilot in an aircraft running down a mental checklist.

Another important aspect of offshore racing is navigation. Good and precise navigation, along with proper observation of the racing rules and the regatta requirements, can mean the difference between a win and a loss.

The 1973 One-Ton Cup is a fine case in point. Rounding one mark in the wrong direction lost the world championship for Doug Peterson and *Ganbare*. Even if everything is set up well and the boat is moving fast, the smallest miscalculation in the navigation or tactics department can lose the race or the series.

Referring back to the selection and setting of sails, a truly competitive boat should have one man with the sole duty of calling the trim of the sails. Unless you have an experienced crewman who really knows the boat and its sails you can't really use effectively the 18 bags of sails that many One Tonners carry. You will never have the right one up at the right time and rarely make the correct change early enough.

For example, think of how many times a boat will go around the windward mark and the call for the spinnaker goes up. Before the chute is set and drawing, people will be rushing around to set the staysail. As soon as the staysail goes up, the spinnaker collapses and the boat loses its drive. It takes half an hour for the staysail, working perfectly, to make up for that collapse. The sail-trim specialist could have prevented that mistake.

Let's put this into some logical form. Imagine that you are the skipper of a 30- to 40-foot offshore racing boat. There are many questions that you should be asking yourself as you prepare for the start of a day race around a triangular course.

Is the wind dying or coming up? This determines whether you would use a heavy genoa or a lighter one. It is better to be overpowered than underpowered, especially around the buoys. If the wind is dying, you might want to start overpowered, because there is nothing worse than getting caught in a leftover slop with lighter air and too small a sail. The loss in changing can be too costly. So, make sure that you can reef the main and start with the larger headsail, because it is always easier to take a reef out than put one in after the start.

The above plan can be modified somewhat if you are quite sure of the wind direction. If the weather leg is very short, it is better to start with a large genoa and lug it through the windward work so the larger sail is up for the reaching leg.

As you sail to windward the trimmer should be directing action with a crewman assigned to each control. It is surprising to see the number of people who are really geared up for racing, having traveled a long distance and spent a lot of money to prepare for racing, get lazy on the boat. The crew shouldn't just sit on the rail and observe the competition, they should each have a task to perform, perhaps with a sheet in hand, because sheets should never be cleated. There is no point in running about making a lot of commotion for no reason, but there are many jobs that can be done if a man knows what his duty includes. This is especially true in light air and drifting conditions. On a puffy day, the crew won't have time to uncleat and cleat a sheet for adjustment on each puff. The sails must not be cleated, but trimmed constantly, whether with a large coffee grinder or with a small sheet winch. If you are going to race, then race seriously,

When you arrive at that weather mark, don't be too anxious to hoist the spinnaker. The skipper or helmsman should call the shots because he is the only one in a position to really see and feel all the factors involved. Whether you ease to round or hoist a spinnaker at the mark, wait for the skipper to give the commands. So often there are close calls as the ascending chute nearly fouls the mark, or the genoa as it is eased almost brushes the mark. No one on the boat can judge the proper timing as well as the helmsman. He has the feeling of the boat and knows what chances he can take at any given moment.

As you go off the wind, it is important to have the sail trimmer pay close attention to easing the sails to increase draft, to trimming the spinnaker and staysails, and to ordering changes in the sails as the conditions require. The helmsman should be able to concentrate on sailing the boat, confident that the crew will monitor all the variations in wind and tactical considerations.

The people on the foredeck must be prepared for a quick tack at the mark, setting the spinnaker gear up to allow for this. As soon as the command for the chute hoist is given, the sail should go up rapidly and be trimmed immediately. The first thing to do is to get the guy and sheet manned as the sail goes up. Someone always seems to be playing with the topping lift, fiddling with the foreguy or working with the inner end of the pole before the spinnaker is even full. First things should come first. Someone should be calling the spinnaker trim to the winch crankers, who can't see anything most times because of the mainsail and jib. Otherwise, you may end up sailing along for a minute or more with the chute overtrimmed, and the foredeck crew taking care of the small details, ignoring the major ones. What's the difference if the pole isn't at the right height? That's a small thing compared to having the sheet eased properly and the sail doing its job.

Sometimes there are certain details that must be attended to right away. If it is a dead run, the pole must come back early and if it is rough going, the vang should be set as soon as possible to prevent a flying jibe. The main also wants to go out fairly soon, but the most important thing is to get the spinnaker up and drawing at the earliest moment. The outhaul, Cunningham, and traveler can all wait until the chute and even a staysail are up and drawing right, unless there are enough crew to do it all at once.

It really is a matter of organization, with each man knowing his job. It also is a matter of having one man calling the shots and the crew cooperating with him. Too many people making too many different decisions can spoil an operation. This often occurs with too many competitive sailors on one boat. It turns into a load of indians with no chief.

Well, let's say we have sailed the reaching leg and are now at the jibe mark. If the next leg is a run, we should be ready with the shooter or blooper. This is a hybrid combination of spinnaker and reacher tacked to the stemhead with about a two-foot pennant, the halyard eased from five to ten feet, and the sheet led to the end of the main boom. The mainsail is dropped about half way or more. The shooter makes up for the loss in area of the modern high aspect main by putting up about two-and-a-half times the area of the main. It also steadies the boat on a run by rolling the opposite direction from the spinnaker. You can use it to sail by the lee much more effectively than the usual staysail.

Since this is a triangular race, the run to the finish is nearing its end and the race is about to be won by your boat and your crew and you, because you were better prepared, made fewer mistakes, and kept the goal of the race in mind throughout.

The winning of the race is always the long-term goal of the sailmaker, yacht designer, and the sailor, but there are other rewards as well. I like to sail and was sailing long before I ever made a sail or designed a boat. I have always liked to race and to sail. I also try to keep that pleasure separate from the business side of things. If I had more time and money I would spend more time racing than I do working in the industry. The men who have the knowledge, money, and time to race continuously are very hard to beat.

On Sails

It is getting harder and harder to win races because of new talent, better boats, and keener competition. I can remember when I could do well in a race with three couples and an extra crew, but you can't do that any more. To just finish in the top ten these days you need a top crew on a hot boat with the best equipment and then practice to develop teamwork and expertise. Skippers are always looking for one-design small-boat sailors to crew, steer, and trim sails on offshore racing boats, because the one-designers know competition.

There have been a lot of so-called improvements during the past ten to fifteen years that are what I would call detriments to progress. The constant trend toward stripped-down racing machines continues moving toward extremes which I think could be bad for the sport. It is a case of history repeating itself. The designers of the old J-Boats kept making them lighter and lighter until the boats would last only a year or so. Then some sort of scantling rules were developed to prevent that. I see the same progression developing with offshore boats today. Competition is getting so wicked that someone will end up building a boat like a model airplane—just a framework covered with fabric and doped tightly. We should try to stop this trend before too many good skippers give up and leave the sport.

What I am describing has nothing to do with what design rule is in effect. It happens that the IOR is the one we are using at present, but the same things would happen under the CCA or the RORC. As long as racing competitors become more fanatically dedicated to winning, extremes of design will continue to develop. In the 1930's, the Cruising Club was initiated because people were tired of having to race in 6-meters, R-Boats, Q-Boats, and the like. They decided to take up cruising boats and establish a less fanatical category of racing. This kind of movement is presently taking place in California and other areas. People who enjoy racing, but not in the super-race category, are finding alternate rules and races. The One-Ton level-rating class is a super type strictly devoted to racing. A boat capable of winning in the class can't have much going for it in the way of cruising ability or comfort.

I really enjoy designing boats—it's a fun thing. I designed my first boat when I was about fifteen. It was a small dinghy, and after I built it I made a sail for it. I guess that was my initiation into the business end of sailing. Designing is strictly an after-hours hobby for me, in spite of its relationship to my primary business.

166

Ted Hood studying the set of a seven-ounce No. 2 genoa in a rolling sea.

The first major boat I designed was a centerboard Finnesterre type in 1959. It is still my most successful boat—at least it won more races in a season than any of my other designs. I try to make the design hobby self-supporting by selling the boats after I use them for a couple of years. Then I do another design in a short time to try to offset any loss. Furthermore, if I went to a major designer for a boat, all the other designers in the area would ask why I didn't come to them. All designers are potential customers for a sailmaker.

I also like to experiment with the rigs of the boats. The rig relates to the sails and vice versa, each affecting the other a great deal. Adaptations of the rig in conjunction with sail changes can make a tremendous difference in the performance of the boat.

It is still a thrill to watch a boat of mine go into the water for the first time, even though I already have an idea for another one as soon as the first is off the drawing board. It is always a problem trying to improve the next design. If you design both a new rig and hull, you really don't know if you will have a better boat or not. If you keep one constant, then you have a basis for comparison.

It is extremely difficult to compare the performance of one boat with another. Out on the race course, a slight difference in wind conditions, different helmsmen, and different sails make comparison literally impossible. Everyone seems to jump to conclusions when a boat is performing a bit better. They might have the right reason, but more often they are wrong, since pinpointing what makes the difference is too complicated.

Tank testing is undoubtedly the best way to compare one hull with another, if you have the time and the money for it. When all is said and done, it is the designer's feel for the data of tank testing, his original ideas of design, comments of others, and last-minute practical considerations that finalize his design decisions.

Despite my comments in this chapter on sailing as a science, it is good boats with good sails, good crews, and good luck that win races. As I said earlier, sailboat racing continues to be more of an art than a science, and let's hope it always remains so!

14. Spinnaker Handling

Spinnaker work represents a tremendously important part of yacht racing, and it is here that many skippers exhibit their greatest skills and their greatest weaknesses. I have tried to perfect techniques with this sail so that every detail of its setting is automatic, and to instill clockwork efficiency into my crews.

It is in light-to-moderate breezes that exacting spinnaker handling becomes critical—much more so than in heavy winds. When the wind is really blowing, your boat soon reaches its maximum hull speed. No matter what additional force is applied, no boat can exceed this optimum, which as you may know, is 1.34 times the square root of the waterline length. Under no circumstances, however, do I recommend the elimination of a spinnaker in hard breezes, except during ocean races in heavy seas. There are always lulls in the hardest breezes in which the spinnaker can be advantageous. In a lull the apparent wind will shift forward due to the spinnaker's relatively large effect on the boat's speed. You should head the boat upwind to maintain speed rather than have the trim changed, although the trim may have to be changed if it is a persistent lull. The opposite is true as a puff comes up. The apparent wind moves aft and you should head the boat off the wind more and ease the sheets to stay in the puff longer. It's vital to realize that in hard winds the spinnaker must be sheeted very hard, making it as flat as possible, to prevent the boat from rolling to windward. When the breeze drops to gentle zephyrs, however, every additional ounce of thrust you can extract from that spinnaker will make the difference between winning and losing.

The downwind leg is where the spinnaker man really earns his keep, and if you have a first-rate man, you are fortunate indeed. This crew member must have the talent for intuitively anticipating the next cat's-paw, he must have the patience needed for making endless minor sail adjustments, he must have a delicacy of touch that permits him to capture every little waft of breeze, and he must be an agile, experienced sailor. You must have complete confidence in him, for while you are at the helm concentrating on your sailing, it is impossible for you to supervise head-sail work. In fact, you are intruding in the spinnaker man's domain if you habitually interfere in foredeck work. Once you are satisfied that you have picked a good man, turn the headsail work completely over to him. Don't try to be both skipper and first mate; it won't work. Voice your displeasure if something isn't being done to suit you, but then leave it to the spinnaker man to improve conditions on his own.

Training and Drill: The Key to Success

As soon as the committee signals your course, you should immediately run the compass course of each leeward leg and determine on which side the spinnaker will be carried and at what angle.

You must perfect the operations of setting the spinnaker, getting it down, and jibing it, and you must try to do these things in the least possible time. Now these things are rather elementary, but let's discuss each operation anyway, for nothing is as simple as it first sounds.

If your spinnaker is drawing a few seconds before your competitor's, you have gained just that much advantage over him. So you should aim for smoothness, speed, and accuracy in setting. The sail should be perfectly trimmed as it fills, and the jib lowered, in one smooth operation. The only way to do this is by practice—continual hard drilling. You must have mentally and physically prepared for setting the spinnaker long before you have approached the weather mark. Plan your tactics ahead of time, so when the order is given the operation will be performed smoothly.

The light or heavy spinnaker gear—whichever you have selected—and the pole will have been rigged before the start. The sheet should be gradually trimmed in as the sail is hoisted. Be sure you don't trim too quickly, or the spinnaker will fill prematurely and be difficult to hoist.

The goal of smartness and efficiency should also hold for lowering the spinnaker. It should come down quickly, without snags or hitches. Simultaneously, the jib should be hoisted and trimmed in one smooth continuous motion. The pole and spinnaker gear must be stowed if there are no further leeward legs to be sailed. Again, anticipate the actual maneuver when approaching the leeward mark, and have everything in readiness for the change of course, including yourself and the crew.

Spinnaker jibing is a powerful weapon in the arsenal of the racing man who can execute the maneuver quickly and properly. Jibing is simple in theory, but in yacht racing, the most hopeless foul-ups happen during this maneuver. You must constantly practice jibing by taking your boat out in different kinds of weather on a simulated racing course. Every man must know his job when going from jibe to jibe.

During the 1958 America's Cup races, *Columbia,* like the old sailing men-of-war, had a written station bill that ensured that every hand knew his position during each maneuver. If necessary, do the same for your boat so confusion doesn't reign. There is really no standard way that jibing techniques can be written down to the minutest detail. Each skipper must work out the procedure that best suits him and is within the capabilities of his crew.

Jibing from reach to reach is usually termed the "free-wheeling" jibe. It is the most difficult jibe of all, especially in a fresh breeze. Precision crewwork is most necessary. In this maneuver the sheet is eased, the spinnaker pole fitting removed from the tack, the pole dipped under the jibstay, and the fitting snapped onto the former clew, which has now become the new tack. For a brief moment during this procedure, the spinnaker is not attached to the pole, and the sail is in danger of collapsing or twisting upon itself unless, by careful helmsmanship, it is kept filled. The tiller must be put over at exactly the right moment. As the main boom swings over on the new tack, the sail should not break. It takes long practice by the crew to make the free-wheeling jib an effective part of your racing repertoire.

In your spinnaker practice sessions, be organized. Keep a critical eye open for methods that are cumbersome and require a lot of fumbling back and forth: simplify so there is no wasted time or motion. Keep a stopwatch from start to finish on the setting, lowering, and jibing, and seek constantly to shave seconds from your time. As I related earlier, during the 1961 International One-Design Class alumni race, when I had gotten together a crew of youngsters from the *Columbia,* including my son, I glanced over my shoulder to make sure we would clear the buoy

Etchells 22's downing spinnakers to round during the 1973 Nationals.

mark for the downwind leg, and by the time I looked forward again there was the spinnaker up and drawing. The setting didn't take the boys over eight seconds: that's my idea of smart spinnaker work!

George O'Day, one of the finest small-boat sailors, has even gone so far as to get a friend to take movies of his boat in action. He then analyzed them, with the crew present, to see how performance could be improved. His record in small boats has proved the efficacy of this kind of attention to fine spinnaker handling.

TRIMMING THE SPINNAKER

There is a knack to trimming a spinnaker so that it pulls most efficiently. You want to get the sail up as high as you can, where it can catch the flow of the least-disturbed air possible. It should be set so that it lifts as high as possible with the wind; when the thrust is forward and up, the sail is developing its greatest pulling power.

The spinnaker man should not gad about the deck during a run, but should stay on the foredeck where he can watch the spinnaker's every ripple. In very light weather he must "play" the sheet with all the subtlety of a violinist, keeping it always full and drawing. He must watch the luff carefully, for it is here that ripples or a breaking of the spinnaker will show the first sign of wind change. The sheet of the spinnaker should be well flowed—eased out so the clew lifts as much as possible. Frequently, a smart yank on the spinnaker sheet will restore the contour of the sail if the airs are extremely light and it tends to collapse.

The spinnaker man should also glance constantly at the masthead fly, or permanent backstay tell tale, to make sure that the pole is always trimmed at right angles to the wind: the wind may back or veer a few points, and the trim must be adjusted accordingly. These flys are the surest indication of the apparent wind. Flys in the shrouds are of no use for gauging spinnaker trim, because stray air currents from the mainsail deflect them and they will not accurately indicate wind direction. These, however, should be used as indicators under reaching conditions.

When the breeze drops to vagrant puffs, the weight of snap shackles and heavy sheets will sometimes prevent the spinnaker from standing. A trick is to remove the heavy gear and tie a light but strong cord to the clew. Hold it in your hand, giving and taking with the varying strength of the breeze. You will be surprised how this will ghost you along when the puffs are hardly discernible.

To be properly set, the spinnaker pole should always form a right angle with the boat's mast. The exception to this is sailing on a close reach: here it is advisable to cock the pole so that the sheet can be flowed as much as possible. On a reach also, it is important to slack the spinnaker halyard slightly until the upper leech clears the jumper strut stays.

The foot of the spinnaker, from clew to tack, and the outboard end of the pole should form a straight line parallel to the horizon, no matter what the heeling angle of the boat. It is the horizon, not the deck of the boat, that should be the line of reference for the spinnaker foot, and adjustments should be made until this is so.

THE SPINNAKER IN HEAVY WEATHER

When sailing a spinnaker reach in heavy weather—the helmsman should sail below his normal course to avoid the unpleasant and sometimes dangerous results of broaching. This can easily happen if the rudder rises clear of the water and loses its controlling force, or if the spinnaker suddenly breaks from the lurching of the hull in violent seas. Remember, with a spinnaker your boat is not always as responsive

Ray Hunt is designer and helmsman of *Chaje II* (24), the 1963 5.5-meter World's Championship winner. His spinnaker is well-lifted and perfectly trimmed. The spinnaker on the second boat is larger and not standing as well. It appears that if the sheet were eased considerably, the sail would lift and be more effective. The sheet on the third boat should also be freed. The main sheet could be eased further. The jib is bound to disturb the spinnaker and should be lowered. Even if the wind were on the beam, the jib would still bother the spinnaker.

and maneuverable as when under normal sail, and you must be psychologically prepared for all eventualities. This quality of alertness is one that yachting constantly demands.

In ocean racing during heavy weather, the genoa jib can frequently be set as a spinnaker. It is of much heavier material and will stand up where a nylon spinnaker of lighter material would break—if it could be set at all.

How to Stop Rolling to Windward

In very strong winds, a boat carrying a spinnaker, with the wind dead astern, will sometimes take violent rolls to windward, slatting and breaking her gear, and seriously endangering her crew. This unnatural leaning can be an unpleasant experience, for many sailors do not understand the forces at work. When the boat you are sailing is narrow beamed, this rolling to windward is accentuated and can be quite detrimental to her speed.

The reason for this rolling is that the spinnaker sheet has been eased too far out and is causing the luff of the sail to cup inwards. The wind from aft drives into the center of the spinnaker, and, because of its great force, is deflected around until it strikes the cup-shaped luff of the sail. Here the wind is concentrated with tremendous force and thrusts the vessel down on her beam ends to windward. The luff of the mainsail

As I have said, this is a disagreeable experience. The men of the ocean racing fleet who sailed to Bermuda in 1958 found this to be so to their dismay. The yachting magazines carried photographs of the many knock-downs at the start. By studying these photos carefully, one could see that each of these craft had been pulled over to windward by the luff of the spinnaker, just as if the wind had been blowing from the leeward side.

In my opinion it was not good judgment in the first place to have attempted to carry a spinnaker in those winds, which were of near gale force, because the advantage to be gained was not worth the risk, where gear must be preserved over a four- or five-day race. But once set, they could have been carried *if the spinnaker sheets had been trimmed as flat as possible.*

When the sheet is brought in, the spinnaker is flattened and the cup doesn't form at the luff. The wind cannot exert any thwartships pressure because there is nothing for it to get a grip on.

I realize it is hard to believe that so simple a thing can make such a great difference, but it does. I used to sail a 6-meter with an enormous spinnaker, and one day this very thing happened to me. I was sitting to leeward, when suddenly we rolled to windward in a heavy gust. The next thing I knew, I was up in the air and actually looking straight down at the water *to windward.* I was certain she would swamp as the water was coming in over the weather cockpit coaming. She righted herself, but the experience was the start of an important lesson for me. I finally realized that the problem was caused by incorrect trimming of the spinnaker sheet. After I learned that it should be trimmed hard in strong winds, this seldom happened.

If you sail 5:5's, 6-meters, Internationals, Lightnings, or narrow-beamed boats that carry abnormally large spinnakers, remember this heavy-weather technique with the sheet. It really works.

15. Tuning the Rigging

If your rigging is not well tuned, your boat cannot sail her best. There are many schools of thought on how rigging should be set up for racing. Most of them agree that a great deal of variation in the set of sails can be achieved by different adjustments to the rigging. I am convinced, however, that the most important requisite is that the mast be absolutely straight athwartships. This can be achieved by either slack or taut shrouds.

I prefer to start tautening the upper shrouds first and then the lower ones. I also like the uppers to be considerably tauter than the lowers, for they will carry the thrust of the major part of the rig. I set the lower shrouds much slacker than the uppers. Only by sighting up the mast with the eye at *deck level,* using the track of the mast slot as a guide, can you see the effect of tautening each adjustment.

The jumper stays counteract compression-strain to the headstay. Tauten them until there is a slight forward bow at the top of the mast. Next, set up the backstay until the mast is perfectly straight fore and aft. This is your zero or maximum forward position of the mast. Incidentally, it is a great convenience for adjustment purposes to have the stays lead to a position on the mast where they can be regulated from the deck. Diamond stays support the upper area of the mast, and in my opinion these stays should be set up as taut as physically possible before the mast is stepped.

After preliminary adjusting, take your boat for a sail and turn the helm over to a crew member. Sight up the mast from deck level to be sure it is straight when sailing on both tacks. There should be no inequality whatsoever.

Every time I sail my boat, I marvel at the ingenuity of Starling Burgess, who developed the permanent backstay rig, which I believe first came into being on his Atlantic Class boats in 1929. It is a triumph of modern engineering design, with each member a vital and interdependent part of the whole. With the exception of the upper shrouds, the whole intricate network is designed for one thing—to tauten the headstay so your boat will work to windward efficiently.

I think there is a lot of confusion regarding the functioning of the rig. If, in our imagination, we can follow the sequence of events that takes place when the permanent backstay is tightened, we can obtain a clear picture of the process. As the backstay tautens, the head of the mast comes aft, tightening the jumper stays. The jumpers in turn apply compression-loading to the jumper struts, which forces the upper part of the mast aft. This after movement of the mast then tautens the headstay.

Another case: as pressure fills the sails, the lower shrouds (which are secured to the mast opposite the jumper stays) and the jumper stays tauten. Again the mast is forced aft and the headstay must become more taut. The upper shrouds stiffen the mast so the full sail does not sag off to leeward. They are, however, completely unaffected by strains on the backstay jumpers and the headstay.

You must be careful not to overtauten stays. The word "tuning" makes some people think that shrouds and stays should be so taut that they "sing" like a violin string: this is not so, with the exception of the diamonds, as mentioned. Too much tightening puts an abnormal compression load on the struts and spreaders. When the sail fills, this stress further increases and may reach critical limits. I think a good rule of thumb is to tighten stays only hand taut (again with the exception of the diamonds), just taking up the slack.

The 12-meters use dynamometers to measure rigging and sheet strains. Simpler devices are available for use in small boats.

EFFECTS OF BOWING THE MAST

One of the great virtues of the permanent backstay is that changes can be made in the shape of the mainsail by judicious tightening and slackening of the backstay. When the backstay is tightened the center of the mast goes forward, thereby flattening the mainsail. You will decide the amount necessary by the strength of the wind. This adjustment is, of course, only made for windward work. The mast should be straight for reaching and running where maximum draft is required. Furthermore, tautening of the backstay in windward work makes the jib stand better because the headstay will be tauter. How much bow you will want in the mast depends on the amount of draft you want to remove from the mainsail at the head or along the entire luff. If in your opinion the mainsail is too drafty aloft, slack off your jumper-strut stays from their normal positions, thereby increasing the bow aloft, which will produce flatness in the upper area of the sail. Bear in mind that other compensating adjustments must therefore be made in the backstay and headstay, to arrive at a new zero mast position. A word of caution: *Do not bow your mast aft unless your upper spreaders can swing aft to conform to the new lead of the upper shrouds.*

When it becomes necessary to replace wire rigging, it is a good idea to make measurements with the turnbuckles opened about halfway. Wire will stretch along the direction of pull as it settles down and breaks in. After new wire has been installed, recheck the tuning frequently, and sight-in the mast again for straightness. Tighten turnbuckles as needed to take up the slack from stretching.

Sheet Leads

The position of jib and mainsail fairleads affect the tuning and performance of your boat. The jib should be trimmed on a line about 10 degrees off the centerline of the boat measured from the jib-tack fitting. If your boat is beamy, you may need to place it along a 12-degree line.

To determine the 10-degree line, measure back 5 feet from the jib-tack pin and then 10½ inches outboard from the deck center line, and make a pencil mark. A string stretched through this point will represent the 10-degree line on which the jib sheet fairlead is to be placed. The lead on a genoa-equipped narrow boat such as a 6- or 12-meter would be reduced to 6 or 7 degrees.

I believe I place my working jib leads further forward than most racing men, for I find it makes the jib stand better and gives the foot of the sail a good airfoil shape. Don't worry if this looks strange—as if the clew were too far inboard; if you try it once, I think you'll be pleased at the way it improves your boat's performance. In harder breezes I move the leads a little aft and outboard. I am, of course, referring to conventional working jibs—not genoas.

The genoa mitre is a good guide for the lead. Normally, a continuation of the sheet should fall below the mitre line. In any event, make certain that the lead is not too far aft; if it is, the head of the sail will not stand.

Because I have found so much uncertainty about the proper trim of genoas, I suggest that the sail should never be trimmed beyond a point where the upper spreaders begin to interfere with the set of the sail.

I am a firm believer in the wisdom of using a wide traveler to carry the main sheet lead block if class rules permit. If the traveler extends across the whole width of the deck clear to the rail, you will have a more effective device for trimming the main than is possible with a single midships lead. By fixing the block to an adjustable slide, you will be able to position the sheet lead anywhere along the length of the traveler.

The advantages of using a wide traveler are several. On a reach it should be extended to its maximum; this will flatten the upper part of the sail, permit a wider trim and produce the same effect as a boom vang. For windward work the traveler should be amidships, thereby producing the greatest draft. As the breeze increases, the traveler should be moved out. This lead will tend to flatten the sail and trim the upper area more efficiently. A high-cut mainsail should be trimmed more amidships than a lower-cut sail. Except for reaching, I have found the traveler to be rather treacherous, and again I caution you to limit your adjustments in windward work to normal movements.

Once you have tuned your boat as well as you can at the mooring, take her out against a favorite competitor. Keep experimenting with the things that you have heard, learned, or suspected about tuning a boat's rigging. When you are convinced you have achieved perfection, assist your competitor while he tunes his boat. I have profited in this way on many occasions by sailing tuning trials with William S. Cox, an excellent helmsman in any size boat, and especially adept in tuning his boats well.

Use a Boom Vang

There is hardly a sailboat that cannot be improved by fitting of a boom vang, or "boom jack," as it is sometimes called. The refinements of sail trim that you can get by using it are many, and it is especially valuable off the wind. If your boat is not already fitted with one, and the class rules do

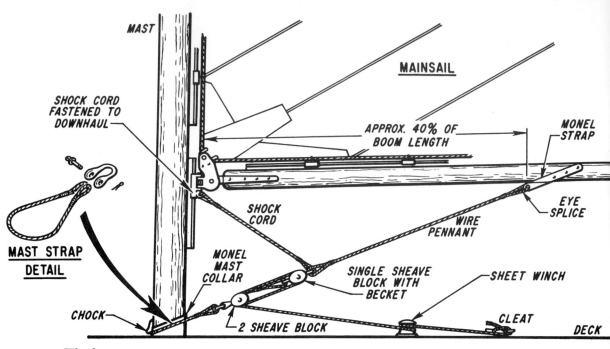

The boom vang.

not prohibit it, I would certainly urge you to try one of these effective devices. The accompanying diagram shows in detail one way a vang can be made and fitted.

The vang keeps the boom from lifting when the mainsail is suddenly filled by a gust of wind or the boat lurches from a violent seaway. It allows the sail to swing in only one plane like a door: all the power that would otherwise be wasted is captured to drive your boat ahead. The sheet can be eased much further without luffing if a vang is used. A mainsail always luffs aloft first, and must be trimmed to remedy this condition. The upper and lower areas of the sail will luff simultaneously if a vang is used, and this is a decided advantage. In light airs you need as much draft as you can get, so do not set the boom vang, for it flattens the sail too much.

Because a boom vang exerts enormous strain on the boom, and because all fittings must have a large built-in safety factor, I would use oversize hardware and through-bolt the gooseneck track and mast. The bolts should be of small diameter and widely spaced so the mast is not weakened by excessive drilling.

Arthur Knapp, Jr., skipper of *Weatherly* in the 1958 America's Cup trials, a man who habitually gets the most out of a boat in light weather, has capitalized on the use of the boom vang more than any competitor I have ever raced against.

16. Building a Winning Crew

To win races it is necessary to bring together an effective, first-rate crew and mold it into a working team. How well this crew functions will be the responsibility of the skipper. He is the most important man in that crew: there can and must be only one skipper. I know personally of some boat teams that make strategy decisions by consensus of opinion after calling what amounts to board-of-directors meetings. While opinions are being solicited, purposeful, well-commanded boats usually drive by to leave these budding democracies in their wakes. In boat racing, even more than in business, deciding and effectively carrying out policy must be the responsibility of one man. Remember that any third-class seaman can steer a ship but it takes two smart captains to wreck her.

A good skipper must have, or must develop in himself, a peculiar combination of talents and qualities if he is to be successful. Paradoxical as it sounds, I believe the ideal skipper should have a mixture of humility and egotism; he must also have an ability to quickly grasp over-all concepts, and he must have a computer-like memory for detail.

The most necessary of all the qualities for a winning skipper is an intense spirit of competition. A competitive instinct and a will to win are the first requirements for racing success. The man who avoids competition, for whatever reason, had better avoid racing yachts. But if you enjoy laying your talents, your skills, and your belief in yourself on the line to defend against all comers, the chances are you will become a good skipper. You must dislike being beaten, you must feel a sense of pleasure at being the best, and you must have an overwhelming drive to win.

A winning skipper also values his own judgment; he enjoys gambling on his educated opinion. Indecisiveness has to be ruthlessly eliminated from his personality, and after having evaluated a racing situation, he must make decisions as quickly, firmly, and casually as he breathes. The responsibility for the results of these decisions must also rest lightly upon him. Whether this choice results in a win or a loss, the responsibility is his alone, and the blame for a loss should never be divided up or shoved off on the crew—although the credit for a win may be.

Frankly, I never selected anyone for my crew in order to make use of his judgment; first, because I wanted to race the race myself, and second, because I didn't want to race against one of my own crew members as well as 25 other skippers in the class. I had no objection to talking over the fine points after it was over, but I wanted no one to tell me how to sail the boat during a race. Thinking back, I've been very fortunate in that respect. I can only remember once when a crew member started to tell me how to sail the boat, and I will never forget him or when and how he offered his advice. I tried not to offend his feelings, but I told him I was in the habit of sailing the boat, that I didn't agree with his opinions, and that I didn't want any more interference. There was no quarreling or unpleasantness, but needless to say, that was his last sail with me.

Of course everyone experiences flashes of anxiety and momentary doubts, and it requires restraint not to solicit the opinions of others for reassurance. It is also painful to be curt toward your friends and bring them up sharply, but in this respect, you must be absolutely adamant. There can be no equivocation, no vacillating, and no back-talk aboard the boat if you are determined to win races. Every order has to be carried out quickly and willingly, and the man who will not do so must be promptly eliminated from your crew.

Whatever the pressures, a racing skipper has to train himself not to let tautness and excitement affect his decisions. It is forgivable if you get upset once or twice, but make sure it doesn't happen habitually. Even when someone has let go of the spinnaker halyard instead of the sheet, and you see your lead on the fleet evaporating, you must express your criticism only in calm tones. It requires monumental control, but it can be done. If you get mad, your anger colors your decisions, and you might as well leave the race and sail back to your mooring, for you have already lost. You have defeated yourself.

Try to develop a good head for detail. As a winning skipper, you must have instantly available a thousand points of information. You must carry a plan of campaign in your head, a timetable of tide and current changes, knowledge of standings in the fleet, and an awareness of wind and weather conditions for the day. To enter competition with a well-tuned boat, you will have to know about hundreds of maintenance needs. Besides this, you must remember race-committee instructions for the courses, and numerous flag and time signals that will be used aboard the committee boat. Much of this information can be written down; some of it cannot. Often it is the little things that determine whether or not a race is won, so try to train yourself to cope with this mass of detail.

I think so highly of patience as a quality that I named my favorite little sailing sponge boat *Patience*. It is an attribute that can be a great asset to the racing skipper. No one can attain perfection at the first try; if one could, the joy of attainment would soon disappear. If a crew member with promise doesn't do his job right the first few times, have patience with him, and you'll probably succeed by explaining again what you want. Have patience with yourself also if you don't reach your racing goals the first few seasons. No one who sails can ever learn everything. Each time I leave the mooring I can truthfully say that, without exception, I learn something new and fresh and wonderful. No matter how long you sail, this constant newness and reawakening of stimulation will remain. It is one of the great attractions of sailing as a lifetime sport.

Perseverance is an important quality in the racing sailor. You will not go far if you are easily discouraged. You will be competing with some of the most dedicated and accomplished men to be found in any sport—men who talk, eat, and breathe yacht racing. You have to meet them on their own terms and keep on striving despite defeats. A dogged determination must pay off eventually. Even champions make mistakes, and as your skill grows, you will be able to capitalize on these mistakes. In the end, the winner is usually the one who makes the fewest. In any field of endeavor, talent alone is not enough to win if it is not backed up with perseverance. The world is full of talented failures.

Self-assurance and confidence will come to you as you race. The easy casualness in competition that distinguishes champions is the result of years of training and doesn't come about overnight. Frequently it is a façade to disguise violent inner tension, maintained with difficulty. So don't worry about lack of confidence: it comes with achievement, the same as with any other endeavor. Always comfort yourself with the fact that your competitors have for certain the same taut nervousness from which you are trying to free yourself.

THE SPIRIT OF THE BOAT

I believe that there is an almost tangible atmosphere that surrounds each sailboat that might be called the "spirit" of the boat. Composed of a complex of many things, it can be a negative, gloomy cloud or a positive, happy aura of jauntiness.

A good-spirited boat is that way because she has efficiency, harmony, aggressiveness, and pride. There is no greater pleasure to me than to sail on such a fortunate craft. On the other hand, the unhappy ship will carry ineptness, dissension, half-heartedness, and humiliation as an unseen stowaway: she is an unpleasant thing indeed and a trial to be aboard.

Now no boat is born on the stocks with this spirit, good or bad, built into her—it requires the personality of man to animate her. So if you would always run a happy boat, make these your goals:

1. *Efficiency*—Every maneuver smart and sailor-like
2. *Harmony*—Every man a friend and a respecter of the other
3. *Aggressiveness*—Every race your finest effort
4. *Pride*—Every rival respectful of you as a competitor

CHOOSING THE CREW

When you put together what will eventually become a winning crew, you must have people who are not only compatible and agreeable, but also able. You want no one on your team who is not a serious and enthusiastic sailor. The social aspect of yachting becomes entirely secondary; you can have that ashore or in your pleasure sailing. When you're racing, you're out to win, and you want the strongest team that you can procure.

Observe a crew candidate closely before you ask him to join your boat. A casual discussion will give some indication of his potential. Then, for example, you might like the way he rows a dinghy, or be impressed with the way he handles himself on another boat. Your aim is to select men who are handy and perfectly at ease around the boat. By all means exclude the chatty type; nothing is more disturbing to the skipper than empty conversation during a race.

I have known wonderful fellows, pleasant and charming to be with, but cursed with the bad coordination and clumsiness of the accident-prone. If you have a friend like this, spend time with him pleasure sailing, but out of respect for his longevity and your nerves, don't, for heaven's sake, ask him to race with you.

Youngsters make wonderful shipmates, for they are agile and eager to learn. In addition, they are usually pleasant and free of problems, which makes them enjoyable companions. Throughout my racing, I have always tried to have one or two youngsters available as crew members. If they are interested in racing at all, they are the easiest persons to train, and you have the added advantage of their willingness to accept direction without question. You will also have the wonderful satisfaction of introducing a youth to a healthy and fascinating interest.

Don't wait until the last night before the race to pick your crew, and don't fall into the habit of picking up someone from the dock at the last minute. Try to aim for a well-organized crew that will be with you all season. Choose two or three substitutes that can fill in when members of your regular crew are unable to race. Take the alternates out and train them to your method of working. This kind of foresight is a lot of extra trouble, but if you are aiming at becoming a champion, it will pay off.

THE SECOND-IN-COMMAND

When you are sailing to windward, even a mediocre crew can trim the sails to suit you. But crew efficiency is a vital factor when you are sailing off the wind: it is here that the crew makes its most valuable contribution toward winning. This is especially so in spinnaker work.

Your second-in-command, or first mate, whatever you call him, must be chosen with a great deal of discretion. Usually the mate is also your spinnaker man. He has to be experienced and thoroughly schooled in foredeck work and every maneuver or sail change that may be required of him. He must know how to get the most out of a spinnaker and understand what delicate adjustments of trim can do to make your boat go faster. Perhaps he has skippered his own boat in another class or perhaps you may have promoted him from the cockpit crew of the previous season. Whatever his background, he should not have to be trained during a race. You must turn over to him the complete responsibility for running the foredeck and bossing spinnaker handling, so he has to be absolutely competent. If it is your misfortune to have a green spinnaker hand, take care to do your training before the race. Go through an exhaustive practice drill so you don't have upsets when rounding the mark or at a critical moment of the race when there is no margin for error.

I was most fortunate in having the talented Everhard (Ducky) Endt as my first mate and spinnaker man for many years. He and William (Boots) LeBoutillier were superior to anyone I have raced with or against, in their thoroughness and great ability at trimming spinnakers.

17. On Crewing

BY STEPHEN VAN DYCK

One of the best-known men in the 1970 America's Cup defense was Steve Van Dyck, tactician aboard *Intrepid*. Steve was the number two man, whose talent speaks for itself. Bill Ficker, *Intrepid*'s helmsman, calls himself a practitioner aboard a boat, steering the boat at the greatest possible speed and depending on his executive officer for many tactical decisions and a constant input of information. He selected Steve Van Dyck, and the combination worked very efficiently.

Steve has had the same sort of job aboard *Charisma* and several other well-known offshore racing boats with the same results, success. Planning, organizing, delegating tasks, and taking on responsibility are his strong points. He coordinates all the specialists on the boat, building them into a single operating unit. Tactician is much too simple a title for the task that Steve does so well. He is a motivational genius and has undertaken a serious study of the human element in a boat's performance.

Much has been written by skippers for other skippers about winning races, yet, on most boats over 20 feet in length, it is the crews who are responsible for the major part of the boat's performance. The crew must complete a wide variety of tasks effectively if the boat is going to be competitive, and the separate contributions of each crew member comprise this team effort. Boat speed increases proportionately as the individuals improve their skills, and to his end I have compiled a list of basic characteristics and abilities that I have observed in good crew members. These attributes can be acquired and developed through practice. If you keep the following points in mind when you go out for either practice drill or racing, you can develop the characteristics of a good crew while learning the mechanics of racing the boat. Also, I believe you'll find that the more proficient you become, the more you will enjoy racing.

Desire to win is the motivating force that keeps good sailors working every minute of short and long races. This desire has to be strong enough to overcome the physical and mental suffering that accompany competitive sailing from time to time. Additionally, you must have an interest in doing the particular job to which you have been assigned aboard the boat. A crew member who wants to win but does not have sufficient interest in his task to do it to the best of his ability will not be an asset.

A winning attitude is an integral part of one's desire to win. The person with a winning attitude feels that there are no excuses for losing. Generally speaking, if you do not win, it is because mistakes have been made, not because of bad luck, for bad luck is most often man-made. In analyzing performance, you must look hard for the real reason why something happened. More often than not this leads to the conclusion that the mistakes could have been prevented. Such candid analysis provides valuable lessons for the future. These lessons should be examined carefully after each race and become part of your experience, not forgotten right after the finish. (Incidentally, there are lessons in winning, too.)

Alertness should be as automatic to a good crew member as breathing. Only by being alert and paying attention to your area of responsibility (be it tactics, the foredeck, or the coffee grinder) can you be aware of what may need changing or what may actually be wrong. Experience teaches you what to watch and listen for. This alertness on the part of the entire crew is becoming more essential as boats become more sophisticated and the number of possible adjustments increase.

Like many sports, sailing rewards those who are aggressive. Much of competitive sailing is physical, so those who attack their crew assignments aggressively will get the job done more quickly and expertly. This *aggressiveness* pertains to tactics as well as sail handling. Take the fight to the competition by acting first, offensively, by setting the chute first or faster than they do, or by being at the line in the best spot at the start. Crews who merely react or act defensively rarely win races. Closely tied to aggressiveness is *initiative*. A good crew member never needs to be told to do basic things, such as easing the jib when the wind lightens, overtrimming the chute when the boat takes a bad windward roll, or checking to see that all the halyards are clear before and after making a sail change. From the time a good crew steps aboard the boat until it is put to bed, fully ready to race the next time, he does 90 percent of all his tasks on his own initiative. No other single factor separates a superior crew member from a mediocre one as much as initiative.

Coupled with initiative is the *ability to anticipate* what actions might have to be taken next. For example, if the boat to windward is closing from behind under spinnaker, you might expect to have to luff to defend against being passed. This might mean getting an extra wrap on the spinnaker-sheet winch on a big boat or readying the trapeze on a small boat. In a hard breeze, the next smaller headsail on an ocean racer should be ready in the hatch below in case the one that is up blows out or tears. You should be as ready as possible for any impending event, no matter how unlikely it may seem. If the crew is well-prepared, what could become emergencies become routine drills instead. The key is anticipation.

Yacht racing continues to grow in complexity and puts a very high premium on *intellectual capacity and curiosity*. People have differing intellectual interests and attitudes, and in choosing a class or one-design boat to sail on, a crew should make sure his own interests will be satisfied. The skipper and crew of a boat must share the same goals and be motivated by the same drive. Curiosity about how and why the various mechanical parts of the boat work is vital to achieving maximum performance. In the same way, the ability to review and understand how and why something happened the way it did is indispensable to improving crew work and overall racing performance.

Most skippers really appreciate knowing before a crew member comes aboard what his interests are and what jobs he feels he can do best. The speed of learning is in direct proportion to personal interest. This *ability to learn quickly* is essential in racing, since the time available for practice and tuning is normally quite limited.

Physical dexterity is helpful in the execution of any job on a boat. The faster and more confidently you can perform most tasks, the faster the boat will go. This puts a high premium on dexterity and coordination. A major part of coordination is getting around the boat with as little disruption as possible, especially in light air. Even though you may be big, there is no reason why you cannot be light of foot. A touch of Nureyev's style is not unwelcome!

Of course, *physical fitness* is a prerequisite to dexterity and coordination, and it's something that few people consider seriously. On small and large boats alike, there are many physical tasks—from hiking out to cranking coffee grinders. Top physical condition is important because it assures that whatever job you tackle, your cardiovascular and respiratory systems will not be taxed beyond capacity. It enables you to do the assignment more quickly, too. You should tailor a fitness program to the type of boat you plan to campaign.

Preparedness for racing includes having a knife, foul-weather gear, sunglasses, protection against sunburn, warm clothes, and any other appropriate items you may need for the duration of the event, whether it be a day or a transatlantic race. Being improperly prepared prevents optimum output and detracts from the balance of the effort. Another aspect of preparedness is doing whatever you can prior to arriving on board to reduce what you have to do on board, such as studying the weather, consulting with the skipper about crew assignments, reviewing the charts of the racing area, checking the current and tidal data, and reading up on past races on the same body of water.

No one likes to have a shipmate who is difficult to get along with. *Compatibility* involves pitching in to get the boat cleaned up, keeping your personal articles stowed, and generally trying to make life aboard pleasant for everybody. You should learn where all the basic gear and equipment are stowed when you first report aboard so no valuable racing time will be lost while you have to ask where something is.

The noises and activity aboard a boat often hinder *communication*. The first step in communicating effectively is listening—something that many sailors fail to do in the heat of competition. When you speak, speak *at* someone, making sure first that you have his full attention. Start by using the person's name: "John, trim the main." John's response should be: "Trimming main." By repeating the instruction, John assures you that he has heard your message correctly. If he cannot attend to the job immediately, he should at least acknowledge your request with "Stand by" or "Wait, please." On larger boats, general commands like "Ready about" should elicit a response from someone forward who is responsible for checking with the rest of the crew involved and then answers, "Ready amidships and forward." This enables the skipper to steer rather than having to look about and check with a number of people to see if they are all ready to tack the boat. On *Intrepid* in 1970 just about all communication to or from the crew went to or from Bill Ficker through the tactician for the express purpose of allowing Bill to concentrate fully on his job of steering the boat on the fastest possible course. Simple hand signals should be used when possible to eliminate unnecessary conversation. When it is necessary to converse, it should be done in a way that least interferes with the concentration of the skipper or others. However, although conversation can be distracting to the helmsman, a certain amount of communication between crew members about sail shape, sheet leads, weather developments, upcoming sail changes, and other relevant information is vital to keeping up boat speed. For instance, on an ocean racer at night, if there is no conversation up forward, it is a sure sign that no one is paying attention to the sails.

Not everyone on board can be a leader, but *leadership* is an important attribute in a crew member. Similarly, the ability to follow leadership is an equally valuable quality. Three men organized and led properly are worth four more expert men improperly led and organized. The skipper should delegate one man to be in charge of each section of the boat; this delegation of responsibilities forms the basis for effective leadership and communication. These leaders should give all major instructions to the men in their respective areas and direct and explain the maneuvers when necessary.

Seamanship ranks first among all the characteristics in a good crew. It is an essential part of getting home first, for unnecessary risks that result in broken gear or injured crew merely work counter to winning races. However, this is not to imply that maneuvers have to be done slowly to be safe. Some of the best seamen are also the best racing crew members because they are able to do things quickly as well as safely.

Once a skipper has assembled a group of able individuals, he must mold them into a working unit. This requires careful organization. Each boat demands different things of its crew according to its size and layout as well as the capabilities of each crew member. As a general rule, the larger the boat, the more people are needed to run it and the more difficult the equipment is to handle. This in turn requires more thorough planning. Regardless of the simplicity or complexity of a boat, the skipper or crew boss should make a crew plan which tells each person what he is to do in each major evolution and what his job is for each leg of the course. If such a plan is not drawn up prior to the race, the crew cannot

Charisma Crew Plan Developed for 12-meter crew tryouts. October 1973 by Stephen Van Dyck

POSITION	WINDWARD		DOWNWIND			
	Basic Responsibilities	Tacking to St'bd	Basic Responsibilities St'bd Pole	Spinnaker Set St'bd Pole	Gybe: St'bd to Port Pole	Take In (Port Pole)
Helmsman	Steer	Steer	Steer	Steer	Steer	Steer
Skipper	Final sail selection / Fine trim					
Tactician	Communication to crew / Sail recommendation / Course monitoring / Tactical considerations / Watch other boats	Monitor speed / Call time to tack / Watch other boats	Recommend spinnaker and angle to sail / Tactics / Communicate with crew	Call hoist of spinnaker & staysail	Recommend time to gybe	
Navigator	Optimum course to steer / Predict apparent wind for next leg		Navigation / Optimum course to steer			Rig take-in line on spinnaker
Mainsheet	Main trim and adjustments	Ease & trim main / Traveller adjustment	Main trim	Main ease / Trim vang	Ease vang / Gybe main	Trim / Vang off
St'bd Coffee grinder & Tailer	Trim jib on port tack / Call halyard tension	Cast off jib sheet	Call spinnaker trim / Trim spinnaker sheet / Call pole position	Tail sheet / Call spinnaker trim	Ease old sheet, clew to stay / Crank old guy until new sheet takes over	Ease pole as necessary / Trim jib sheet / Cast off guy / Tail jib sheet
Port Coffee grinder & Tailer	Trim jib on st'bd tack / Call halyard tension	Trim jib sheet	Tail afterguy	Tail afterguy	Crank afterguy; crank new guy as necessary / Take up new sheet on coffee grinder / Trim spinnaker	Over trim sheet and cleat / Take in spinnaker
St'bd cranker	Crank st'bd coffee grinder / Tail port secondary sheet	Run clew aft / Trim port secondary sheet	Crank sheet	Crank spinnaker sheet	Tail afterguy; square pole / Crank guy as necessary / Trim staysail	Put take-in line on / Crank pole as necessary / Cast off staysail sheet / Main outhaul and downhaul

POSITION	WINDWARD		DOWNWIND		DOWNWIND	
Port cranker	Crank port coffee grinder Tail st'bd secondary sheet	Cast off st'bd secondary jib sheet Crank port coffee grinder	Trim staysail Crank guy as necessary	Ease jib Crank guy as necessary Ease main downhaul & outhaul	Cast off staysail sheet Ease new guy forward Take up new guy; tail guy Move to crank sheet	Over trim sheet Take in spinnaker Crank jib sheet
Aft side mast	2nd crank port coffee grinder Tail jib & spinnaker halyards	Crank port coffee grinder	Tail halyards Pole in board end Foreguy Foredeck boss	Inboard pole end up Tail halyard Hoist staysail Foreguy	Lower staysail; pole inboard end up Trip pole; foreguy Hoist staysail	Lower staysail; hoist jib Drop spinnaker; crank jib
Fore side mast	2nd crank st'bd coffee grinder Main downhaul & outhaul Crank jib halyards	Clear jib at mast	Spinnaker pole lift Crank halyards	Help connect spinnaker pole inboard Adjust lift Drop jib	Gather staysail; lower lift-raise Help hoist staysail	Main outhaul & downhaul Gather staysail; hoist jib Drop inboard end of pole
Bow	Tacking line, jib Cunningham Spare sail ready Crank relief	Tacking line	Rig next sail Rig jib sheets	Connect sail Pole outboard end Feed chute Gather jib Halyard on staysail	Take guy forward; gather staysail Connect guy; crank lift Halyard on staysail	Gather staysail; halyard on jib Break connection; pole on deck Check for clearance to tack

function smoothly and get the most out of the boat during racing conditions. When each man arrives on board, he should be able to consult the crew plan and know what he will do. He can then check out the gear he is responsible for—and familiarize himself with it if need be—long before leaving the dock. An even better system is to mail a crew plan to each person, especially if there are new assignments or new crew members involved.

This form of organizing a crew implies that everyone has a clearly defined role to play. It is essential, however, that each man actually do what he is assigned to do, acting on his own initiative within his area of responsibility to see that his job is executed properly. This means the navigator navigates, the helmsman steers, the jib trimmer trims, and the cranker cranks. While this may seem rather elementary, it often happens that the spinnaker man tells the navigator how to navigate or the mainsheet man runs forward to kibitz with the foredeck crew. Although there must be some flexibility during extenuating circumstances, for the most part even special situations can be provided for in a crew plan. Ocean racers should have a special category in their plans—"emergency drill"—which assigns people to stations in the event of fire, man overboard, dismasting, and so on. The key assignments here are the radio transmitter, flares, and the life raft. In man-overboard situations, it is vital to designate one crew member to watch the man in the water. By assigning emergency-drill stations, the skipper can usually prevent further disaster and possibly tragedy.

Once the organization of the crew has been established, the crew needs to develop close team work through practice. The very word "practice" makes some sailors want to jump ship to a less serious boat; and in some cases they have good cause, since practice is often unproductive. So the objective is to make practice both productive and rewarding. Here are some suggestions:

1. Before leaving the dock, the skipper should have a plan for practicing, based on the weather conditions of that particular day, and review it with the crew. Included in early practices should be general maneuvering to familiarize each man with his area of responsibility; practice starts at a buoy so the skipper and tactician can practice timing; tacking, with special emphasis on the way the boat is turned to minimize speed loss; difficult spinnaker sets that require either tacking just at the mark or jibing just after it; quick jibes; spinnaker take-ins at the mark with a

jibe, a tack just after the mark, or windward take-ins; and appropriate sail changes.

2. Start practicing when the boat leaves the dock. Each man should be at his station, concentrating on making the boat go fast; in this way, everyone gets used to working together—for example, jib trimmers become accustomed to the helmsman's way of steering. Treat each maneuver as a racing one, executing it just as you would if the competition were all around. In other words, all the proper trim adjustments—outhauls, Cunninghams, light-weather sheets, and so on—should be made continuously. Racing should become a natural way of sailing the boat. This will greatly reduce tensions during races and dramatically improve the boat's performance.

3. The skipper or crew boss should see that each maneuver is properly understood before it is executed, so that it can be done smartly and effectively.

4. All discussion or criticisms should be saved until the maneuver is completed. Be sure to take time to review the operation fully before going on to the next one.

5. Treat practice seriously. It is helpful for the skipper to announce to the crew when a break begins and when he wants practice to resume.

6. When possible, it is a good idea to practice going around the course of the race to become familiar with the wind phases, sea conditions, and navigational aids.

7. Each crew member should make suggestions for improvements during the wrap-up session that follows a practice drill.

8. The tactician or skipper can use practice sessions to time a variety of operations—for example, rigging for spinnaker sets, changing headsails, jibing and tacking one full circle—so that during a race the advantages or disadvantages of doing something can be intelligently evaluated.

9. Even one hour of practice before a race is better than no practice at all.

I doubt if there is a skipper alive who would balk if his crew asked to leave the dock early in order to practice before the starting gun. There is always something to be learned through practice, and the more you know about the boat you are sailing and your shipmates, the better equipped you will be to handle any eventuality.

In preparing for race day, the ideal crewman takes his job just as seriously as does his skipper. He directs all his efforts toward winning, and this dedication begins the day before the race, when he is in the sack early—sober. First thing in the morning, he checks the weather forecast and map, regardless of his position on the boat, as this information will help him prepare mentally for the day ahead. He arrives on board well ahead of the scheduled departure time and checks the equipment in his area thoroughly; he oils spinnaker-pole fittings, reeves off the running rigging, verifies chart inventories, and packs spinnakers. Once the crew has checked and rechecked all the equipment on the boat, they should review with the skipper what is to be expected that day. (If your skipper does not suggest a meeting, then you should!) The weather should be discussed and the navigator ought to explain the course if he knows it in advance. The skipper or crew chief ensures that everyone knows his assignment and that there are no questions. Safety-equipment locations and man-overboard procedures are reviewed in the pre-race meeting. The crew can make sail either in the harbor or well before reaching the starting area so that there is ample time to sail to windward to check windward compass courses, to discern any wind phasing patterns, to make a quick spinnaker set or other practice maneuvers, and generally to familiarize everyone with the conditions. At this time, the designated crew members adjust halyard and Cunningham tensions as well as outhauls and downhauls until they achieve the exact desired shapes in the sails. These adjustments are then noted carefully so the crew can reconstruct them on the final approach to the line without any further trial and error or any instructions from the skipper. (If you put marks on all the sheets, halyards, and other gear, you will easily be able to repeat these adjustments.) Once the course is announced, the skipper can put the boat on the compass courses of the various legs of the race so everyone can take note of the apparent wind angle. This avoids a discussion of what angle of sail a certain leg will be just before the mark (provided, of course, that there is no shift in wind direction or velocity). The spinnaker gear can be pulled around to the proper side. The halyard and outhaul adjustments ought then to be slacked off to obtain maximum reaching speed needed during the starting maneuvering. If each crew member approaches the balance of the race with the same type of intelligent planning and continuous effort, you should find yourself up with the leaders instead of in the middle or tail end of the pack.

In many respects, you have the best of both worlds as a crew. You have the chance to participate in a challenging sport without the headaches or expenses of ownership. Additionally, by not owning a boat that

Charisma in the 1973 Admiral's Cup with Stephen Van Dyck as tactician and Bill Ficker at the wheel.

you feel committed to using every available moment, you can do a wide variety of sailing, especially if you like to sail on both ocean racers and class boats. The obvious shortcoming to not owning the boat you sail on is that you are usually not its skipper. But this can be offset to some degree if your level of competence improves to the point where your skipper relies on you for more than just doing what he tells you to do. On the best-sailed boats, the important tasks of making tactical decisions and increasing boat speed are delegated to the crew more than ever before. This is partially because boats are becoming harder to steer and mechanically more sophisticated, but mostly because there are more talented crews available. For those who want to become top-notch crews, this offers great opportunities to exercise their abilities to the fullest extent.

197

18. Match Racing

The following situations have been set up in an endeavor to demonstrate some of the possible maneuvers that can occur in match race starting. With these as a base, many more less fundamental maneuvers may be developed as the attack and defense continues.

In match racing, the start is all important. Your competitor must be controlled through various techniques so that your boat will be in the advantageous position when the line is crossed; and *when* is not important as long as your sole competitor is behind you. In fleet racing it is desirable to be on the line at the starting gun and also in the favored position. In match racing you can start as late as you desire, but you must have the other boat covered.

Practically all of the many maneuvers in match-race starting are controlled by the Golden Rule—and forcefully supported by North American Yacht Racing Union Rule #2, Appeal #63.

In the match race start you must be the aggressor. Don't let your competitor have this opportunity. You must be the one to get on his stern, a psychologically strong position to be in. He is upset, surprised and maybe even unnerved when you attack. Your technique and tactics in this tailing operation must of necessity be precision perfect. Even a touch on the wheel or an improperly trimmed mainsail or jib can cost precious position. As in all racing, you must know the rules perfectly and how to use them to your advantage on a second's notice. You must constantly anticipate the possible movements and positions of the other boat. Your decision must be instantaneous and, of course, correct.

This is all fine, so long as you are the aggressor and in control. The important question, however, is "How do you get your boat there?" Difficult as are fleet starts with some 30 or more boats, timing the start in match racing is, in my opinion, even harder. In the former, no one is trying to prevent you from starting (with the exception of a barging situation at the windward end of the line). In match starts, each boat is endeavoring to control the other.

Because it is a more intricate operation than regular starting, management, thought, and endless practice is more necessary. It is important, of course, to understand techniques and maneuvers, but it becomes entirely different when you attempt to execute them in actuality. This, of course, is no different from any other activity.

Those who love golf, for example, in looking at pictures or experts in actual play, think they can take many strokes off their own game until the heartbreak comes when they try to put into practice what they thought they had learned. To practice properly you should have a friend who is a sharp helmsman, knows the rules, and has a good understanding of match starting. These are severe requirements, because very few realize the demands for this type of starting. Nevertheless, endeavor to find a skipper that wants to learn, if an experienced man is not available. Study the fundamentals, then go out in two one-design boats for your actual practice.

You will find, as my son Corny and I did, that it can be the most interesting and thrilling department of all the wonderful phases of racing, perhaps even as advanced as chess is to checkers when compared with fleet starts. However, before entering into actual practice, you must familiarize yourself with certain fundamentals that are most necessary in "tailing" maneuvers.

One of the rudiments in match starts, and even more valuable than in fleet starts, is the ability to judge the sailing time for various distances and at various speeds. The importance of this cannot be overemphasized. Practice this continually. Know your tacking and jibing times, especially reach-to-reach. Regularly test your judgment for time on approaching buoys, anchored boats, boats dead in the water, and driftwood. Always use the stem in judging times and in assimilating actual starts. Learn how to slow her down if you are early, either through violent course variations or easing the jib, which can usually be more easily controlled than the mainsail. On a big boat, always know your exact speed on the speedometer, a very important factor in your judgment of time and distance. Be aware of what your loss in speed is in a jibe or tack. Learn how long it takes to regain full speed.

It is necessary to practice incessantly to learn when your stem is on the line. In large boats it is especially difficult to be accurate in this regard. When the helmsman is 50 or 70 feet aft of the stem, he will find the angle surprisingly difficult to measure. For large boats, I recommend having a man on the stem to assist in starts. He should be a helmsman himself with the ability to judge speed and distance. A good man in this spot is invaluable to the skipper. In the tailing operation, he can also be most helpful in determining overlaps and the boat's ability to swing clear. He should also have the knack of using psychology on an opponent. For example, he should call the overlap with great emphasis. He must loudly and repeatedly caution the opposing skipper not to bear off after you have obtained an overlap. Furthermore, you or your navigator should immediately call out your course, loudly and clearly, as soon as the overlap is established. This, too, is extremely important psychologically, and could be useful in the event of a protest.

In endeavoring to get on the stern of your competitor, meet him on an opposite course, widely separated to permit you to start your turn early, well before you are abeam. This would be when he is approximately 45 degrees on your bow. The distance between the two courses should be three to four boat lengths, permitting you to maintain speed on a gradual slow jibe or tack. Should you be fortunate and have timed your turn well, you will be approximately a boat length astern. A course slightly to leeward of your opponent's will permit you to control him. If he luffs, you should do likewise and prevent him from tacking. If he bears off, you will gain an overlap and not allow him to jibe. Then, maintain this controlling position until you are certain you can jibe or tack for the line, with your competitor in an unfavorable position. Remember, *when* you start is of no consequence as long as you do so in a controlling position. If in control, don't start until you are satisfied that you can maintain this advantage at the start.

If you are unable to gain the controlling position and more than a boat length separates the boats, your competitor will of course attempt to escape your efforts to control. He will luff and tack, or bear off and jibe, continuing this circular course in an endeavor to prevent you from getting an overlap. You must follow, trying for this key to your control. In this

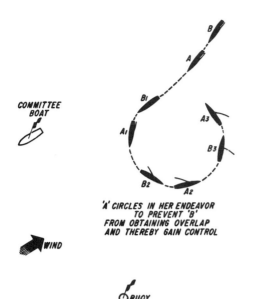

A, endeavoring to prevent B from obtaining an overlap and control, enters into a circle.

'A' CIRCLES IN HER ENDEAVOR
TO PREVENT 'B'
FROM OBTAINING OVERLAP
AND THEREBY GAIN CONTROL

WIND

BUOY

situation you must have previously determined the time required for a full circle—in both light and fresh breezes. At the start of a circling maneuver, make certain you or your navigator know the exact time and check off each full circle. You must decide as each circle ends whether the time calls for another circle before the start or whether you could leave your competitor and permit him to be on your stern, with your getting to the line without being early for the gun, thus having exactly the position you have been striving for. Naturally, you must also judge, when the circling starts, the time required to get to the line—so you will not be early.

The circling maneuver is extremely confusing and requires the utmost concentration. It is not an exaggeration to say that it can be as bewildering as a small boy spinning with his eyes closed, wherein it is impossible to maintain equilibrium or direction when ended. Because you are in such a state of concentration on your own boat and your competitor's, on occasion you will not know where the line is, let alone where its two ends are. For this reason, you must have assistance from either the navigator or a member of the afterguard who is concentrating solely on time and position.

You will, of course, have determined the favored end of the line, if any. Needless to say, you should attempt to start in that area when you have the choice.

After the start, the match race becomes like any other race, with certain important exceptions. Following are some pointers for racing.

Always cover your opponent. If he double tacks, you must do the same.

However, if he triple tacks in an effort to get clear I believe it better not to follow, because you will have an opportunity to gain two to three boat lengths as a result of his almost complete loss of way. If you are the leeward boat and covered, you will, of course, reach off a little in your endeavor to get clear. Under the present rule he cannot bear off to prevent your doing so. There are no other boats to worry about, so tack as often as possible. Try to tire his crew out, or hope for a bad tack on his part.

Incidentally, in your tacks, free up your mainsail and jib to aid you in gaining speed. If you are covered and decide to sail wide, make certain your boom vang is set taut. It will be of enormous importance in quickly building and maintaining speed. Adjust its set to the strength of the wind. Be wary of tacking under his lee bow, especially in a bigger boat. You should be able gradually to gain a position to backdraft him. But if you don't and he is sufficiently clear of you to windward, you are really locked. If on the starboard tack, I believe you are better off to cross him and tack on his weather quarter, clear of his disturbed air. If on the port tack and you would be forced about, go under your opponent's stern and tack on his weather quarter, and as aforementioned; clear of his backdraft. In both cases you are then in control.

In a tacking duel watch for false tacks. If he falls back on his tack, do likewise. However, make certain that you maintain maximum way on your boat. Your tacks should be slower than normal, but after getting head to wind, fill her away quickly, because after this point you are gaining nothing to windward.

When you are the weather boat, immediately after being filled away on your new course be sure to read the compass heading. This will permit you to disclaim any charge of your bearing off. Your navigator should constantly take bearings on the other boat to help you decide on the need for sail adjustments, and to consider whether you should sail her finer or wider through the seas.

If you are ahead when you get to the lay line for the windward mark, under no circumstances overstand. It only brings your competitor closer, and you have given away the precious distance earned to windward. Say you both go by the lay line: your opponent, when you tack for the mark, reaches in your wake with his wind clear, whereas he would have been in your backdraft had you tacked on the lay line. If he continues on his course he will have to reach off for the mark, thus sacrificing valuable distance. This may be elemental, but it is surprising how many experienced skippers will continue to cover their opponent after reaching the lay line. The skipper of the leeward boat is hoping for such a situation when he goes by the lay line.

Before the start you will presumably have run the courses of the reaching and running legs to determine the jibe for the run and the possibility of a spinnaker on the reach. If you plan to carry the spinnaker on the reach, then as you proceed on the windward leg, you and your navigator must watch for any change in the wind direction that would affect your spinnaker decision for the leeward legs. Study wind direction by observing the compass while you are head-to-wind in tacking, by looking at the water over the compass at other times, or by knowing how close to the wind your boat can sail in points or degrees. The latter is especially accurate after you and your navigator have previously determined how many degrees off the wind she will sail in various strengths of winds.

There may be opportunities for special maneuvering at the weather mark. For example, say the boats are overlapped and not laying the mark which must be left to port. The leeward boat is maintaining her position because of having her wind clear. The weather boat skipper, although he is ahead, is not in the lead because of his requirement to give room as they tack and reach the mark. He therefore decides that if he goes by the lay line, he will be in a better position to break the overlap as he tacks and reaches back to the mark. The leeward boat must be adroit in tacking simultaneously to maintain a relative position. In fact, when endeavoring to obtain this advantage she should gradually luff to bring the boats as closely together as possible before both tack for the mark.

When the boats are overlapped on the starboard tack, and very comfortably laying the weather mark to be left to starboard, the helmsman of the lee boat—with luffing rights—may see an opportunity to reverse the positions and gain an overlap at the mark. He luffs his opponent to weather of the mark, continues a sufficient distance to permit himself room to jibe, and return to the mark with an overlap. Probably his greatest advantage is that he has done the unexpected, causing great turmoil on the weather boat. It is likely that the skipper of this boat, in his surprise and confusion, may become "frozen to the handle bars" and continue on course until he has lost his only opportunity to maintain his former advantageous position. In this circumstance he should, as soon as he sees he will be taken to windward of the mark if the bow of the leeward boat overlaps the mark, tack and jibe without letting the jib sheet go. This will bring the boat around quicker, and the jib will be filled and ready for easing on his short reach to the mark. The leeward boat's position requires most accurate timing and judgment in this maneuver. For this reason both conditions should be prepared for in previous practice. These maneuvers are not far-fetched and should be expected to occur regularly in match racing. If such situations do develop and advantages are not fought for, the helmsman is being too casual in his effort to win.

Remember again there are no other boats to be concerned with, and a fierce competitor will go to any length within the rules to win. Extreme as this situation may appear it is one with which you may well have to contend. You may well find an opportunity to employ it yourself.

If the next leg is a reach, few opportunities for trading positions will occur, because both boats are likely to be of equal speed in most match races. However, if the leeward boat is being overtaken she should luff as long and as far as possible. Her one hope is to get far enough to windward to jibe, set her spinnaker and obtain the overlap at the second mark. Presuming the boats are of equal speeds, the entire leeward legs must be sailed to gain the overlap. This is especially true on the spinnaker runs, the dead runs of windward-leeward courses in particular.

On the leeward legs, especially the runs, there is more room and opportunity for maneuver. You will start your run on the jibe that you have previously determined to be correct. The following boat will attempt to get on the wind of the leader by steering a course exactly for her masthead fly. If the leader is being bothered, he will sail higher to get free wind. Both boats, therefore, quickly get well above course and plans must be made to jibe. This should be anticipated first by the following boat, so she can make an opportunity to cover the leader after the jibe.

As they run their distance and approach the proper angle for the new course, the following boat should bear off, hoping to do this so gradually that the purpose will go unnoticed. The leader, of course, must eventually jibe. If the following boat has been able to get over far enough, she will be in a better position to cover when both jibe. The leader will repeatedly jibe in her struggle to get clear. This is exactly what the following boat should endeavor to induce, as the maneuver is all in her favor. The leader can make a poor jibe and have the further disadvantage of her adversary coming down with new breeze. Furthermore, she is being attacked, which, in itself, can be disturbing psychologically.

If the following boat is successful and does become close, careful plans must be made. In the event that another windward leg is to be sailed, she must program everything around obtaining an overlap at the leeward

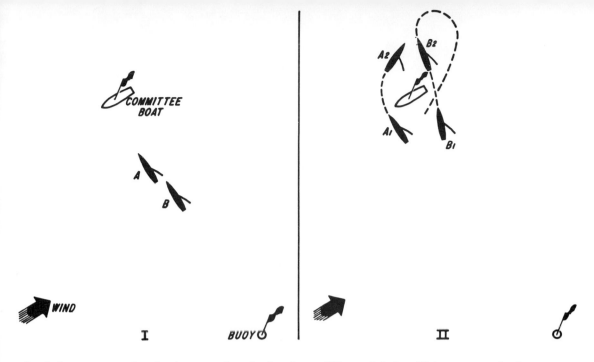

Both boats are early. A plans to absorb the time differential by jibing around the committee boat. B prevents this by bearing off to leeward of the committee boat.

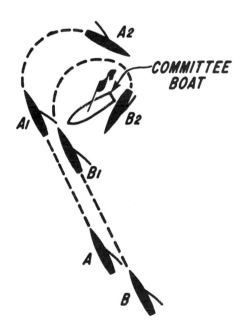

B, in control, prevents A from dipping the line to make his start, forcing A to windward of the committee boat, then jibes himself, which A must follow.

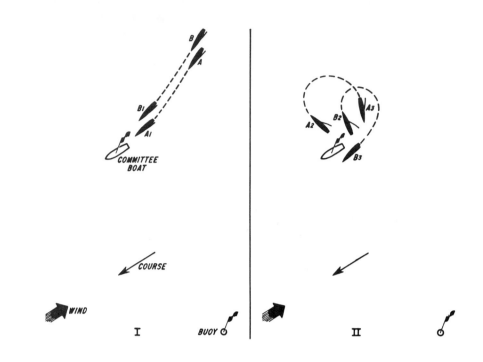

I.   The hazard of "running time" in a match race start. "Sitting duck" B, running time, observing that he will be attacked by A, returns a minute early to upset A's plans and allow himself maneuvering time. Having obtained his desired position under B's lee bow and realizing that B's premature return will make him early, A, in his confusion, sets out to luff B to windward of the committee boat.

II. Because B has returned early, there is a minute extra to be absorbed. Judging poorly, A has elected to luff B to windward of the committee boat. This decision places A in an awkward position to reach the starting line favorably in relation to B. B should now tack and jibe, employing the remaining time, and approach the line with the right of way.

When A tacked under B's lee bow he was in control. He could kill the extra time and maintain control through better maneuvers than luffing B to windward of the committee boat. They are:
1. Realizing that both were early, A could luff B almost head to wind to pass the necessary time.
2. A could take several luffs to break the overlap, cross the line, then tack and jibe around the committee boat.
3. A could sharply luff and bear off, making certain he gets no further to leeward than a point which would permit him to approach the committee boat with right of way under the anti-barging rule.
4. A could jibe and tack as he reaches the line to leeward of the committee boat.
5. A could run down the line regulating his speed so B will remain overlapped to windward and as close aboard as possible. As both sharpen for the start, A can then lee bow and back draft B. In this circumstance A cannot put B across the line. If he did, B could then tack and dip the line. A could only follow or jibe and tack; in both cases he would be in B's wake.

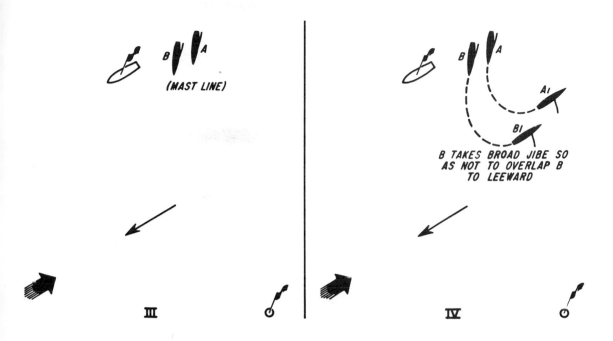

(MAST LINE)

B TAKES BROAD JIBE SO
AS NOT TO OVERLAP B
TO LEEWARD

III   IV

III.   A in his endeavor to place his boat under B's lee bow has misjudged his timing and B has obtained "mast line" on A.

IV.   As A jibes to escape the mast line position, B takes a broader jibe in order not to overlap A to leeward and be locked. B is now in control of A and will win the advantageous starting position.

A is in control, and tacks for the line a little early for the distance involved, placing B in control. However, A overcomes this by regulating the speed of his boat to the distance involved, keeping B in his wake.

COMMITTEE
BOAT

COURSE

WIND

BUOY

OBSTRUCTION
BOAT

A   B

COMMITTEE
BOAT

COURSE

WIND

BUOY

Endeavoring to get free of B's controlling position, A plans
to jibe around an obstruction boat which is not under way.
To prevent this, B bears off to pass under the stern of the
obstruction.

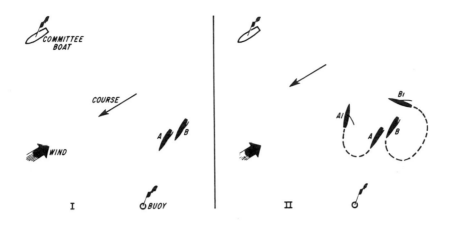

Mast line situation.

I. Both boats are early, A with controlling mast line position. B jibes to get free.

II. A must be cautious of tacking because B, coming out of his jibe, with right of way, could put A across the starting line prematurely. The alternative could be for A to take a wide jibe and place himself on B's weather beam. Naturally, these maneuvers must be judged in accordance with the time remaining to the start.

mark. The leader will naturally make every effort to prevent this. The one situation the following boat must avoid is getting in an overlapped position where she can be luffed, permitting the leader to jibe and be in command. Here the attacking boat, as she draws close to getting an overlap to windward, may jibe instead, again introducing the unexpected. She is then free to maneuver and is on the right side for the overlap. If the leader jibes, she will presumably be covered. She must therefore, continue her course and jibe later, but she will then be on the outside at the turn. Such an opportunity to do the unexpected must never be missed.

The leader must be prepared to luff his opponent to weather of the line, and then to jibe and return.

In the foregoing situations and in the following starting maneuvers, it is suggested that the reader set up matchstick models for purposes of clarification.

VARIOUS MANEUVERS IN MATCH-RACING STARTS

B in control. A, in spite of an effort to slow his boat, approaches the committee boat and is early. He plans to leave the committee boat to starboard and jibe around it, expecting B to follow. B should stay to leeward of the committee boat to prevent A's jibe. B should then jibe for the line, or—if it is still early—stay to leeward of A, jibing when time dictates.

A obviously cannot jibe around the committee boat until permitted to do so by B. If he attempted to do so, he would risk disqualification for barging, as A would meet him on starboard tack after completing his jibe. A is in an unfavorable position either if he eventually jibes astern of B or—worse—if he tacks.

In such a situation where both boats are to windward of the line, B must keep A in this position of line until he (B) can jibe around the committee boat. A must follow and, in consequence, be in B's backdraft as the windward leg commences.

B must exercise proper caution and not bear off for the line, thereby permitting A to do likewise, dip over the line and be in the favored position at the start.

When both boats are to windward of the line, which presumably is square to the wind, and both become free (neither in control) to run off for the line, a reaching course should be faster rather than a dead run. Furthermore, greater speed can be maintained for sharpening up on the wind. If there is a favored end of the line, you should naturally start in that area to be in the advantageous position. Remember the time of your start is completely unimportant. It is *where* you are in relation to your adversary.

When your competitor is running time for his start, he becomes a "sitting duck" for attack. Running time is therefore not advisable.

Defense for a "Sitting Duck" Position

A plans to force B to windward of the committee boat.

B should foresee his problem. He should return to the line very early, expecting to make A early also. B can control the time of his start by regulating the speed of his boat.

In this situation B should permit A to luff him to windward of the committee boat until he (B) has reached a point where he can tack and jibe for the line and not be early for the gun. Delicate timing is required on the part of B; otherwise A can bear off and start. (Barging rule.)

Adroit maneuvering is necessary on the part of A when he places his

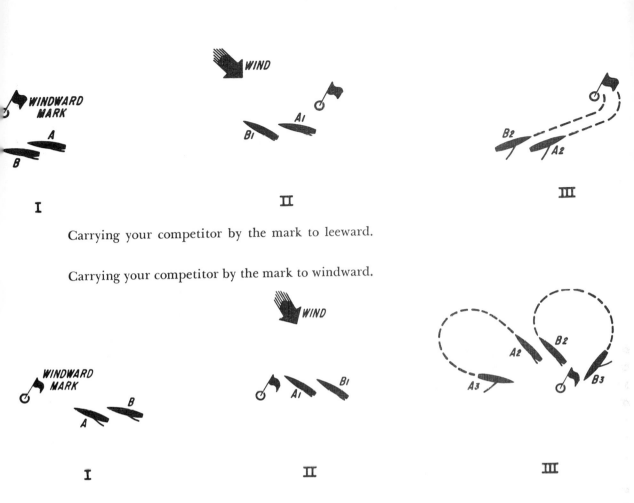

Carrying your competitor by the mark to leeward.

Carrying your competitor by the mark to windward.

boat under the lee bow of B. B is probably at full speed if he is running time and might well go on by A and obtain "mast line." He would thereby defeat A's plan to force him above the committee boat. A would probably jibe in an attempt to get free, because he could not run off with B on his wind at the start. So when A jibes, B would follow suit, become the "tailor" and be in control *(see diagram)*.

It is risky for B to tack, as he might meet A coming out of his jibe with luffing rights.

If your opponent, in his strenuous efforts to get on your tail, has a possibility of doing so, if the time is only two to three minutes until the start, and if there is sufficient distance from the line, an interesting opportunity may occur—either by design or accident—on which you could

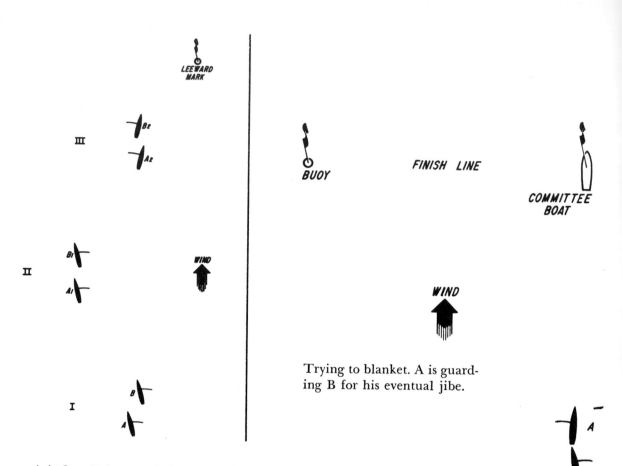

Trying to blanket. A is guarding B for his eventual jibe.

A is first. B is second. In a surprise jibe, B prevents A from obtaining a controlling position.

capitalize. Your eager opponent could well fall into a trap in which you permit him to become the "tailer." If you do this, you must be in a position of freedom from which you can get to either end of the starting line. Obviously, if you were headed away from the line, you would be completely controlled. In this situation, however, in spite of the fact that you are the "tailed," you are in control—provided, of course, you are far enough away from the line to control your speed and decide when you want to reach it. If he rides up to windward, you can luff. If in other words, to leeward, you can control him through the mast line rule. With only several minutes to the start, and after various courses in which neither boat has been successful in obtaining control, A permits B to become "tailer," thereby putting himself (A) into position to reverse the control, through regulation of his speed and freedom of maneuver, and gain the favorable position at the start.

Some skippers, in their efforts to avoid being tailed, have evolved a plan that has worked out to a degree, but that is in my opinion quite risky for both boats. Here the skipper delays breaking out his genoa until just before the start. If his opponent had set his jib, the opponent is not in a position to tail because of the greater speed of his boat. If both boats remained jibless, the control of each is materially reduced and fouls are more likely to occur. For this reason I consider it a rather hazardous procedure in the circling and other maneuvers attempting to gain control. Furthermore, I believe that a skipper should not take the defensive, but should become the forceful aggressor at approximately seven minutes (in large boats such as twelves) before the start.

To avoid being tailed, keep your boat moving at the greatest speed that wind will allow. On opposite courses, pass as close to your competitor as possible to deny him tacking or jibing room to get on your stern. If you are in control and your opponent plans to jibe around the committee boat or another of moderate size (not underway), prevent him from doing so by going to leeward of the boat he intends to go around. You can then keep your control. Some reduction of your speed may be necessary, as he may start his jibe and thereby reduce speed. If you don't slow down, you are likely to become overlapped after you pass the obstruction boat. A's defense would be to tack after B has overlapped the obstruction boat.

Aside from circling (a defensive move) the skipper of a controlled boat may luff head-to-wind very sharply in an effort to kill way and make the controlling boat shoot by or become abeam as the controlled boat loses way. To kill your speed under this circumstance, secure the spinnaker halyard in the grommet for the brail tacking line in the center of the jib foot. The forward part of the jib will then brake your speed as the halyard is hoisted. He can then go on one tack only and must not fill away on the other at the risk of disqualification. If the maneuver works out as planned, the controlling position could then be reversed. The same situation could prevail if the "tailee" *bears off* sharply and is overridden by the "tailer." In this case, make every effort to be on starboard jibe.

Nothing is lost in this effort by the "tailee," as he may at least be permitted to go into a defensive circle. This may give him an opportunity to go for the line when he elects, whereas previously he was controlled and was prevented from freedom of maneuver.

If by fortune you find yourself with "mast line" while you are reaching for the start, the courses may be such that your opponent cannot get up to the line *(see diagram)* . His only defense is to jibe immediately and save as much time as possible for further maneuvering. He then might be clear on the start, and, if sufficient time remains, he might even be in a position to put your boat over the line *(diagram)* should you tack simultaneously with his jibing.

19. *Match Racing and Other Ruminations*

BY BUS MOSBACHER

Bus Mosbacher is one of the most modest men I have ever known. He always gives credit to the boat, sails, crew, and weather before he accepts any for himself. Aboard a boat, Bus is composed, calm, without any of the emotional display so often associated with a very dominating skipper. Two of his most important traits are his penchant for organization and his total composure. Bus manages to stay well-organized ashore as well as afloat, a most important quality in an America's Cup campaign. Everything around the race course is well thought out beforehand with Bus, from the start, through the windward leg, and all other maneuvers.

Bus is the kind of sailor who will always give his opponent more than an even break and would never take advantage of another sailor. I can't remember Bus ever filing a protest. This includes several occasions when he was obviously fouled and the other fellow did not withdraw.

I am a very fortunate person in many ways. It is not everyone who is privileged to skipper not one but three 12-meters in as many America's Cup campaigns, and it is not everyone who is privileged to be surrounded by a crew—and a team of technical advisors—that made it possible to be selected the defender and to win two of those matches.

However, these triumphs are the direct result of more of my good fortune, not the least of which was being born to a father who was as avid a sailor as I will ever be. For example, in 1931 or 1932, when I was only nine or ten, he gave me a Star boat—at that time one of the hottest classes going—which he had acquired from another rising skipper, Howard McMichael, for me to race in the midget racing group. Subsequently, when I grew old enough for junior sailing, I moved up to the 30-foot Atlantic class. During this period, my father also raced his two *Susans:* the first a Sound Interclub and the second an International one-design, acquired when the class was formed in 1936 and retained in the family for twenty-three years. I raced the second *Susan* myself pretty heavily— and I'm happy to say successfully—from 1950 through 1957. That indicates a measure of the support I enjoyed in learning to sail, support which afforded me two of the prime ingredients required to become a successful sailor: time and opportunity to sail.

But my good fortune didn't stop at mere time and support. I was also given the opportunities to race with, and get my ears pinned back by, men who really knew their way around the water. For example, during the summer of 1949, I went to England with an American 6-meter team. The boat was *Llanoria*, Olin Stephens' newest 6. During that year, I was able to learn from very knowledgeable people, people who thought about it and worked at it, people who really knew design, balance, tuning, sail shapes, weight distribution, and all of the things that count when you begin putting it together. I learned the things that make you go a little faster than you did before you knew they mattered. And that, of course, is one way of saying that successful sailboat racing is really paying attention to a great number of small things, and as the kids would say, getting it all together.

This is perhaps one of the reasons that we were so successful with the International. All of us knew *Susan's* every detail. Almost automatically, we had every variable aboard the boat correctly adjusted for the prevailing conditions, and as anyone who has sailed one can testify, when an International is right she is a joy, but when things aren't quite up to snuff she is anything but. Having sailed aboard her for many years, we usually had the boat nicely balanced and going her best right from the start. This gave us a healthy edge, and I say "us" advisedly because outside of singlehanded sailing I believe the crew to be a very, very important factor in winning—a factor that becomes increasingly more important as size increases and becomes absolutely critical in boats the size of a 12.

And it is here that I have perhaps been most fortunate. Having had some success early on, I was able to attract good men to sail with me. This made the later successes easier to achieve. This, in turn, helped make it even easier to attract still better people. The 1967 *Intrepid* campaign was perhaps the epitome of this progression. In my opinion, there has never been a better crew on any boat. Some of their sail-handling evolutions were sheer beauty to watch. Having a crew like this aboard made racing *Intrepid* easy. During the match itself, I never once had to give any thought to whether or not the crew could keep up in an involved tactical situation. I just went ahead and did what I thought ought to be done with the boat and they kept right up with me. In fact, they were usually one step ahead, anticipating and being ready to perform whatever evolution was required. Anyone (which means all of us who have ever raced) who has been frustrated tactically, or even strategically, by inept sail handling or by a foul-up that seems to take forever to untangle will appreciate fully what I mean when I say that I didn't have to take the crew's capabilities into account in planning or executing tactics. If the boat was capable of it, they were too.

But crews who can function like this do not just happen. Ten assorted sailors, excellent though each one may be, cannot walk aboard a boat and expect to perform as *Intrepid*'s crew did in 1967, *Weatherly*'s in 1962, or *Vim*'s in 1958. The 1958 match was, of course, the first post-war organized racing for 12's and it was the first time that the America's Cup had been raced in 12's. We went into it with what was presumed to be the slowest boat (she was the oldest by twenty years), but also with a full deck-load of savvy, agile, and eager small-boat sailors. None of us knew much about how 12's were supposed to be sailed, so we merely adapted small-boat, closed-course sail-handling techniques to *Vim* and thereby surprised a number of more traditional-type sailors. I am also pleased to report that, helped by these new techniques, we were very competitive. In any case, we gave *Columbia* a good run for her money.

In 1962, with *Weatherly*, we again had a boat that was not, in reputation at least, up to the others. But lopping 2½ feet off her stern, getting rid of a 300-lb. boom, and making many other minor modifications, we improved her considerably; but the big edge we enjoyed was in crew and this was a result of a new and arduous program that we had started in 1958, developed further in 1962, and brought to maturity in 1967 for the *Intrepid* campaign. As fully developed, our crew training consisted primarily of what we called a short-course race (which we sailed alone) between two of the buoys on the Newport Torpedo Range. We'd make a start, sail up a 200-yard or so weather leg (making half a dozen or more tacks in the process), round the mark, set the chute, make at least two or three jibes going downwind, round the leeward mark, dump the spinnaker, set the job, tack up wind, and so on and so on until everyone was ready to drop.

After a short break to catch our collected breaths—and iron out any problems that might have surfaced—we'd do it all over again. And we'd keep on until we simply couldn't continue any longer. There is no question that everyone was in as good physical condition by the time the serious racing started as any professional football player is for the Super Bowl—maybe even better. And we never had serious foul-ups. Naturally, things would go wrong, but we had run through all the possible evolutions so many times that even the foul-ups began to fall into a pattern. When something wasn't right, the foredeck bunch seemed to know instinctively where and what to look for.

They made sailing a 12-meter look easy, when, in fact, it is a tough, hard sloop to handle, with big, heavy gear that requires a nice combination of brute force and intelligence.

And, while I've been given a great deal of credit for winning two Cup matches, the truth of the matter is that without the crews I had aboard I would simply not have come close. In match racing, particularly aboard big boats like 12's, there is no question that the biggest single key to success is the crew and their ability to handle the boat and her gear. No matter how clever, how savvy, how brilliant the skipper, his ideas cannot be executed without the crew. Match-racing tactics, as you will see shortly, depend almost entirely on instant response and split-second timing on the part of the skipper; but his responses and timing, no matter how exquisitely planned or flawlessly executed, are of no use whatever unless, and only unless, the crew can respond equally as fast.

While the other aspects of fast sailing (the boat, the sails, tuning, and what not) are important, the one absolute necessity in match racing, in my opinion, is an expert crew. This truth was clearly demonstrated to me in the 1958 *Vim* and the 1962 *Weatherly* campaigns.

The reasons why the crew and its training are so important are intermeshed with the nature of match racing itself: Match racing is almost wholly a race of tactics with few if any strategic considerations.

This is in direct contrast to most other forms of sailboat racing. Long-distance racing, for example, is at the opposite end of the spectrum: Most long-distance races are pure strategy in that—with very few exceptions—

each boat is sailing its own race to get home as quickly as possible. Sailing near another boat during a long-distance event is usually a matter of mere happenstance. Since the chances are high that the boat you happen to be sailing near rates differently, whether or not you finish five feet in front of him or five feet behind him is of little importance. The most important benefit of inching past a boat alongside is the lift it gives to crew morale.

Normal, closed-course, one-design fleet racing fills the middle of the spectrum. There are a number of strategic considerations (wind shifts, current, effects of nearby land) which must be taken into account, but tactics play an equally important role. It is important to inch by a boat, as many boats as possible, but the balance of tactics and strategy will change as the race progresses. For example, in a race with two weather legs, the first, opening weather leg will most often be a strategic one, a leg in which the more important consideration is getting to the weather mark as quickly as possible. What the other boats do is of lesser importance. (The other boats, however, should not be totally disregarded since playing the role of the lone wolf is most often a bad idea.) In contrast, the second weather leg, which is usually the last leg in the race, ought to be guided by tactical considerations. If you're leading at the final leeward mark, you really have little choice but to cover the fleet. If, on the other hand, you are well down the line, your logical choice is to go where, anywhere, the leaders don't. If you are in the middle, the optimum choice is to cover those behind and split with those in front. In other words, preserve what you have while trying to get more.

These concepts are, of course, simplistic and far easier to write down than to accomplish, but they do serve to provide background for match racing which is entirely a game of tactics. In contrast to offshore racing, in which time is the key element—the quicker you finish the better—in match racing, finishing at any particular time is of no consequence *provided* it is in front of your opponent. This makes match racing fundamentally different from all other forms of sailboat racing.

Strategy may have a role in match racing if the matches are held on confined waters where currents can vary or winds can shift around a particular point, but they have almost no role in the America's Cup, which is held ten miles at sea. There is rarely, if ever, much difference between one part of the ocean and another, at least not across the limited area involved in a race.

As all sailors should, we routinely kept abreast of all available weather information, and we were quite aware of what the current was doing at any particular time. The latter, however, was primarily for navigation while the prime use made of weather information was in sail selection, in itself another vital element of success in Cup racing. Beyond that, there was little to be pre-planned. Once the sails were selected and bent on, and the rest of the boat and crew ready to do battle, there was nothing much that could be done until the starting area was reached and the match about to commence.

Certainly more has been written about the commencement of America's Cup matches than many other sporting events. It isn't all that mysterious or brilliant, nor were our starting tactics all that unusual, although in 1958 many thought they were. Mike Vanderbilt had used much the same evolutions and for the same reasons in the 1934 *Rainbow-Endeavour I* match. *Rainbow* was the slower boat and this made a tremendous difference in how the start was played.

With a boat known to be slower, being on top at the start can well mean, probably will mean, the whole race. Since that is the essential, all other considerations must be subservient to being directly on your opponent's wind when the starting line is crossed. This requires aggressive tactics, tactics which carry with them the ever-present danger of fouling out.

If, however, you have a known faster boat such as we enjoyed with *Intrepid* in 1967, starting on top of the other boat assumes less importance. A start somewhere on the line with clear air is sufficient. This is not to say that we did not try to be on *Gretel's* wind at the start, but since we could count on the boat doing at least half the work for us, we were far less inclined to take chances that were not essential to the success of the match. Our posture at the start of the 1967 races was definitely more defensive than offensive.

The reverse was true, of course, with *Vim*. In 1958, we were all offense and aggression. During that summer, my heart spent more time in my mouth than in its usual location. Driving a 12-meter at top speeds with your stem head within a very few feet of another's transom has a tendency to make anyone nervous. If you have the slower boat, though, that is what is required.

The prime object in pre-race maneuvering, if aggression is indicated, is to get directly behind and close to your opponent. It doesn't make too much difference what direction you're going in when you accomplish this, although the preferred direction is reaching away from the starting line on the starboard tack. Since your opponent will be well aware of your intention, he will probably harbor visions of sitting on your transom. As you turn toward his stern, he will, no doubt, turn to chase you. The result is an interminable merry-go-round, a circling maneuver which can continue for quite a while before one or the other succeeds in breaking it up. Hopefully, you will be able to get close enough to prevent him from tacking or jibing under the rules (boat on a tack has right of way over a boat tacking or jibing). Rather than sitting in irons, he will have to bear away, and if your response is quick enough you can run up close on his transom, thereby preventing him from doing anything but going straight ahead away from the line. If your responses remain sharp you can drive him as far away from the line as you like. If he attempts to tack, you can head up inside of him and force him back. If he elects to try and jibe back toward the line, you can easily bear off and block him from that. If all this takes place while reaching on the starboard tack, your task will be relatively easy, because even if he succeeds in completing a tack or jibe, you will still be on starboard while he is now on the port tack and hence the burdened boat.

If, however, when the circle breaks, you are both on the port tack and reaching away from the line, your task is more difficult. It is at this point that your tactics must approach the dangerous if they are to succeed. You *must* remain close enough to prevent him from completing a tack or jibe. If he completes one, he will have right of way and your position will shift rapidly from giving chase to being left out in the cold. To block his moves requires instant response on your part and the part of the crew. A moment's hesitation or even a tiny fluff may well mean letting him get away. All of this underscores the importance of having a superbly trained crew. Without it, none of these maneuvers is possible.

If all goes well, you will be able to keep him heading away from the line until you decide to tack and head back toward the starting line at a spot of your choosing. He will be forced to wallow across in your wake.

Sometimes, however, you may find yourself astern of your opponent when you are not reaching away from the line. You may, for example, be to weather of the line, or you may still be on the right side of the starting line, heading closehauled and about to cross—what then?

Just keep on going is the answer. But in the first case, it is wiser to be more to leeward than behind your opponent. If you can keep him to weather, you will effectively block him from getting back to the line, until *you're* ready to do so. Under the rules, he cannot bear off without fouling you. He can, however, tack. Your response is to tack also and re-establish your position to leeward, thereby continuing to block him from bearing away for the line. After the gun, you can bear away at your convenience, barely dip the line, and start. He will have to take second best.

It might be well to point out again that the starting signal has only one function: You can't start before then. How much after it you start is of *no importance whatever*. The important fact is your opponent's position, when you do cross the line, whether it's with the gun or a half hour later. If he's behind and/or to leeward, you are three-quarters of the way home free. If the positions are reversed, you are truly in hot water.

Actually, you are in *very* hot water since, all things being equal, the race is over and you've lost. Provided the leading boat responds correctly and quickly, there is quite literally no way out once you're behind in a match race.

The bright side, if there is one, of being behind in a match race is that the trailing boat has the initiative. The leading boat's posture is almost entirely reflexive, responding to and covering every move made by the trailing boat. Here, again, the crew is crucial. We have made as many as forty tacks in a single leg. If each of these tacks had been even minutely less well-executed than our opponent's, he would have broken the cover and perhaps gone on to win. Match racing is primarily a battle between crews, secondarily between boats and skippers.

The options open to a trailing boat on a weather leg are few. He can tack and keep tacking or he can try false tacking—that is, a tack is started but never completed. Unfortunately, succeeding with either of these maneuvers depends on the boat ahead fluffing, a most unlikely possibility in America's Cup racing. When you are behind, you must try, and sometimes—particularly if your crew is better drilled—a tacking duel will pay off for the boat behind. Obviously, the crew's physical condition plays a major role.

If the options for the boat behind are few, the options for the leading boat are even fewer. The skipper's role is to respond to the moves made by the trailing boat, staying squarely between it and the next mark. With two races in the bag, Sopwith forgot this maxim in the third race of the 1934 *Rainbow-Endeavour* match. He let Vanderbilt get away and thereby lost the third race, and subsequently, the match.

The only exception to this procedure, and it is only a partial exception, is when conditions vary over the course and you feel you might gain more of an advantage on another part of the course.

A good example of this was with *Intrepid*. We felt that she was a better boat in a slop than *Gretel*. It was quite obvious that the waters near the spectator fleet were sloppier than elsewhere. We encouraged *Gretel* to sail where we wanted her to by simply sitting all over her hard when she tacked away from the spectator fleet, but allowing her a little air when she sailed toward them. I hasten to add that we never let her be completely uncovered. There is a difference between tacking directly on a boat's wind and tacking so that the following boat has more or less clear air.

On the leeward legs, the following boat has more advantages. She is then the weather boat and can, if she's close, put the leading boat in her wind shadow. Of course, the leading boat has a considerable number of possible responses to anything the trailing boat might do. The skipper of the leading boat can, in fact, stave off an attack by an even faster boat for some considerable distance. In contrast to fleet racing, he has only one boat to be concerned about. There is, however, only so much that can be done when the trailing boat is faster. This was illustrated by the magnificent way *Gretel I* sailed past us on *Weatherly* during the 1962 match.

So far, we have talked primarily about aggressive match racing. There is the conservative approach. One of the best examples was Mike Vanderbilt in the 1937 races against *Endeavour II*. Vanderbilt knew he had a better boat (many referred to *Ranger* as the "Superboat"). His whole approach to the match was conservatism personified. In the pre-race maneuvering, Vanderbilt's only objective was to keep *Ranger*'s air clear, and after the start, to point her in the right direction. *Ranger* did the rest.

Similarly, with *Intrepid* in 1967, we played a very careful game. Our objective, like Vanderbilt's, was to clear *Intrepid*'s air and let her do her thing, which in anything above true light air, she did superbly.

This conservatism extended beyond simple maneuvering. For example, sail selection was on the conservative side. If the wind was light but expected to increase, we would probably start with a heavier jib, whereas with *Vim* we started with the lighter weight and hoped that the whole thing would hold together through the leg. Similarly, we routinely squeezed everthing we could from *Vim,* but we tended to take it a bit easier with *Intrepid*. Backstays were never socked up to the ultimate degree unless we were forced to do so. We thus reduced the risk of carrying away a spar—an ever present hazard on 12-meters because of the constant demands put on them.

This conservatism points up a fact of life about 12-meter racing that isn't usually fully discussed. All match racing requires close combat, but with boats the size, heft, and complexity of 12's, close maneuvering and fighting for every inch have about them an element of danger that any prudent skipper must try to minimize. One purpose of crew training is obviously to win, but another is to keep every member of the crew in one piece. An untrained, uncoordinated crew is not only a liability to the race, they are a liability to themselves. Serious physical injury from flailing wire jib sheets or spinnaker guys is always a distinct possibility.

Is it any wonder then that we did not push to the nth degree for minimal potential race advantages at the expense of increased risk of physical injury? While I take considerable pride in having been the leader of three teams to campaign for the Cup, I take even greater pride in having completed three such campaigns without one serious injury. And this is as it should be. Winning is wonderful, but a skipper's first job is to bring the boat, her gear, and most importantly, everyone aboard home to a safe harbor. Since man first went to sea, this has been the skipper's main responsibility. Hard as it might be to accept, sometimes the race has to take a back seat to seamanship and safety.

In fairness to all involved in our quest for racing success and safety, I must say that in our three campaigns we were blessed by having the best possible gear and sails. In 1958, for example, we had the advantage of Ted Hood's sails—and Ted himself—on board. We had sails in a far wider range of weights and materials than anyone else. In 1967, as far as I remember, we were the first to have a half-ounce spinnaker. It is true that this is a sail of limited usefulness, but it gave us a great advantage when conditions made it the only chute that would fly. This is just one example of the material advantages that made so much difference to the three Cup campaigns I was involved in. The latest equipment was always made available to us. From 1958 to 1967, for example, mainsails went from 13-ounce monsters that required six men to lift, to mainsails of 6 ounces or less.

Racing equipment developments are of great benefit to the sport of sailing as a whole. Without the spur of the Cup and the truly vast amounts of money that people are willing to spend on winning or defending it, developments in sailing would be fewer and much slower in coming.

Sails are a prime example, but in many smaller ways this Cup spinoff has helped the sport. Sail-handling techniques and devices are definite benefits. To mention smaller, more plebian items, the lightweight, extremely strong shackles and other fittings that were first used on the 12's are now available at reasonable cost to every sailor.

The real exotica, such as titanium mast sections and carbon or boron reinforced materials, will probably remain expensive and limited to owners who feel winning is more important than money. The critics of America's Cup racing say this is wrong.

Maybe, maybe not, but the America's Cup simply would not be the America's Cup if the boats weren't of the biggest and best open-design class available. Cup racing, perhaps, could be made even more useful by shifting to an open class of boats that would be directly competitive in, say, offshore racing, after their Cup days were over. It has been suggested that the IOR could be used, thus making the design work that goes into building a Cup yacht directly transferable to all offshore racing yachts. This would create what someone would surely label the Twelve Ton class.

Whether this happens, or whether the Cup continues to be raced for in 12's, I hope it will always be a prime crucible for new and important developments in sailing. The Pacific Coast Congressional Cup has developed into a series that produces new ideas, new techniques, and a whole new breed of sailors, weaned on and marvelous at match racing. The winner of any Congressional Cup would be a very worthy opponent in any match race. I am sure these winners would agree with me on the importance of acquiring the best possible crew and training them until their actions are automatic.

There are no secrets, per se, to match racing. I have no bag of tricks unknown to anyone who has been involved in match racing. Success at match racing lies not so much in what you know, as in when and how well you apply what you know.

I am sure that a high percentage of you who are reading these pages can sail quite well, but you should ask yourselves these questions: Can you sail without the burden of excessive deliberation? Have you sailed long enough and often enough on your boat to respond to headers and lifts without much if any conscious thought? Can you say "hard alee" and not worry about whether the jib is going to be sheeted-in swiftly and to exactly the right point? Can you approach a weather mark without the slightest concern about preparations for hoisting the chute? Can you contemplate a heavy air spinnaker jibe with equanimity?

If you can do these things, you will be free to concentrate fully on tactics in a match race and exert your best efforts against your opponent. This freedom puts you well on the road to victory.

If achieving the abilities just outlined sounds like it requires a great deal of time and effort-consuming work, please be assured that it does. No one knows better than I just how much work this means, but I also know that these abilities are necessary if victory is to be yours. And, what that is worthwhile in life was ever easy?

20. On Helmsmanship

The subject of helmsmanship embodies what is probably the most important single principle of successful sailboat racing. The sailor who grasps this principle will be well on the way to becoming a champion. It is this:

The helmsman does not assist the progress of the boat through the water; he impedes it.

Here is why I make this seemingly heretical statement. A boat is making her best progress when she is sailing herself. When the forces of lateral resistance in the keel or centerboard exactly balance the thrust of the wind in the sails, the hull is traveling at the greatest possible speed, considering the force of the wind and the potential of the hull.

When the helmsman corrects with the helm to make the boat follow a predetermined course, he is using the rudder as a brake to alter the natural direction of sailing. Therefore, it follows that the less a skipper uses the helm, the more efficiently he is sailing.

Now we all like to think that it is our magic touch on the helm that causes us to win boat races, but the reverse is true. The man who can balance his boat to sail a given course with the fewest possible helm adjustments is the better sailor. Naturally, during the race, he must put her in the proper places, and for this his good judgment merits credit.

Perhaps the most important element of helmsmanship is the ability to know when a hull is moving well. There are many devices that measure the speed of a boat, but there is none that is sensitive enough to register minute changes in a sailboat's speed. A fortuitous sail adjustment can sometimes affect speed by one-tenth of a knot, and this will not register on speed meters. It is a combination of experience with a given boat, and an intangible "feel" that permits the sailor to mentally sense the increase.

True, a certain amount of innate sensitivity is necessary to learn to steer a boat properly—I don't believe that someone with defective coordination or an inability to sense relative movements could ever become a champion helmsman—but performance can be improved by training.

I think that the best way to develop this "feel" is to sail with a companion boat for comparison, carrying an observer along. When open water is reached, the helmsman is blindfolded and forced to sail the boat without benefit of sight. The observer can guard against accidents and take over if a serious situation develops.

I suppose that a blind person at the helm for the first time would immediately do better than a person with sight. It is not that vision reduces efficiency, but the blind person will have trained himself to be aware of bodily sensations as an aid to orientation. We have gotten into the habit of relying on our sight and ignoring the nerve messages of our other senses. I think that with the proper training a skipper can make himself utilize more of these signs of the boat's performance.

An excellent way to attain feel is to sail at night. In the darkness you do not see swells and surges off the bow, and you must allow for them instinctively. A good nighttime helmsman is a good daytime helmsman.

I believe that talent at the helm of a boat is like any other talent—part of it is inherent. But talent without training and perseverance is of little value. As I have stated elsewhere in this book, the world is full of talented failures.

It is important to work on acquiring feel if you would become a successful racing skipper. When the boat is going properly, she feels "proper" and lively. Although she is pointing up high into the wind, she does not hesitate or stagger when she reaches the top of a crest. She carries her way through it gracefully even if she is hit by a lurcher.

The Two Major Faults

When the Sailboat Training Facility's programs were inaugurated by Herman Whiton to provide a kind of postgraduate training ground for sailors who wanted to become better skippers, I was privileged to act as observer and advisor. During the races I would watch the starts from the committee boat and then hop into an outboard runabout to tail the fleet throughout the whole race. It was an excellent opportunity to watch the skippers in action, and I learned a great many invaluable things. One of the striking facts that became apparent was that not one skipper in ten was sailing the proper heading for the existing conditions: supposedly experienced helmsmen were consistently sailing either too high or too low.

The most common of the two errors was sailing too high. Now the reason for this is easy to understand: in their excitement to beat competitors to the upwind mark, the skippers were sailing their boats too close to the wind and "starving" the sails. The pinching was not flagrant, and probably the loss of speed was barely perceptible, for an experienced skipper would be aware of any obvious luffing. But it was sufficient to prevent those boats from carrying maximum way for the given conditions of the sea. A simple glance indicated the boats were not moving properly.

When a good breeze causes chop to strike the weather bow, it is absolutely necessary to sail your boat wider than you would if there were no disturbance. You must "feel" for those seas, and work her through them. If there is any indication that they are slowing you down, then you must free her up: free up the jib, free up the main a few inches, and let her develop enough power to pull her through the seas. If you do not, you will not only be knocked imperceptibly to leeward, but you will also lose way. I find that many experienced sailors are unaware of this basic principle. They sail to windward in disturbed water with the jib and main strapped in much too hard.

Conversely, it is obvious that on the opposite board we sometimes sail too free. We have no resistance from the waves on the weather bow, but we are sailing with the jib and main trimmed the same as for the other board. Again, by way of illustration, with the wind from the same direction as before, we are now going to windward on the other tack. We are riding gently over the waves instead of slogging into them; we do not need as much power to drive her through them. Now we can strap her a little harder. The important principle to remember is that the two boards of a windward leg will be different and must be dealt with differently: one board or the other will always present more of a problem with the sea.

Another mistake that comes under the heading of sailing too wide is failure to take into account the course you must make good. To illustrate this point: I once sailed a Bermuda Race with a sophisticated helmsman who thought that "the course to Bermuda is 8 knots." We were sailing an exceptionally high-winded boat and could have made good a course much closer to the rhumb line than our actual course. As a result of this fallacious thinking, we must have sailed many miles longer than necessary. That skipper was lured by the idea of speed-through-the-water instead of course-made-good-over-the-bottom. The same error can occur in day-racing, too. Remember that the winning boat will be the one that gets first to the mark: do not sail too free merely for the sake of attaining hull speed.

ON TELL-TALES AND WIND PENNANTS

I can't stress too strongly how important it is to sail by the tell-tales on the shrouds and the backstay. Particularly in light airs, it is extremely difficult to gauge the wind direction without an indicator of this sort. If you know some skipper who says he sails by the luff of the mainsail or jib and doesn't need tell-tales, look at his standing in the fleet before you emulate him—you might learn that he has more to learn than most of us. Perhaps the only reason my long-time rival and friend Arthur Knapp smokes that great chimney pot of a pipe is to find out what direction the wind is from.

Don't use ribbons for tell-tales; they flutter too much. And because of their heaviness, they are not sensitive enough to lift with light airs. I use black thread, since it can be easily seen against the sky. Put a tell-tale on the backstay for the runs; a tell-tale in the shrouds will be useless then, for it will be deflected by turbulent air blowing off the mainsail. Your masthead fly is also valuable on the runs.

WHERE TO SIT

In light airs, and when carrying a genoa jib, it is preferable to seat the crew and to steer from the leeward position. Putting the weight on the leeward side when the breeze is not quite sufficient to heel the boat allows

This International is laying over so far that much of her rudder is out of water, causing her to broach. This can be avoided if in hard breezes a median course is steered slightly above the next mark. Your boat then may be held off in the hard puffs and brought back to course in the lulls.

the sails to assume their proper set, and of course you can see the luff of the genoa better.

When the breeze is strong, it is preferable to steer from the windward side. It is a more pleasant sensation, you can observe the seas, and work her through them better. Even when carrying a genoa, I think it is a more

231

comfortable and pleasant place to sit, although many skippers do not agree. Also there is some advantage in having your weight to windward in the smaller boats.

If you are working to windward, keep your crew low in the boat to lessen wind resistance. A few upright bodies present a lot of area to push to windward.

21. Desire to Win

BY TED TURNER

If the yacht-racing game has an exciting maverick it
must be Ted Turner. The outspoken Atlanta corporate
head and champion one-design and offshore racing helmsman has sailed in almost all major races, around the world,
winning more than his share with the converted 12-meter
American Eagle and the One-Tonner *Lightnin'*. He also
campaigned the famous *Bolero,* nearly losing her in a fall
gale off the East Coast on the way to an SORC series. His
great spirit of competition has taken him to starting lines
everywhere to risk his fame against the top skippers and
nearly impossible problems of logistics.

Ted Turner, in his business life and sailing career, has
managed to be most successful and put together winning
combinations of people and things. He is not adverse to
taking risks such as crossing a towboat line by heeling the
boat over and bluffing the tug skipper into slowing down
to make the towline sag, or by doing nearly the same thing
crossing a reef to take miles off a leg of a race.

Ted was sailing a Tempest at the Yachting One-of-a-Kind
regatta at St. Petersburg when I first saw him in operation.
I was watching him as he rigged the boat, worked on the
mast tune, and adjusted different bits of hardware. He
would start to walk away to take his lunch, then return
again. He did this several times. I don't know if he ever
made it to the lunch line. It's that extra effort that makes
him the champion that he is, taking that extra look, making that extra modification, giving that extra thought.

233

Sailboat racing offers a perfect opportunity to break away from the increasing complexity and resulting frustration of our everyday lives.

When Christopher Columbus discovered America, it was his idea entirely. He decided to make the voyage, promoted the money, bought the boats, and assembled the crews. Then he led the group of three boats, sailing one himself, and discovered the place. Finally, he worked his way back to Europe. Altogether, it was a gargantuan task.

A few hundred years later when Neil Armstrong went to the moon, he was only a passenger. Perhaps 15,000 people worked on that project for almost fifteen years, so it wasn't really his idea. He was just the rider in a computer-driven piece of scientific equipment, and that's similarly true of men in the business world today.

There is little opportunity for one man's personal efforts to produce any tremendous effect very quickly. I.B.M. might involve itself in a new computer project that will take five years to research and develop and another five years to prove successful. Thousands of people are involved at one time or another. What happens to any single one of them? The individual sense of personal accomplishment disappears or is at best diluted.

A sailboat race often takes just one day. You either win or lose, and you know exactly what you've been able to accomplish—then next weekend you have another race coming up. I think that's basically the reason sailboat racing has grown in popularity as much as it has in recent times. There is no ten-year commitment to a project without knowing how it's going to work out. Racing a sailboat presents a different challenge each time, and every individual race is plenty complex. In fact, I have always maintained that we have a relatively low level of performance in the sport because it is so complicated and involves constant decision making.

Compare yacht racing to automobile racing, for instance. In auto racing, you have a track that you go around. This track is 30-odd feet wide, and you circle the same course over and over again. The track doesn't move or change. At the most, you have two alternate drivers, maybe a pit crew of four to six, and just one machine—that's all. The machine has an engine and a steering wheel. The engine of the car, if it is properly prepared, will go faster if you step on the accelerator. In other words, it is basically a pretty simple operation.

Now consider the course of a sailing race. You don't have a track that is 30 feet wide. You can go anywhere to the right or left of the direct, straight-line course. The propulsion unit of your machine is the wind. There's nothing more fickle than the wind. It will blow this way or that way all day long, and all night long too. Sometimes it doesn't blow at all. What about the propulsion unit's partner, the sails? You have your choice of 25 different sail combinations to accommodate the fickle wind and the infinite number of courses available to you.

Then there is the competition. In a horse race, you have one man on one horse in a field of eight or so. On a football team, even though you have eleven players, you are only competing against one team at a time. In a yacht race, you might be, as in the 1973 Fastnet Race, going against 290 boats in one event. The chances of winning the football game are 50 percent, because you only have to beat one team, but your odds are only one in 290 in the sailboat race.

In offshore sailing, you usually have two watches, like football teams with offensive and defensive platoons. The coach on the sailboat has to be asleep half the time. Can you imagine a football game that took three days with the coach spending half the time sleeping?

As you can see, when you compare yacht racing with other sports, its complexity boggles the mind.

How about navigation? In ocean racing, you don't know where you are a lot of the time. Not only that, you don't know where the competition is! In an automobile race, your pit crew posts a lap chart to let you know how many seconds behind or ahead you are, so you'll know exactly what time you have to make up. In an ocean race, you can't even see the competition. You don't know whether they're beating you or whether you're beating them. In automobile racing, if you are winning, you want to win by simply holding the front position. You never press your lead too hard because something might break. In sailboat racing, who knows how many boats have gotten into trouble because a hurricane was blowing and they thought they needed gear that they wouldn't have used if they knew their position. You might be out in front on corrected time, but you can't tell. For example, in a transatlantic race you've got to keep the spinnaker up regardless of the conditions, because you don't know where you are in relation to the rest of the fleet. If you knew you were ahead by five hours, you would probably play it a little smarter and safer to avoid the chance of breaking something.

So from every aspect, the currents (often you can't tell how they are affecting you), the wind, and the competition all add up to one complex problem.

Then there is the human side of sailboat racing as well. In the 12-meter program, one of the biggest problems we had was too many people wanting to sail on the boat. I could have manned a square-rigger with a 70-man crew. It's pretty hard to say, "Gee, you know, we're pretty well full," to men that I've known for a long time and who I know are good sailors. Under normal circumstances, I'd be tickled to death to have them on board. I'm always worried about hurting their feelings. It's tough, the personality side of things. Most guys have trouble coming up with crews for offshore racers; our trouble is coming up with too many. The final decision is usually made in that best decision-making tradition: just fumbling your way along. I don't write any lists, but I guess my mind does it unconsciously. This man has these strengths and these weaknesses, and so forth. You have to have a wide range of different abilities aboard a 12-meter; some adept crewmen on the foredeck and others with a lot of physical strength for grinding. The personality aspect is a major factor to consider, and one that I sweat over when selecting my original crew. It's such a critical point; in fact, it's almost the primary consideration.

I try to run both my business and sailing operations in a similar fashion. My philosophy in both areas is that if you have good enough men (and it's essential to get the very best), you should give them responsibility. Give them as much responsibility as they can handle, then you don't even need to be there. Get the best people with plenty of experience and simply supply a work atmosphere that is rewarding to them. Then everyone shares the victories or the defeats as integral members of one team.

We don't run the "professional" operation that some of the other boats do, with a bevy of sailmakers on board because the owners are buying a load of sails. My crews don't get tickets or travel money for sailing events. Many times they'll be selling their cars to get to Australia or England or wherever. We just have a good "go-go" type of operation, and the guys enjoy sailing on a boat just for the pure fun of competition. It makes everyone a lot happier having all the crew in on the expenses and knowing that each one carries his own weight.

Of course, there is another factor: Crewmen aren't going to "bust their chops" to sail on a boat that either isn't fun to be on or doesn't have a chance to win. If you have real competitors in the crew, they want to be on a winning, well-run boat. If the boat isn't winning or isn't well-run, how are you going to get a crew? I might own the boat, but everything else is US.

I often think back over the summer of 1973. Just the logistics of getting *Lightnin'* to the various races, from the SORC, to the Annapolis-Newport, across the Atlantic to the Skaw Race, and then to the Admiral's Cup and down to the One Ton Cup in Sardinia, would have thrown most people into a tizzie, and came close to doing it to us. I had one of my most faithful and capable crewmen work out the transportation, and everything had to click right on the minute. There was no time for contingency plans. If we missed anywhere along the line, the whole system broke down.

It all went pretty well until the Fastnet. It was one of the slowest in history, but we couldn't do a thing about it. We had a truck standing by in Le Havre and we had a yard in Plymouth ready and waiting to put the propellor, shaft, and strut (which had been removed to increase rating for the Admiral's Cup) back on in order to cross the English Channel. That was the tightest one, getting from Plymouth, England, at the finish of the 605-mile Fastnet Race, to Porto Cervo, Sardinia, for the start of the One Ton Cup. In fact, the boat arrived with only one day to spare. We had to get the boat out of the water to put on the prop and equipment, which had arrived by truck from Lymington. We put all the extra gear on board and pulled the boat out of the water on the first high tide after the finish of the race. The crew worked all night putting all that material on and getting it set. They put the boat in the water the next morning and sailed to Le Havre. In Le Havre, the yard was standing by and so was the truck, which had been waiting there for days. Within 24 hours, they left for Marseilles. They had to do all that to get to Sardinia on time.

I was already in Sardinia, and I'll tell you, it was really pretty frightening because we had to get all the gear off the boat and we barely made the start.

Lightnin' had to be remeasured also. Within an hour-and-a-half of the Fastnet finish, there was a measurer on board, and we were cutting the spinnaker pole down to size and doing other jobs. It would have given the average person a nervous breakdown just attempting it. Compared to all that, the 12-meter operation should be simple. The America's Cup program doesn't frighten me from a logistical standpoint, although we are taking nothing for granted.

Ted Turner at the helm of his *American Eagle* during the 1971 SORC.

We are dealing with a group of people who have had a lot of experience; there are no amateurs involved. George Hinman is heading it up and has a world of experience. Bob Derecktor has built boats to deadlines, and although he is a very busy builder and designer, I think he will give the 12-meter project first priority.

There are a lot of people on-site, and that makes a difference too. We're not conducting the campaign 10,000 miles away, as the French and Australians must; it's going to be within shooting distance. And then I've got crewmen who have been well-tested on *American Eagle.* We know how to fix things on the boat ourselves and don't need a yard to do winch repair. We will be able to do many of the little jobs ourselves. So, assuming that we don't run into any real serious problems along the way, something wrong with the boat or rig that needs really serious work (we're even geared up for major hull modification at any time), we are well prepared.

There is a lot to be said for the experience that one-design racing brings to offshore sailing. The level of competition is different, though. I've got a Flying Dutchman in the garage, but I just haven't had a chance to use it over the past year. I really don't have a great wish to get back to it because it's so hard to find good competition on a consistent basis. We have a little fleet of eight Dutchmen here in Atlanta that sails on the lake, and there are one or two regattas, but just not enough regular competition to make it really interesting.

I guess what I am saying is that in the past few years we've been at all the big ones. There is always a major ocean race going on somewhere in the world, and we've gotten used to large fleets and top competition with all the best sailors. That's the best way to go as far as I'm concerned. Even so, you can really learn a lot from one-designs: sail trim and the nuances of making the boat go fast. There is the practice of constantly trimming the sails, and I know that is not a new idea, but seven or eight years ago when we started there wasn't nearly as much focus on that in ocean racing. It was mostly a group of older guys sailing wooden boats like *Bolero* and *Windigo* and they were really easy to beat because they weren't that well organized. They were just doing it on a lark.

The main lesson I've learned from one-design racing is the need for practice and perseverance. There is absolutely no substitute for establishing a familiarity with the boat under all possible conditions. There aren't many people with any special intuitive feeling about a boat. Lots of time aboard, racing and practicing, tells you where to put a deck lead or what sail to have up at any given time or how high you can point. The more you sail, the better you should get. Perseverance must be one of the major attributes of a successful sailor either in a one-design fleet or in offshore races. In the first nine years that I sailed, I never won a fleet championship. I sailed in Penguins, Lightnings, Y-Flyers and never really won anything important, but I kept working at it. That is the only secret of success that I know of: hard work and then more of the same until success begins to come—then loads of additional effort to remain in that pleasant position.

You have a tremendous number of men, good men, now racing sailboats. Offshore racing has become a big deal in the last decade, and a lot of people have gone into the boat business who wouldn't have otherwise, because it was just too small an industry ten to fifteen years ago. More and more people, like John Marshall and Lowell North, who would have been exclusively small-boat sailors a decade ago, have become involved in the big boats because there is a lot more money in them. An offshore boat owner may spend $50,000 a year on sails while a new suit for a Flying Dutchman would run $1,000. All the best talent is gravitating to the bigger boats, where there is a lot more money. One-design racing just hasn't grown nearly as fast as offshore racing.

Today you will find very few stock offshore boats that are truly competitive at the highest level. But, competition on the second level has improved a great deal in the past few years with bigger and better boats and sails.

Back in my office after a summer out there racing, I am sharply reminded of things left undone, so much backlogged work to get through. And then my thoughts jump ahead to the next race and the next summer. Maybe that's the only secret formula for success: Neglect your wife, your family, your business, spend every minute on the water, and you'll improve your chances of being a winner.

22. Some Thoughts on Ocean Racing

I have had my greatest successes in triangular-course day racing, but I have been no less interested in the subject of ocean racing. It is a wonderful experience to prolong the intensity and excitement of the 10-mile triangle to a 4- or 5-day race. It is a precious gift, unique to the yachtsman, to relive in some measure the same experience and emotions felt by those who sailed the great tea clippers, who for economic reasons were compelled to make fast passage. An ocean race will be a long-remembered event in any man's life.

I have sailed many Bermuda Races, and I have by great fortune campaigned on two of the finest ocean racers afloat, *Good News* and *Bolero*. Reflecting on my experiences in this kind of racing, I have come to one overwhelming conclusion. I think the reason more ocean racing skippers do not do better is because they do not continuously race: in most cases, after the first six or eight hours, the race deteriorates into an off-shore cruise.

Now, this may seem like a harsh judgment, but believe me, I have seen it time and again and I know that I am right. It is only human to let down after an extended period of intense effort; we all know that. When the ocean racer is out of sight of the rest of the fleet for days at a time without the constant spurring of the sight of competitors, it is the natural order of things for efficiency to slip.

But if he is to be successful at ocean racing, the skipper must prevent this loss of efficiency at all costs. The great ocean-racing skippers like Olin and Roderick Stephens, Carleton Mitchell, Richard Nye and Hugh Long have learned this, and from all reports I have heard from men who have crewed for them, the concern for never letting down is constant and fore-most in their consciousness. These men are champions, thanks to that phi-losophy. Carleton Mitchell, especially, has proven it by the feat, un-equalled in yachting history, of winning the Bermuda Race three times in succession.

Here is an example that will prove my point. In 1946 I took the *Good News* to Bermuda; after five days of sailing, we crossed the finish line at Saint David's Head only minutes behind the winner. Without the slightest doubt, we could have won that race had we not lost many, many minutes each day because of slack helmsmanship. Understand, the helmsmanship was of a high order, but sometimes we lost minutes because it was not the best we could possibly do.

And so it goes: minutes are lost in a watch, an hour is lost in the day, and the lost hours lose the race. How does one go about remedying this human failing?

A PHILOSOPHY FOR THE RACE

I think there is a simple, but perhaps not easy way to cope with the common problem of the let-down in ocean racing. The solution I offer is this—*treat every watch as though it were one leg of a triangular-course day race and sail it with supreme concentration.*

By maintaining an attitude of this sort, a certain effect is achieved, and here is why this solution is not easy. In a day race the distances are short; every board of a windward leg must be fought tooth-and-nail. The best man at making that boat go to windward is the windward helmsman. The same holds true for the reach and run—the finest hand available is the one that must coax everything possible out of the boat; the tautness is main-tained until the end. It should be the same with every watch of an ocean race.

Again by way of illustration: in one Bermuda Race, we had passed through the Gulf Stream and it was one of those beautiful sunny days you so often get in those tropical latitudes. We had gone through some bad wet weather and were drying out. The wind had fallen very light, and the minute I came on deck I had the impression that purposiveness had somehow inexplicably vanished and that the whole ship had the atmosphere of a cruise. Sure enough, when I looked aft, who was steering but the junior crew member, and he was simply murdering that boat!

Now he was one of the most able youngsters on deck, but he was not a racing helmsman. What he was doing to that boat was so heart-rending that I couldn't stand it. It was unpleasant to do, but I had to take him off the wheel immediately, because the speed of the boat meant much more to me than his personal feelings. I hated to think of the precious time that inexperience had cost us. I hope to heaven that as long as I live I never again hear the words, "Would you like to take a stab at steering for awhile?" aboard a boat actively engaged in racing. No one should touch the helm who has not been chosen for his skill and appointed to the task.

THE WATCHES

No matter how you set up the watches, whether four-hours-on-and-four-off, or any other system, this principle should guide you: each watch should have a watch captain in whom you have complete confidence. He should have equal, or greater abilities than yours, and he should be a first-rate helmsman. If, because of heavy weather and a limit of physical endurance, a relief helmsman is necessary during the watch, the relief should be the next best man in the watch; and he should be supervised by the watch captain.

It is in the nature of things that one must go below occasionally for a cup of coffee or whatnot, but the watch captain must never absent himself for more than a few minutes, if at all. He should never leave the deck until he is certain that the helmsman is doing well. I also believe that a boat should not sail shorthanded in an ocean race, because every member of each watch should be available on deck during his whole tour of duty. In this way men are available for necessary chores and the helmsmen can pay strict attention to the steering.

It is vital to place your best helmsmen in the night watches. Sailing in the darkness requires a good hand and steady nerves, especially in heavy weather. It is in the long night watches that the poorest sailing is done. And now, of course, the inevitable question arises: "How do I know who the best helmsmen are when this is the first time I have sailed with them?"

The answer to that question is that you must sail with them before the race. The best of men need a period of time to settle down to a routine, to learn the ways of a strange boat, to know what is expected of them. And the first few days of an ocean race is not the time to begin this process of breaking in; by then it is already too late; the race has started and everything must be improvised by trial and error.

THE SHAKEDOWN

If you are serious in your desire to win, you must somehow find time to spend three or four days in a shakedown sail. When I was asked to campaign the *Good News* in 1946, I wanted to do everything in my power to win, and yet I was faced with the prospect of a grueling 700-mile ocean race on a strange boat with men who, although most had sailed with me before, had yet to learn their duties. I, too, had to learn about ocean racing, for although I had my own ways of doing things, I needed the practical experience aboard the boat to test them and to apply them to the *Good News*.

It seemed to me the best way to obtain this experience was by actually going to sea for three days and simulating a real race. In effect, this would be more than racing, because in racing, you can sometimes stay on one tack for days on end. But we did everything that I thought would be necessary during a race, and some things that I hoped would not be necessary, like man-overboard drill and damage-control practice. We reefed and shortened sail, shook out the reefs, tacked, set and doused spinnakers, jibed spinnakers, changed from working jib to genoa jib, and made so many sail changes during those three days that I began to fear the boys would have no enthusiasm for the actual race.

We stood regular watches, we cooked and served hot meals, and since we were way offshore we had plenty of opportunity to test our navigation. It was early June and there was plenty of heavy weather to deal with, to try men and gear, and we learned an awful lot in those three days. By the time we crossed the starting line at Newport, bound for Bermuda, we were a pretty rugged, seasoned bunch aboard that yawl. Most important, the shakedown gave me a chance to observe the hands in action, and I now knew where both our strengths and our weaknesses lay. The experience was extremely valuable. It is astonishing to me that this is not regular practice in offshore racing.

I have often thought that the greatest ability one can have is the ability to recognize ability in others, and this is certainly true of the ocean-racing skipper in the selection of his crew. This kind of training session, with the hands learning to know and work the boat, affords an occasion to evaluate the crew's potential and to form the men into the most efficient watches.

As I stated before, the two or three best helmsmen should be chosen captains of the port, starboard, and middle watches. The three next best should be ticketed as relief helmsmen, one to each watch. The balance of the crew is best assigned so that there is a good seaman-sail trimmer for each watch.

During the shakedown racing, you must make judgments, not only as to ability, but as to character. You must eliminate from your ship any man who is ill-tempered or quarrelsome. Five days or a week cooped up in a racing sailboat with an antisocial personality of this type can be very disturbing; morale will sink and with it your chances of success. Try to pair off men in the same watch who get along well or whose personalities complement each other.

If it is at all possible, two men should stand no regular watches—the navigator and the cook. The navigator, if he does his job well, will be up and down at all hours during the night searching for star sights to obtain a line of position. During dirty weather when the sky is overcast, he may have to wait for hours to grab a quick sextant altitude through the scud. He also needs a certain amount of time to work up his sights and maintain his records. During the day and in clear weather, he can be called upon for assistance if necessary, but his job is to get you to your destination accurately, with no interference.

As for the cook, if you have a man who can reef, hand, and steer, who is immune to seasickness, and who can turn out good hot meals in a wet, lurching cabin that's dripping damp and laden with the assorted smells of a small boat battened down in a blow—and still remain cheerful—then hang on to him for dear life. Treat him royally, for every skipper in the ocean-racing fleet will be after him when the word passes around. It is really a difficult job to turn out three meals and innumerable snacks a day under ocean-racing conditions for a crew of ravenous men. So, like the navigator, the cook should be relieved of the added chore of standing regular watches. He deserves it.

The Indispensable Man: the Navigator

Aside from the skipper himself, the navigator is the most important man aboard an ocean racer. Upon the skill of this vital crew member will depend the success or failure of your ocean-racing campaign.

It is for this reason that the choice of navigator is even more important than the choice of the crew. A good crew will avail you nothing if the boat cannot be accurately pinpointed each day and if you are unable to lay a course that will, at noon of each day, put you in the most advantageous position for the next day's run.

You should know the potential navigator, and though it is possible to pick one by reputation, it is better if you have sailed with him. He must be a man who understands the subtleties of ocean racing; a man who can just lay a "steamboat course" is not sufficient. There is the windward ability of the boat, and the effects of leeway, currents, and many other things to consider. Again, he must be a chap who will be a compatible member of the organization. No matter how great his talents, be sure he meets this requirement, because he will be under pressure night and day. Five days at sea can seem an eternity if he is not compatible with the other crewmen.

After you have picked your navigator, for heaven's sake leave him alone and let him do his job. Once you have committed yourself and given the man the berth, remember that he is head of his division, and accept his decisions without reservation. Don't be the type of skipper who is constantly popping topsides armed with a sextant and a stopwatch to work sights of his own and who then proceeds to interrogate the navigator. He might assume that you do not fully trust his ability, and this tends to make navigators unhappy.

Naturally, you will want to understand the navigator's thinking on certain matters. In the case of the Gulf Stream, for instance, you might want to know what the navigator had allowed for drift. If he allowed 30 miles, the skipper might not agree because of some special knowledge about the boat's performance—for example, the knowledge that the wind is from a quarter that would not knock your yacht unusually far off course. This is a rare example of when a skipper may interfere in the navigator's work.

If you have no confidence in his ability, it is better to relieve him of his duties completely. But the rule should be that the navigator's decisions are final, because if you don't have confidence in him, you might as well leave your boat at the mooring.

We have spoken about the skipper's "choosing" of the navigator. In effect, however, this is not often the way it works. You will find that the best navigators usually pick their own boats. The reputations of successful navigators keep them in constant demand. They will only ship aboard yachts where they find the skipper and crew congenial, where they will unqualifiedly head their divisions, and where there will be no attempt to interfere with their decisions. The skipper of an ocean racer has enough work running the boat and sailing her fast without trying to do the navigating as well.

Passing on the Reckoning

When I began ocean racing, I developed a custom that I think is a practical one. The watch is required to record the boat's speed by the log every fifteen minutes. The speed of a hull can vary a great deal during the course of an hour, and I do not believe that reporting the speed once an hour, as is customary, is often enough. There are plenty of unpredictables in ocean racing as it is, without introducing any unnecessary ones. A record of speed for fifteen-minute intervals will give the navigator a basis for calculation that is bound to be more accurate than an hourly record.

Navigators are a breed of men in themselves, and like skippers they have their temperaments. I suspect that the navigator considers his daily work a creative act—and it is, too. All creative people should be allowed a few idiosyncrasies, so if your navigator should turn into a bleary-eyed, mumbling monomaniac because Venus has been perverse enough to stay hidden behind a layer of cloud throughout a whole night, you must, above all, be discreet and softly whisper your condolences. After all, it is a kind of desperate, unrequited love, this star-crossed profession.

23. Anticipation and Objective Appraisal— The Basic Keys to Racing Success

BY ROBERT BAVIER

The late Robert Bavier, Sr., was a renowned racing sailor from 1905 to the mid-1940's. His 60-foot *Dragoon* was the winner of many offshore races. He was one of the original International class owners in 1937 and I remember well his remarkable five firsts that won the Larchmont Race Week Series. He won a Bermuda Race in his New York Yacht Club converted yawl, *Memory.* In 1938, he was helmsman on Clinton Crane's J-Boat, *Weetamoe,* during the trials to select the America's Cup defender.

His son, Bob, Jr., carries on this winning tradition. Some of his early racing was done in the famous Herreshoff 12-footers. This is still a great boat for racing and day sailing, but I do wish they would break tradition and allow a Marconi rig.

Bob, Jr., served as an officer in the Navy from 1940 to 1945. In his first year of sailing after his service years, he won the Atlantic class championship. The very next year, he did the same thing in the Lightning class. He then raced his father's International and regularly finished with the top sailors in the class.

As the publisher of *Yachting* magazine and author of many books, Bob Bavier has contributed greatly to the advancement of sailing and racing the world over. His approach to racing has always been very practical and down to earth, as you will see in his chapter.

Bob was invited to sail Olin Stephens' *Courageous* in the 1974 America's Cup trials. His successful defense of the Cup in 1964 at the helm of *Constellation* certainly speaks well for his selection by the *Courageous* syndicate.

By the time you read this, the 1974 America's Cup will be history, but I am sure Bob Bavier will still be a dynamic force in the world of yachting.

What are the basic keys to racing success which set the very good sailor apart from the fairly good one? This book and other books give excellent advice on tactics, tuning, helmsmanship, and sail trim to the point that there simply are no secrets. The answers are there for anyone willing to study and to practice what they have studied. Still better for learning than any book is the opportunity to observe and then to try to emulate the successful sailor. If you can figure out why he wins, maybe you can too. And yet the same people keep winning, joined each season by a small group of newcomers.

It's certainly not a question of intelligence. I've known men who have graduated from college with high honors, who have been huge business successes, who can steer a boat as fast as anyone, who own a fast boat, who try hard and have a real will to win, and yet who year after year finish well below the top. While it is certainly not lack of inherent intelligence which keeps them in an also-ran status, I suspect it is a gap in their thought processes, a lack of objectivity, and a failure to use their minds to even a fraction of their capacity. If only they knew why they weren't winning or why the leaders were winning, maybe a reversal could come. Could the answer be to train your sailing mind to focus on two traits which every top sailor has—anticipation and objective appraisal of why (*really* why) they won or lost?

Anticipation on the race course takes so many forms. It begins even before the race. The good sailor knows there can be delays or foul-ups getting to the starting line and hence leaves earlier than his basically smart opponent. If the latter is delayed, even though he will probably make the start, he is allowed insufficient time to case the course, or plan his start or his initial course.

Anticipating changes which might occur in the weather will help select the right sail to bend on. And I've been caught with light sheets bent on and then hit by a sudden increase in the wind, which I could so easily have foreseen if my mind had been geared to anticipating that possibility.

Anticipation is particularly important at the start. If one end of the line is favored greatly, you can bet your bottom dollar that there will be a big jam of boats there. Knowing that, you can then decide if you wish to join the jam in hopes of being top boat among it, or avoid it by being somewhat up or down the line, near the favored end but clear of the crush. The latter is usually the best tactic and becomes especially so if you anticipate a wind shift which after the start will offset the initial advantage of being at the favored end. All really good sailors know that it's where you are a couple of minutes after the start rather than at the start itself which determines whether or not you got a good start.

It's almost laughable how many people get fooled by current at the start. If there is a strong fair current, you can be sure that some boats will either be early or killing headway during the seconds before the gun in order to keep from being early. Knowing this, hold back well below the line, look for a hole, and then come steaming through at high speed. You can almost invariably shoot into clear air and a lead. Equally important, you remove the possibility of being over early and taking an eternity to recross against the current. Under these conditions which invite a premature start, the savvy sailor is never early because he knows the damage from being early will be so very costly. Never was this better illustrated than in the start of the 1973 Fastnet Race. There was a gentle head wind (about 4 to 5 knots) and a 2- to 3-knot fair current. All boats had engines which they could use up to the prep signal to get well up-current behind the line. We did this on Bob Derecktor's *Salty Goose* and when the gun went, we were about one length shy of the line, hard on the wind with the current lift adding to the apparent wind strength. A few other boats did the same, but when the gun went the bulk of the fleet was broach reaching at slow speed trying to keep from being swept over early. Within seconds, we were out in clear air and winging. A few boats were early and unable to stem the current to return. They remained anchored for *hours* while the fleet sailed literally out of sight. Through lack of anticipation, they had put themselves out of a 600-mile race right at the start!

Anticipation becomes important on a reach. Every good sailor knows it pays to bear off in a puff and sharpen up in lighter air, but too few carry this reasoning far enough. In addition to this short-range action, it pays to think in terms of the whole leg. If you anticipate the wind to increase steadily over the course of the leg, sail high in the early stages. This will help you moving at high speed for the light air. You can then bear off at good speed when the wind increases. Just the reverse should be done if you expect the wind to decrease. This philosophy can apply to a two-mile reaching leg or for one of 200 miles in an ocean race. In the latter case, your anticipation is more long-range and is determined by weather forecasting rather than looking at wind on the water, but the principle is the same.

Anticipation becomes particularly important when approaching a mark in a closely packed fleet. The boat which has an inside overlap will pick up immeasurably on the one which is on the outside of, say, four boats rounding together. Knowing this, the smart skipper will plan ahead so as not to be caught outside. An alternative, if you see lots of boats sailing high to gain the inside berth, is to sail low and reach up ahead of the pack as they slow down on a poor sailing angle to get down to the mark. The latter maneuver takes courage because if you've timed it poorly or have misgauged your chances, you could wind up blanketed on the outside. But the main thing is to plan your approach to the mark well ahead as there is much to be gained or lost at this time.

There are so many examples of the reward of properly anticipating or the pitfalls of failing to do so that I could go on and on. Relax, I won't, but here are just a few quick points. Knowing you can get a spinnaker wrap is all you need to never have one. Just rig a net when conditions are such that it could happen. On *Salty Goose* in the 1973 Channel Race, we noticed the spinnaker sheet had frayed a bit. We bent a second one on as a lazy sheet. Sure enough, the original one did break an hour later, but we lost nothing in the process. If a headsail blows out, you will lose something, but not much, *provided* a replacement one is already on deck, bent on, and ready to hoist.

Before we leave the subject of anticipation, let me tell you about the last race my father ever sailed. It was in the late forties on the New York Yacht Club Cruise. The course was from Edgartown to Newport. At the start there was a light leftover nor'wester. Under those conditions in that area of the coast, everyone knows that a sou'wester will eventually come in. Therefore the entire fleet but one beat along the Martha's Vineyard shore in order to be up to windward when the sou'wester came in. The one exception was my father. He could see a better breeze and what looked like a header under the Elizabeth Islands and took a long port tack over to them. When we got there we were headed, flipped onto starboard, and despite rating below the middle of the fleet had, after six miles, a full-mile lead over the next boat. The rest of the fleet, seeing us, tacked to port belatedly and headed for us. The breeze was still stronger to the north, but abating gradually. My father, realizing that this abatement was the prelude to the advent of the sou'wester, never tacked back into the northerly but held starboard tack even though the whole fleet crossed our stern to get into the stronger breeze which had given us our advantage and was now plain for all to see.

We had some anxious moments when we fell flat and they held the old breeze. Some 20 minutes later, it died out all over and soon thereafter came the most beautiful sight you can imagine—the hard sharp line of a brisk sou'wester south of us, with the entire fleet more than a mile to the north of us. We got it 15 minutes sooner than the second boat and were reaching at hull speed while the others were having trouble keeping steerageway. We won by over 20 minutes, an unheard of margin in a day race and not a bad finale to a truly brilliant racing career. You may call it good weather forecasting, some might call it luck, but I choose to refer to it as anticipation that the norther would last long enough to give us an initial advantage, and that the important thing thereafter was to get in position to take advantage of the inevitable sou'-wester.

All of which brings us to the other absolute essential to racing success. In the title of this chapter, I refer to it as objective appraisal. That's a rather high-flown phrase for the ability to avoid wishful thinking, to recognize a situation for what it is during a race, and to learn after the race both from your mistakes and from your successes. During a race, you may have decided port tack was best. If after a time it's not working out, you've got a big decision. Many get stubborn at this point and sail themselves completely out of contention when an honest evaluation would tell them they had goofed and had better admit it and get over onto starboard tack and join the group which had been smarter. Hans Fogt was exemplary in this regard in the light and fluky weather which prevailed in the 1973 Soling Class Atlantic Coast Championship. Usually he took the right initial tack and was well-placed soon after the start. But on two occasions he chose the wrong tack and was in mid-fleet soon after five minutes. On each occasion, he took his medicine, tacked under the leaders, and then proceeded to grind them down. Had he not quickly admitted his mistake, he would soon have been out of it. The difficulty, of course, comes in trying to evaluate if your initial tack, though starting out wrong, might pan out eventually. Hoping it will work out never seems to work, but if your eyes and instinct still tell you that it will in the long run, then stick to it. The point is you must be objective and honest—neither too stubborn in your conviction nor too quick to abandon a preconceived plan.

There's even more to be learned by an objective appraisal after a race. If you won or did well, analyze carefully just why you won. And if you stank up the course, there's some solace from the opportunity this affords you to learn and thereby correct the next time. A friend of mine who is a good sailor has a chronic habit of overstanding. He invariably sails right to the lay line or beyond and gets killed by either a lift or a header. Why doesn't he learn from this?

When I was young, my father would often watch me racing. At the dinner table, he would ask me if I knew what I had done right, what wrong. He would ask if I knew how and why the winner had won. Luck enters into yacht racing, but to a far lesser degree than most of us realize and that was one explanation Dad would never accept.

While this is Monday morning quarterbacking, it gives a superb chance to learn. I've made every mistake in the book, and believe me, I still make some, but it is mighty seldom that I don't recognize them. When I was sailing *Constellation* in 1964, we used to have an oral review of the race each evening with trained observers who had been watching every move from our tender. They would start out by citing the mistakes they had noted and it was seldom that I did not have the same list of mistakes in my notes (mental or written) and frequently I had one or two they hadn't detected. By recognizing what you did wrong, you build a subconscious storehouse of knowledge which will make reoccurrence less likely. That's experience, but only if you recognize it.

It's also important to recognize that you did little wrong, but still lost. A number of years ago, we were sailing a Lightning and for the first half of the season had a great record. When we went into the district championship, we barely qualified for the nationals. Despite not putting my finger on what I had done wrong to warrant an also-ran finish, I concluded that I just must have sailed poorly. When we went to the nationals, we found out that our boat speed was shot. Sure I know we were in keener competition, but boats we had beaten earlier were also there and they were in contention and we out of it. After returning to local racing and doing poorly, we finally realized that the draft in our mainsail had so shifted that we had a bad case of the slows, a fact confirmed the following year when a new sail got us going again. I was stupid in not realizing this and correcting it before going to the nationals.

But far more prevalent is the inability to recognize the sailing and tactical mistakes one makes or the failure to realize the things the winners did that you didn't. It is all too easy to ascribe it to boat speed, which, of course, is important and can make you look smarter than you are, but the very best way to be smart is to be objective, to realize how dumb you've been, to recognize the mistakes you've made and thus build up a reservoir of information in your mind which will make it less likely that you will repeat those mistakes in future races. It doesn't take much intelligence to develop this trait of objective analysis, but failure to develop it can make smart men look stupid. Worse still, it will keep them also-rans on the race course.

24. Racing and Weather

As a racing sailor, you will have a vital interest in weather phenomena; you must change your thinking from that of the landsman who can make do with a look out the window or the sketchy forecast sandwiched in between the evening's television news. The needs of the sailor are more sophisticated, the necessary information more detailed than that required by the average person.

There is probably no need for a complete knowledge of meteorology, for this is a complicated and exacting science; but the sailor must work, at the least, on becoming "weatherwise." You must learn as much as you can out of self-defense, for if you are unable to read obvious weather signs, your better-informed competitors will have a decided advantage.

The study of weather, like the study of the other faces of nature, has always fascinated me, and I have spent many hours training myself to notice the skies and to understand the "why's" of change. Beyond a doubt, it has been invaluable in helping me in my racing. Ask yourself these questions, and see of you can really answer them:

Why is it cold in January? What is different between January and February weather? Why is it different? What conditions cause June to be fine and fair and January to be drear and unpleasant? What is rain? Where does the wind blow from? I wonder how many of us are really competent to answer these seemingly infantile questions.

Racing and Weather

The difference between the average man and the creative scientist is precisely the intellectual curiosity with which questions as simple as these are pursued. A child asks, "Daddy, why is the sky blue?" And we are embarrassed because we must answer with an oversimplification that is a half-truth. So it is with these other simple questions, for when something simple is explored to the end, it generally no longer remains simple.

We are interested in general weather patterns because they will be the largest influence upon our local conditions. Because of the work of the gifted Norwegian meteorologist, Bjerkenes, we now think in terms of large "packages" of air that are the "factories" that produce weather. The characteristics of a mass of air thousands of miles away will interest us, for sooner or later its effects will be felt in our own area. Though we are primarily concerned with local conditions for the day of our race, we will also find it to our advantage to become acquainted with over-all weather patterns throughout the world.

Some of the things that we must explore are the characteristics of high- and low-pressure areas, the meanings of warm and cold fronts, the names and significances of cloud formations, the all-important use of the barometer, and familiarity with the weather map. In this chapter I want mainly to discuss weather as it applies to yacht racing, since it would be impossible in the space available to cover the field of weather completely. I suggest that the beginning racer buy a good meteorology textbook to learn terms, principles, and methods of weather forecasting. One that is done in an entertaining manner, and that is complete but not overly technical, is *Eric Sloane's Weather Book.** Sloane is an artist who is also interested in meteorology, and his drawings are imaginative and illustrate the text clearly.

I would like to divide this discussion of weather into two parts, the first a discussion of conditions that prevail over the nation, and the second a discussion of purely local weather. When I talk about national weather, it will have application to racing men no matter where they live; when I speak of local conditions, I must, of necessity, refer to those that prevail mostly in the North Atlantic states, since this is where I have gained most of my experience. But the yachtsman must bear in mind that for every sign of the coming weather particular to my section of the country, there is a similar sign applicable to his.

In my talking about observations concerning Long Island Sound, the

* E. Sloane, *Eric Sloane's Weather Book*, (New York, Duell, Sloan, & Pearce).

value will lie in illustrating the kind of weather portents one should be on the alert for. In my discussion of the characteristics of winds from different quadrants especially, the reader will have to bear in mind that they are meant for my own area. For example, a wind from the north will have different characteristics on the Gulf Coast from what a similar wind would have on the Middle Atlantic coast. The main thing to remember is that the wind from each separate quarter has its own individual identity and will bring conditions that are peculiar to it. This holds true no matter where you live.

For example, southeast wind of any duration on Long Island Sound is a poor weather sign and usually produces rain. Southeast wind on the east coast of Florida results in the best weather.

Westerly wind on the Sound predicts good weather, whereas on the east coast of Florida it is almost certain to bring rain the next day.

THE WEATHER MAP

We have mentioned that large masses of moving air will behave as gigantic "factories," building the varying conditions that we call weather. In general, because of the rotation of the earth, weather tends to move from west to east. The rate at which this weather moves depends upon the velocity of the air mass, as well as several other factors; but in general, it will advance at a rate that is roughly 500 miles per day in summer (750 in winter). So in all likelihood, we should expect that on Tuesday night, New York City will have the same weather that existed over Chicago on Monday. During advance planning of a weekend race, we must take cognizance of weather in the far west, because high- and low-pressure systems and cold and warm fronts there will eventually make their influence felt to the east.

Weather does not always move in a true easterly direction. Sometimes a high-pressure area will merge into a low-pressure area in another direction than east, or a front will dissolve, but in general, we can expect weather systems to follow this easterly course.

The daily weather map is a graphic representation of weather conditions that exist throughout the nation on a particular day. One thing you must remember is that the weather map you are reading in today's paper is really a picture of conditions as they were yesterday. Therefore, a weather map that pictures a cold front 500 miles to the west is already obsolete; by the time you read your paper, the front is overhead. Despite this lag, the weather map is the greatest aid we have for predicting the weather.

The passage of a front will be accompanied by rain and probably by strong- to violent-winds, depending on the season, nature of the front, and how close together the isobars are. I suggest you learn the characteristic clouds of both cold and warm fronts, because you must be able to recognize the approach of these weather systems when you are out on the water. As you look over the weather map, pay particular attention to the spacing of the isobars—isobars are lines connecting stations of equal pressure—for this is your surest indication of wind strengths within a pressure system. Also note the positions and directions of movement of high- and low-pressure systems. Remember that in the northern hemisphere, winds will blow clockwise out of high-pressure areas into low-pressure areas, where they will reverse direction and blow counterclockwise. The small arrows on the map show wind direction, and the feather barbs show the force in 5-knot increments.

Another aspect of large masses of air that concerns us, but that is not usually labeled on the weather map, is the nature of the air mass—that is, whether it is tropical maritime (mT), polar maritime (mP), continental polar (cP), or one of the five other types. Each type has distinctive properties, and except for minor modifications acquired as it moves will retain those properties. Thus winter cP air from Canada will be cold, dry, and of high density. When this strikes against warmer mP air already over an area, a well-defined cold front will be formed—with accompanying cloud formations, precipitation, and high winds.

So we see that the weather map is a picture that—if you can read it properly—will show you the general weather characteristics to come. Forewarned is forearmed, and the man who studies the weather is in a position to exploit what he learns.

On the morning of the race, we consult the weather map and move the positions of the highs and lows 500 miles to the east. Now we note which side of the high or low we will be on, what direction the wind can be expected from, what the strength will be, and how dependable it is likely to remain. If the high or low shows a good, well-defined pattern, we will be able to count on a steady wind. But if the isobars are far apart or, in other words, if the gradient is gradual, then the wind is likely to be uncertain and undependable.

THE BAROMETER

After the weather map, the barometer will be your next most important source of weather information. The barometer measures the weight of the atmosphere, and since a fairly good instrument is relatively inexpensive, it is a weather aid that you can have right in your home. The words *stormy, rain, changeable,* and *fair* that are printed on most barometers have no value or significance for the sailor or meteorologist. What we are interested in is not so much the pressure at a single reading, but the pressure tendency over a period of time, with the tendency during a three-hour period immediately preceding a radio weather report holding the most meaning. From this record we can ascertain whether the barometer is rising, falling, or holding steady.

If a man sees a high barometer, it is probably a 10 to 1 chance that there will be little wind of any strength that day; whereas a low barometer is an equally sure indication of vigorous winds. This is, of course, an oversimplification, but it is an oversimplification that will prove correct often enough to provide a good rule-of-thumb.

I think that a yachtsman who fails to consult his barometer at least twice a day doesn't deserve to win races. It is amazing the information that instrument is waiting to tell you if you only learn to interpret it. I would no more think of coming downstairs, morning or night, without noting the barometer and setting it, than I would of not saying my prayers; both habits are good.

ON CLOUDS

It is wise to study cloud formations and spend time recognizing and naming them. Clouds are beautiful to look at, and they are weather indicators. The cold front, the warm front, the thunderstorm, and the squall all have their typical cloud formations. Get the *Manual of Cloud Forms, Circular "S,"* published by the U.S. Weather Bureau, available from the Superintendent of Documents; it has excellent photographs of the major cloud forms. When you have learned to name clouds by referring first to their altitude and then to the ten genera of the formations themselves, you will be surprised how easy it will be to recognize and name those over your own area.

259

When utilizing clouds as an aid to weather forecasting, remember that it is not an isolated layer of clouds that is important so much as the kinds and number of formations that have preceded and will follow a particular time of observation.

On the Winds

If sails are the engine of a sailboat, the winds are the fuel that moves it. As a racing skipper you must learn as much about the nature of the winds as is possible, and no one is ever able to completely master all there is to know. For the landsman, wind is just wind—something to do battle with for an umbrella or a hat. For the sailor, each wind is an individual, with an identity of its own, having a face and personality he can recognize. Like persons, too, winds from some quarters are inconstant and fickle; others are hard workers, steady and reliable.

In my area, when the wind blows from a particular quadrant, I know pretty well what to expect from it, both in the way of weather and sailing conditions. As I have said, the greater part of my experience has been on the Middle Atlantic seaboard, and I will have to confine my statements regarding winds to that area. I believe, however, that a listing of the characteristics of the winds that blow over Long Island Sound will have value to the general reader. This value lies in the example such a listing gives of the kinds of information that you should try to compile for your own area.

Because of the different rates of heating and cooling of the earth's surface, the nature of the winds will modify slightly during every month of the year. In practice, however, we can think of modification as occurring only four times a year—in spring, summer, fall, and winter. The typical behavior of wind from a given direction will vary in intensity, steadiness, and temperature with the changes of the seasons. Your list—or wind analysis, let us call it—should take this seasonal change into account.

Analysis of the Winds

The northwest wind is common in Long Island Sound and is characterized by its dependability during the time it blows. In my opinion it is an unpleasant breeze to sail in, because despite its constancy, it will be spotty and full of holes, even in the hardest northwesters. In the winter the northwester will often result from a cold front and the winds will approach gale intensity; in the warmer months they are less severe.

Once it sets in, a northwest wind will blow steadily, depending upon the force with which it starts: the harder it is, the longer it will last. If you get a good hard northwester at 12 to 15 knots in the morning, it will last throughout the day, at least until sunset. If it sets in at 15 to 25 knots, it is almost a certainty that it will carry over into the next day and you will have two days of northwest winds. In northwest conditions on the Sound, I have found it best to plan my strategy so that I cross the Sound immediately to obtain the fresher puffs. As the northwester changes its characteristic, it most often hauls to the north.

The northerly, which usually follows the northwester, is a very undependable breeze. In both winter and summer, despite its morning promise, it is likely to die out in the afternoon. It can be a beautiful morning with the northerly blowing a spanking 15 or 18 knots, and you'll think, "What a wonderful wind for today's race." But by afternoon there will be no wind at all, for it will fade out or move to another quarter, probably east. The northerly, despite its flukey nature, is fun to race in because you never know what will happen. I have found in working to windward in a northerly that after getting halfway across the Sound it is an important advantage in favoring the east, because the tendency is for puffs to come approximately north by east. This produces sizable starboard tack lifts.

I imagine that everyone has his favorite breeze, and mine is decidedly a lively northeaster. It is the most delightful wind that we have in the Sound, and it is too bad that it is not our prevailing wind instead of the humid southwesters. I am often teased because of my enthusiasm for northeasters, but people are more susceptible to the influences of the weather than they realize. I can go to bed troubled, weighted down with cares and anxieties, and when I awaken—they are all blown away. I look out the window, and sure enough, there is that weather vane pointing northeast. The barometer is high, the air is light and dry and I can't help but feel exhilarated. The northeast breezes are true, not full of holes or spotty, and are perfect to sail in. They raise a good lump of a sea that is fun to contend with and that adds interest to sailing.

In normal good weather, when you are sailing in a northeaster, you must watch for any sign of the wind beginning to wane, for this is a sure indication that the wind will veer around to southwest. If you see a good 18-knot northeaster drop down to, say, 12, or a 12-knot breeze fall off to 6 or 8, you can be certain that the southwester is making up. Sometimes the southwester will advance across the water with the northeaster still blowing. It is important to watch for this condition, because it can get you into trouble with your racing strategy. We are often fooled by this sudden change of wind direction; it takes you completely by surprise. So in a waning northeaster, always watch for signs of the southwester. You can see these signs in other sailboats, in smoke rising from a fixed point, and most important, in the appearance of the wind itself on the water.

Also, it is imperative that you realize that a sailboat is not an automobile or a power boat; you cannot bear off and cut cross "lots" looking for the new breeze. You'll lose if you do. You will run out of the waning northeaster and wallow around in the doldrums while waiting for new wind to come to you. Meanwhile, the other skippers have stayed in the old breeze and kept their boats moving toward the new, and will almost surely obtain it first.

When racing in shifting winds, therefore, the idea is to stay with the existing breeze as long as you possibly can. In Long Island Sound, when we have this situation, with the northeaster about to change to southwest, we hold up in the northeaster till the last minute, even if it means we are being taken far above our course. The boat must be kept moving with what wind there is and in a position to pick up the southwester when it arrives. Again, keep in mind that you must *stay in the old condition as long as you can; keep your boat moving until you reach the new wind.*

We seldom have a true easterly wind, but we often have a southeaster; this is our most undependable breeze. We don't have them too often, and we all get fooled by them. They come in with a beautiful sparkly ripple, and then, after an hour or so, we are left becalmed, probably to slat around in the motorboat swell for hours. Even the southwester can't be depended on to come in in this weather condition.

A southerly—that is, a wind from due south—is very, very rare in the Sound. It is a nice breeze, solid and without holes in it. I have found that the best way to work a southerly is to move to the west and try to take advantage of starboard tack lifts.

The southwester is the wind that we have to contend with the most, and unfortunately it is not a good breeze except in the springtime. During this season, southwesters come across Long Island quickly, and they are solid and delightful to sail in. But as the weather warms, they don't come across the Island, though they are beautiful and sparkly on the ocean side of the Island's south shore. The southwester will, in May and June, blow steadily and true. But it will be spotty and full of holes. The warmer the weather gets, the more unreliable the southwester becomes.

Since the southwester can fool us regularly, it is always a problem in sailing across the Sound whether to go straight across to the south or to work to the west. I have evolved a formula that has been quite successful. If the southwester is strong and true, I will sail due south across the Sound, and thus capitalize on port tack lifts to the weather mark. If, on the other hand, I have any doubts about the reliability of the breeze, I work to the west. It is especially necessary to go to the west if the wind is a little west of southwest. If another class or other sailboats are ahead of you, watch in the west to see if they are obtaining starboard tack lifts; if they are, then it is safe for you to follow suit. Under these conditions, if you had gone straight across, you would have been lifted and would have rounded up under the whole fleet—needless to say, a most undesirable spot to be forced into.

Incidentally, on a flat calm day, we have a peculiar indication that the wind will go around to southwest. In certain atmospheric conditions, a kind of dark haze will develop in the southwest. It has a similarity to the look of the sky when a northwest squall is making up, although more grey than black, but it does not mean squall conditions. It does indicate that a southwest wind is in the area and if conditions are right, it will reach you.

I don't know what causes this black, cloudlike sign of wind. Perhaps it is smoke or pall being blown along in front of the new wind, but I do know that throughout my racing in Long Island Sound, it has meant the presence of a southwest wind. Whether or not it will come in is another matter. But it must be watched.

As I said at the beginning, only sailors who race in this particular area will be directly benefited by this discussion; but it can be of value to racing men no matter where they operate. If you live on the southern Atlantic Coast, the Gulf Coast, the Great Lakes, or the West Coast, you must try to build up a working knowledge of the behavior and peculiarities of your winds from each quadrant. When I leave my home grounds for national or international racing, I always make certain that I inform myself about the characteristics of the winds in the strange area. The skipper without this knowledge will find himself severely handicapped.

SOMETHING ABOUT SQUALLS

A squall, no matter where it comes from or where it is going, is a very violent, localized wind system, and it can be a fearsome thing indeed. I think that the man who dismisses squalls contemptuously is either a fool or has never been exposed to a fully developed line squall. When talking to the juniors, never be off-handed in your references to squalls, for they can be really serious; and the youngsters should never be taken unawares or unprepared. For that matter, they are serious for adults as well; not only can they destroy a race, but they can badly damage your boat.

When I was younger, I had the attitude, "Who's afraid of a squall? If you're going to swim, you're going to swim; and if you're going to sink, you're going to sink." But I know now that my attitude was the bravado of ignorance coming from my never having been caught out in a real squall. Since then, however, I have gone through many of them, and it is a downright unpleasant, even terrifying experience.

When the ominous black roll cloud that precedes a squall appears, make sure everything is secure. With your crew, review your plans for how you plan to weather it. A line squall in the northern hemisphere is a manifestation of a fully developed cyclone, so don't get into the habit of referring to a summer thunderstorm as a "squall."

The worst squalls on Long Island Sound are always those that come from the northwest. I have never seen a westerly, southerly, or easterly squall blow more than 30 knots, whereas a northwester can blow from 30 to 80. Sometimes they are very localized: I remember one that registered 50 to 80 knots in New Rochelle, and at Rye, a few miles away, there was not a breath of air.

Occasionally a northwest squall will break up before it reaches your area. Keep looking at the center of the blackest part of the squall cloud, and if there appears to be a slight lightening of the color toward the dull gray of a rain cloud—as compared with that awful blackness—it is breaking in half. In a matter of minutes, the blackness can dissipate; and in as little as three to five minutes the whole cloud can break up and disintegrate. This means that the intensity is waning and the storm center is moving off elsewhere. There is still the likelihood that you will get some vicious gusts and, of course, rain, but the immediate threat is gone for the present. However, it can re-form.

It has always been an awesome thing for me to watch this mountainous mass of air forming, re-forming, and collapsing with such tremendous speed. It is exciting to see and certainly reinforces the sailor's respect for the gigantic forces that nature can muster.

WEATHER OMENS: FACT OR FICTION?

Now if you are the kind of person who will accept knowledge only from the latest scientific sources, I suggest that you omit this section. But it will be too bad if you do, for you will not only miss some of the romance of tradition, but you will also skip some information that might just help you to win races.

There is a great deal of wisdom in the weather proverbs that have come to us through the centuries, and most of it is founded on practical experience.

"Red sky at night is a sailor's delight. Red sky at morning, sailor take warning!" This is how one proverb has come down to us today, and its truth is such that it is still included in texts for Naval officers. Much of this folklore can be easily explained by scientific theory, but some of it cannot and must be taken on faith.

In every section of the country there is some old-timer who will state, "we're in for a spell of bad weather." Skeptics laugh away this statement as pure mysticism, but most probably the prophet is merely more aware of tiny imperceptible signs than those of us who have had the faculty of of weather-awareness blunted by living in concrete cities. However, if you are racing sailboats, it is a wise idea to retrain this awareness back into your consciousness. Here are some of the weather signs that I have noticed in the East. There will be similar ones for your area as well.

When, on a summer's morning, there is dew on the grass and flat surfaces, it is almost a certainty that a southwest wind will come up some time during the day.

On a still day, when the light is right, you can sometimes catch sight of gossamer strands in the rigging. I don't know why or how they appear, but they do. They have the appearance of minute strands spun by a spider, although no spiders are involved, I am sure of that. In our area these gossamers are a sure sign of a coming southwest wind. In other areas they may predict something else.

Here is a passage from *The Sea and the Jungle** by the fine writer of the sea H. M. Tomlinson: "Gossamers in the rigging today led the captain to prophesy a storm before night." At the time, the *Capella,* Tomlinson's ship, was lying in the Amazon River.

* H. M. Tomlinson, *The Sea and the Jungle* (New York: E. P. Dutton & Co.).

The appearance of opening crocuses is unfailing in predicting northeast winds. The wind will come either on the day the flowers are first sighted, or the following day. Again, I don't know why this should be, whether it is the nature of the northeast air or what, but crocuses always mean northeast winds for me.

When seabirds cluster inland in large groups and are reluctant to fly, it is a sign of an approaching storm. The reason for this is obvious. The air is thinner within a low-pressure system; it is harder to fly in this air, and storms accompany low-pressure systems. So the birds stay close to the earth where the atmospheric pressure is highest. Birds are much more sensitive to pressure changes than human beings, and behavior like this is a sure indication of future foul weather.

Morning summer fog is always an indication of a beautiful day.

The appearance of porpoises on the eastern seaboard almost always foretells a northeast wind. Why, I don't know, unless, like me, they just love that sparkly northeast air. I have been teased about this belief of mine, but I have consistently gotten back my licks at the porpoise-scoffers.

During one Annapolis-Newport Race in John Nicholas Brown's *Bolero*, the wind was southwest, making the course down the coast a dead beat. We were on the starboard tack and headed off shore. It was my watch, and around nine o'clock that night my friends the porpoises suddenly appeared. We were beating off Montauk and taking a long board offshore because the wind would not allow us to lay the mark, the Chesapeake Light Ship.

I told the afterguard, "We're going to get a northeast wind, and we're foolish to depart from the rhumb line. I think we should go on the port tack to get closer to the course, so that when the northeaster arrives we can set our spinnaker and steer for the lightship." Well, we did just that, and within two hours, the northeaster came in strong. That was the year that we beat *Baruna,* our great competitor, by 24 seconds in the 350-mile race. From then on, the *Bolero* crew always believed what the porpoises told them.

While not strictly a weather sign, there is another phenomenon that I have observed. Very often at the turn of the tide, when it begins to flood, the wind will also pick up. When maximum flood is reached, the wind will slacken, and when the ebb starts, it will often die out.

When a wind shift is imminent, it often takes place when the tide is at the flood. In the summer, I've noticed that an easterly will shift to southwest at the very hour that the current tables tell you the tide will be at flood. I've talked about this ever since I have been racing, and I have never heard anyone else who has had the same thought; and I have never been able to find a completely satisfying answer myself. The best I have been able to do is assume that the rise and fall of that enormous body of water raises or lowers the atmospheric pressure enough to trigger the natural wind changes. No one has as yet refuted my theory.

Now, you might think that all the foregoing is a lot of superstitious nonsense. If you do, try keeping a weather log, as I have done. At the end of the year, when the gossamers and the porpoises have done their work, and when you begin to think of having a new mahogany breakfront built to hold your silverware, I will be happy to welcome you to the ranks of the Order of Mystical Weathermen.

One thing is certain; if a skipper dashes out of the house to his boat, glances quickly at a falling barometer, wets his sneakers in the dew on the lawn, brushes the gossamers in the rigging off his face, and then squints up at the sky and says, "I wonder what quarter the wind's going to come from today," he most definitely doesn't deserve to win.

25. *Melges Methods*

BY BUDDY MELGES

If I had to pick one "best" helmsman in the world, it would have to be Harry "Buddy" Melges. I say that for the simple reason that he enjoys competition—racing against anyone, anywhere, anytime, in any boat—and also because all his successes have been in one-design boats.

Just imagine, he won three straight Mallory Cups, the North American Men's Championship; two Olympic medals, a gold in the Soling keelboat, and a bronze in the Flying Dutchman centerboard dinghy. He races very successfully in scows, iceboats, Solings, and in any class that will give him top competition. Buddy is also an excellent duck hunter and extremely knowledgeable on the subject of waterfowl and upland game. That is about the only way to get him away from boats.

An example of his dedication to the pursuit of excellence and personal achievement on the water comes from the 1972 Olympics where he won the Gold Medal. He told me that he was unhappy because he hadn't had the opportunity to beat Paul Elvstrom in a heavy breeze, and "that's something that I really wanted to do." That kind of drive, the sort that cannot be satisfied by merely winning a series but requires something more at all times, is a sure sign of the champion.

My father was employed at the Bouvais Boat Company in Williams Bay, Wisconsin, when I was six years old. The firm not only serviced the many pleasure motorboats on Lake Geneva but, during the winter months, scow-type sailboats were constructed. The hulls were planked with white cedar on white oak ribs, Sitka spruce stringers, and, of course, Sitka spruce spars. From that date until this, construction techniques have changed very little except for the usefulness of epoxy glues, new longer-lasting varnishes, and so on.

As I remember, it was always a big thrill to accompany my father to work on a Saturday or whenever we had a vacation from school. It was very exciting for me to walk through the factory and observe the boats being built, to smell the cedar lumber, and to see the shiny, new hulls in the final stages of construction. These senses are with me yet as I walk through our own factory and enjoy seeing these beloved scows being produced.

In 1936, Dad brought home a 10-foot, Penn Yan dinghy, canvas covered over cedar planking. She was gaff-rigged with round bilges, and as I remember she was a very sporty dinghy. The bigness of the boat impressed me at first, and it seemed to handle me, rather than me handling it. In those early days, I spent every possible moment in this dinghy. I became well acquainted with her little quirks, and I soon found out how to get to my friend's house in the least possible time using wind from any direction. I guess you might say I had my first touch of racing. Although it was not boat against boat, it was my dinghy and me against the wind in order to get to Jimmy's house as quickly as possible.

My early relationship with the dinghy was marred by many capsizes. After the first summer, we used to test our skills by sailing on the bitter edge and watching the water trickle—and sometimes pour—over the lee rail. It was always a test to see how long we could maintain stability with the dinghy one-quarter full, one-half full, or almost with the gunnels awash. Needless to say, this somewhat unfair abuse took its toll on the dinghy, the rigging, and the sails.

In the middle of the second summer, it was obvious that the sail had to be replaced. How to do this became a problem. Our family was suffering, as many did, from the depression, and there was just no money available for my fun. It was then that I decided to make a sign and hang it on the willow tree at our Delavan Lake, Wisconsin, home. The sign read: "Sailboat Rides—10¢." As I remember, the sailboat rides usually lasted from one to two hours—depending upon how long the person wanted to stay out. I worked very hard that summer, the sail was becoming more and more tattered, and each day I would take it to my mother's sewing machine for repairs. With her looking over my shoulder, I would stitch it back up as best as I could. On one occasion, I remember driving the needle through the nail on my forefinger. In jerking back, I broke the needle off the machine. It evidently wasn't a very serious wound, for I remember inserting a new needle and completing my repairs. By September 1937, I had a bank account that was almost sufficient to afford a new sail. By shoveling snow the next winter, I was able to make the final payment on a new sail to Joy Brothers in Milwaukee, Wisconsin.

In those days, outboards were not only scarce, they were a complete luxury. My dinghy was my means of transportation around Delavan Lake. I did not even own a bicycle until 1943, so I relied heavily on my dinghy, my ice skates, and eventually, the little iceboat that Dad and I made in 1939. Although the dinghy was my very own, I shared the iceboat with Dad and even ventured out alone under ideal conditions. I think the iceboat first gave me confidence in being able to use the wind as propulsion. I find that my own sons—ages six and seven—are also able to comprehend the technique of iceboating quickly and without complications. I believe iceboating helps the summer sailor best on offwind techniques—reaching and running. Confidence in the ability to steer sailboats is a result of my upbringing on both scows and iceboats. I found that these experiences allowed me to fare well when I ventured from the Middlewest to keelboats and other types of sailboats.

Though iceboat races had given me some experience, I had to learn that yacht racing was different. It was in my first summer race on Lake Geneva, Wisconsin, that my iceboating experience prevailed. In iceboating, the start is a standing start at the leeward mark—usually a left-over Christmas tree. Nowadays, you draw for numbers; half the boats go on the port tack, half on the starboard tack, and the starting line is at right angles to the wind. In those days, it was common practice to start between the dock and a buoy moored at 90 degrees to the shore, regardless of wind direction.

On this first race day on water, the wind was from the west, parallel to the starting line. It seemed strange to me that everyone was jockeying for positions in near the shore at the end of the dock. I elected to start on the port tack and left the starting buoy to port, rather than to star-board as I should have. I sailed on port tack all alone to the center of Lake Geneva, tacked to starboard, and crossed the entire fleet. My father instructed the judges not to recall my start, for it would only con-fuse me at the tender age of nine. Upon completion of the race in fifth position, I was taken ashore onto the clubhouse front porch. With the aid of salt shakers, knife, and fork, I was quickly straightened out as to the proper starting procedure in yacht racing.

The summer went on, and it was not until mid-August that I won my first race in the junior program. Even to this day, I can remember almost every tack and every wind shift. I became an enthusiastic sailboat racer. Whenever it was possible, Father would observe the races from a "putt-putt." Upon its completion—no matter what the circumstances, win or lose—we would always resail the race. I should say, he resailed the race for me and corrected the many mistakes I had made. Even in winning, it seemed that I had committed as many or more errors than I did in los-ing. Dad would recommend that I go to the end of the line, sail close-hauled, and observe as best I could the favored end. Because of the yacht club dock starting technique, in many instances the favored end would be further from the windward mark than the unfavored end. This situa-tion added another decision. Would it be more beneficial to start at the unfavored end and hope for a slight lift to fetch the first mark, or was I to start upwind and hope to power over a pinching boat?

During these races, we sailed a 16-foot Inland Lake X-boat—a "beamy" chine-built that could be considered a cross between a Snipe and a Comet. The boat was stiff and quite heavy at 500 pounds and carried approximately 120 square feet of sail area. The boat was stable and when on her beam's end, about to capsize, she would turn abruptly into the wind. Because of these traits, she was quite safe, although per-haps lacking the sensitivity achieved by dinghy sailors from a "hot skil-let" technique of sailing. The X-boat was simple. You hoisted the main to the black band at the peak. You set the downhaul at the black band at the tack. You pulled the foot so that the clew met the black band on the boom. The jib was hoisted so that the full load of the rig was on the jib luff, and the forestay became slack. The centerboard was carried maximum down, and the rest was up to the skipper and crew to trim the sails and steer the boat. I believe this simple rig has much merit for one learning the fundamentals of racing.

Too often our sailing schools for young people teach too much theory and put too many thoughts into young heads concerning sail adjustments, tune of the boat, and so on. They do not dwell heavily enough on the set of sail with regard to sheet tensioning, nor emphasize the most significant aspect of helmsmanship—simply, steering the boat properly to take advantage of every wave upwind and to surf on every ripple off the wind.

My simple lesson in steering the waves came early. Father said: "Up the wave up, down the wave down." Translated for you, this means that as the boat starts into the wave, you should head the boat into the wind and get the lee bow on the rising wave. In so doing, the wave action drives against the hull and centerboard to put the boat upwind. As you cut the wave, the helm is pulled sharply to windward to start the boat away from the wind and down the wave. As I remember, my first impulse was to try to speed the boat up as the wave approached; but by having the boat on a more offwind attitude as I neared the crest of the wave, I was pushed severely sideways. I could never make up this distance on the downside of the wave by pinching the boat for its hopeful surf down the backside. In later years—1956, to be exact—when I first ventured from scows to the Mallory eliminations, Jack Vilas of scow and Luders fame took me for a sail in my first keelboat—the Luders 16. During this sail, he reminded me of the technique Father had taught: "Up the wave up, down the wave down."

Being a scow sailor, I knew little about how to moor a Luders 16. Jack had a simple technique—take one boat length away from your mooring and while running before the wind when the transom is at 90 degrees to the mark, buttonhook to the mark. The sharp turn action will kill your forward momentum. I have found this technique to work in any length of keelboat.

We sailed our first keelboat series successfully, defeating Joe Dowry of the Chicago Yacht Club. From that semi-final, we went on to Seattle and sailed against Bus Mosbacher, Teddy Hood, Gilbert Gray, Bill Ficker, and others. I feel that one of the things that Father taught me has been forever a help, and that is to resail every race no less than three times in your mind to pick out your good points and bad points, to think about sail adjustment, boat tune, helmsmanship, course position, and so on.

The first Mallory in keelboat competition was certainly a new thing for me. The standing start, so familiar with scows and dinghy-type boats,

272

left me on the starting line looking at the cockpit sole and wondering which way they went. Teddy Hood's technique of sharply turning his Blanchard Knockabout up the wind and down the wind to cross the keel in the water, and in so doing slow up the boat, is an art that can be used in any sailing craft on the starting line—whether it be a displacement or centerboard type. The other thing about this series that has been imbedded in my mind—my so-called "sailing library"—was that you must keep your cool in light wind to perform well. Never say die, there is always one boat to pass, think of consistency and the ultimate gain. On the other hand, it was hard for me to sail in this new position—seventh or eighth place, or actually last and second to last. The fact that we mentally resailed each race gave us a chance to accumulate more knowledge. In spite of this, we still finished sixth in our first Mallory championship.

It's fun to reminisce about what we have gained from each of our friends and very good sailors. We traveled up that steep road to success. The top seems a long way off and may never be reached, but just getting nearer to the peak is all I need to keep me active in competitive racing. During my years in the scow classes, I learned speed over the water and some tactics. However, we were behind the rest of the country and world when it came to fine tuning and the gadgetry of boom vangs, Cunninghams, adjustable outhaul, adjustable jib luffs, and so on. These refinements were brought to our attention during Mallory semi-finals and finals. We took these ideas back to the scow country and immediately experienced improved performance because of the gadgets and improved sailing techniques in general. Needless to say, these, together with our years of experience gained in the Mallory, helped us to achieve many scow championships.

Our first Mallory win came in 1959 in Texas. The field was not as star-studded as it had been in the past. Maybe this gave us more confidence to come on somewhat stronger and to be more aggressive, or possibly just being in two previous Mallorys gave us the confidence to pull out the stops. In 1959, Jack Shether joined Dick Reynolds and myself. Jack was the necessary additive that put a clinch on the technique that is necessary to win when it counts. Jack's idea of saving one tack until the bitter end was excellent. In short, if you are behind, never sail to the layline, for your competition shuts the door on any possible advantage you gain from wind shifts or an additional tack to get him out of position, or even from the use of a finish line angle. Always tack short of the finish line or layline in such a manner that you can, if necessary, bring in a third boat to use as an offensive weapon to beat your fleet leader.

As I remember the series at Kemah, Texas, the first race had a poor windward leg in light air. Though we seemed to have boat speed, we were not very successful in choosing the right side for wind shifts. However, on the top reach, we immediately started to move by our competition. With the course shortened to the bottom mark after the two reaches, we just edged out a boat for third place. Considering that the windward mark had us in eighth, we felt thrilled to have done so well. Immediately, Jack cautioned me that we had received quite a break on the finish line with a wind shift and a "flub" on the part of our competition. He said: "Buddy, you'll find in many races that your breaks will never go completely against you, nor will they go completely for you. If you start to sail or shoot the corners for the breaks, your average of wins will be cut drastically. When you do win, it will be by a light-year, but these wins are not as rewarding as a well-sailed race with the close infighting being the final determining factor of the outcome." That series in 1959 ended up with a very close, breathtaking finish. Warner Wilcox of Long Island Sound won the last race, and we had just few enough boats between him and ourselves to finish as overall champion by one-fourth of a point.

The next year, we were pleased to have the Mallorys in inland lake scows, and as they say: "This is my football, and you play my game." The point is that we were at home in our inland lake scows. However, here again, Jack Shether's tactics won two races that we might have lost had they not been well thought out to position our boat tactically to gain the upper hand as much as one-half mile on up the boat course. The 1960 Mallory was one series in which I sailed with all the confidence in the world. I had a great tactician in Jack Shether when I needed him; we were at home on our E scows in inland bodies of water; and it was water I could read for wind velocity and for wind shift. As I progressed in experience, it became ever more evident that consistency was the real factor in winning sailboat regattas. Harry Nye—a world champion ice-boater, inland lake scow champion, and, finally, a world champion Star boat sailor—proved that consistency is the best weapon in large fleets by winning a world's championship with his best race being a fifth.

In scow sailing, as in iceboating, the yachts are quick to respond to wind speed, wind direction, trim of the sails, and the steering of the yacht. In the scow, I feel I've gained the most sensitivity for offwind sailing that anyone can experience. While sailing a scow on a reach (even a big A scow), head up 3 or 4 degrees and you may pick up more than enough added boat speed to offset the greater distance to be sailed. The apparent wind moves rapidly forward, ventilates the sails, and you take off with amazingly quick pickup. In this way, I developed my scalloping downwind action. When reaching, bear away on the puffs, which is only natural, and freshen up again in the light spots to maintain a consistent offwind speed. The feel that a scow can give a person in how far to follow the puff and when to come back fresh is hard to explain in words. It is better felt on a boat.

In iceboating, where the sailing is always with the wind forward of the beam, you will find the sails are never eased as they are in soft-water sailing. In water, we round the windward mark and sail off the wind at 135 degrees or more. On your downwind course, it is two jibes; on your upwind course, it is two tacks. In many cases where the lake allows it, you sail nothing more than a diamond course. Boat speed is of the essence, and little sailing knowledge is needed to win. When you sail down the wind in an iceboat, if you go too far away from the eye of the wind, the boat will die. It must be headed up to bring the apparent wind back forward. This one instance is where most sailors break down when they try iceboating. They will not ease the sail, freshen, and bring the apparent wind forward and peel off and follow back on the normal course. What I'm trying to say here is that through iceboating and scow sailing, I have learned to ventilate sailboats off the wind. Keep the boat moving by having the air pass over the sails at the greatest velocity possible to maintain a course to the next mark. In many cases, tacking downwind can give fantastic gains in lighter air when the hull will not in any way reach her best speed by running dead before the wind.

Not being a big-boat sailor, I do it by feel, not by compass. I would offer the following words of advice if a person feels that tacking down is in order. Follow the masthead fly on the first tack away from the rhumb line. Then, jibe back toward the rhumb line and your competition so that you will be sailing at a closer tack for greater speed. You must observe your competition at this point to determine your gain or loss. If it was a gain, you may now jibe back onto the first tack and sail a greater distance away from the rhumb line on this angle following the masthead fly. Remember your angle for the jibe back so as to fetch the lee mark at the best possible speed.

On the other hand, if your first tack back to the rhumb line proved to be a negative gain and you are bound and determined to continue tacking downwind, I suggest that you maintain good speed to the left side (if you have been on the right side of the rhumb line on the first tack), continuing to the left side of the rhumb line for a considerable distance—but not enough to completely sever connections with the fleet—jibe, and return to the rhumb line. Again, gauge your positive or negative gain on this maneuver. If it is positive, you may now tack back out to the left side. If it is negative and you have already experienced negative on the starboard or right side of the rhumb line, forget your tacking down the wind and go for the mark.

I do not have the guts to use iceboat leeward leg tactics in summer sailing. In the 1967, 5.5-meter Worlds while sailing with Gordon Lindemann of Milwaukee, Wisconsin, we watched Robin Aisher of England successfully sail what I would consider an iceboat leeward leg—a long starboard tack and a long port tack—in three of five races. On the other hand, we were very successful and less inclined to gamble, using my technique of short tacks off the rhumb line. Though the long tacks can be successful, they parallel too closely the practice of sailing to the laylines on windward legs.

The 1961 Mallory was held in Dragon class sloops. We were to win our third straight Mallory this time with consistency. Lake St. Louis must be considered an inland lake, which had to be to our advantage. Though we got off to a good start by winning the first race, we placed third in the second race, and ended the day close behind Bob Mosbacher, who had a first and a second. Don McNamara was also close aboard with a second and a third.

In this series, the most outstanding piece of work was accomplished by Don McNamara—reaching with a spinnaker very close to the wind. By doing so, Don was able to sail from a fifth position at the windward mark to a substantial lead, which he never relinquished thereafter. As they say: "When you're hot, you're hot!" Donnie had his main, his jib, and his spinnaker flying beautifully. It was in this series that I found a good rule of thumb for reaching—to carry the spinnaker pole at 90 degrees to the headstay. Most spinnakers will fly their best with this pole height to open up the spinnaker leech and give the greatest slot between spinnaker leech and main leech. The boat must be sailed in the upright position with the crew hiking 100 percent. The main should be slightly over-trimmed when possible to open the aforementioned spinnaker slot. The upper one-third of the jib must be soft. This is accomplished with a soft trim on the jib clew. Barber hauls should be used if possible to widen the angle of trim.

We had experienced good downwind speed in all of this series but nothing as awesome as that mustered by Don McNamara in this particular race. Nevertheless, we successfully retained the Mallory Cup for the third time. I refer to "we" because it was a crew effort, and in every boat I've ever sailed I've felt that way.

We received from "downwind" George O'Day a lesson in sailing that we immediately put to work on our scows, which I've talked about so much about up to now. It is actually easier to pass a boat while running free than it is while beating to windward. Many people, when approaching the windward mark, have a tendency to reach for the cooler, the Coca-Cola, or the ham sandwich. Actually, they should be more serious about sail trim, wind direction, and keeping the boat moving through the means of ventilation and use of every wave. In a hobby horse boat, such as keelboats, I like to have the crew sit cheek to cheek when going to windward and spread out going down the wind. Here, the theory is not to resist wave action on the wind, but to resist it off the wind so that the boat will sail faster under each condition and the sea will be put to one's aid, rather than opposition.

We returned to the scow family the next few years after 1961, and in 1962 I became interested in Olympic competition. Bill Bentsen and I chose the Flying Dutchman as the boat we felt we could do the best job with, considering our background in scows, iceboating, and so on. In getting into this program, I found out for the first time in my life what real practice was all about. We felt our general knowledge equalled that of those in the class. In our first regatta, we realized that our real deficiency was in plain boat handling. Fortunately, Bill and I were quick to realize this. We did not blame it on sail shape, hull shape, or on our knowledge, but on our boat-handling capabilities. We returned to the waters of Lake Geneva alone, without the aid of a yardstick or a boat to tune against, and we began to sail ourselves into shape. We tacked, we jibed, we set spinnakers, we took spinnakers down, we capsized the boat, we did every exercise that we knew of for any situation that the elements could put before us. Immediately we started to see results as we campaigned the regattas around the country.

The Flying Dutchman class did not have an active fleet at Lake Geneva and the Chicago Fleet was just starting and did not offer the competition necessary to prepare an Olympic crew. In the ensuing two years, we hauled the boat by trailer over 50,000 miles to enter regattas in Canada and the United States that would help develop our effort for the final 1964 games. The Flying Dutchman required physical training as well as mental conditioning. The physical must be considered primary, for if a crew cannot last the duration of a race and be fresh and strong in body, the mind will not cooperate in sharpness. Although you might lead the entire race, losing it on the finish line is a fault of conditioning, rather than the poor breaks we so often hear about in the parking lot and during the cocktail hour. Bill Bentsen used the Canadian Air Force Exercise Program, increased his biceps $1\frac{1}{2}''$, ran six miles a day, and gave 100 percent throughout each race.

Other than the conditioning and the tacking and jibing—comparable to tackling and blocking in football—the simple fundamentals of sailing are an important factor. Our thoughts in 1964 were to "get to the Olympics, get to the Olympics, get to the Olympics." Little thought was put on achieving the Gold once we got there. When we made it, a subconscious relaxing mood set upon us. We were not the bloodthirsty, hungry sailors that we had been in the States.

In Japan, we seemed to have as much speed as the others, and we maintained good consistency. However, one breakdown in a heavy-air race cost us a Gold Medal. This breakdown might not have occurred had we had our senses about us, inspected the boat more closely, and used better techniques in the final rescue after breakdown. It all points to one thing—if you don't race and race often, you're not going to finish well. Books are fine to read, but without actual practice and time on the boat so that man, mind, body, and boat become one, the gain will be slight.

When the Olympic Games of 1964 were history we set about licking our wounds and preparing for 1968. Resailing the 1964 Olympics many times in our minds to see how we could have achieved a Gold Medal made us even more determined than ever. In 1967, we went to Winnepeg to sail in the Pan American Games in furnished boats, using our own sails. We won these games with six firsts and one second. We were to go on to Montreal and again sail on Lake St. Louis. However, the boat was not prepared, as was proven in the 1967 World's Championship.

The fact that we arrived in Montreal with a poorly organized, untuned boat against the best in the class was mistake one. Mistake two was arriving in Montreal with business on my mind, rather than sailing. Finally, a disgusting light-air series was to be the crowning blow. The "what-not-to-do's" of the 1967 World's far exceeds the positive recommendations I might have for the reader. Our boat speed over the water was on a par with some—but not all. John Oakley of England was fast, well-organized, and ready. When the wind was fresh, we seemed to be able to sail with anyone. What took place in the very light air was the most disgusting experience of my entire career. The first incident was at a reaching mark when I was inside on starboard tack, leading the race. At this point, another boat sailed higher on the starboard, jibed over— even though it was evident he could not cross us—and beat us to the mark. To do so, he began sculling his boat in such a vigorous fashion that the spinnaker actually folded on each side of the jib, then out to the sidestays, and fluttered like tell-tales on each side of the boat. As he passed in front of us, I hailed: "Do you need a paddle?" He returned: "Yeah, do you have one?" This was the start of what was to become a week-long fiasco.

In the next light-air race, we arrived at the windward mark in first place. John Oakley was in second, and he simply rocked his boat on by. We challenged John, and he retorted with the fact that he, too, had challenged this technique at the European Championships. He said he even had movies, but the technique was condoned abroad. I was to watch many fantastic rocking techniques the rest of the week, including outright sculling. When I left Montreal, I vowed never to return to the Flying Dutchman class if this was the technique needed to win in light air. Granted, I'm the only one to suffer, for I've dearly missed the thrill of sailing a Dutchman in high-speed conditions and even the fun of sailing in light air against the elements without means of false propulsion. At that point I was beside myself on how to handle the situation, so I decided that the best way was to give up sailing for awhile and look for another sport.

Training Labrador retrievers was to be my bag for the next two years. Being an ardent hunter, I'd always loved dogs, and I took a keen interest in field trial work. However, the love of sailing was too much to resist.

In 1969, we returned to the scene, in a Soling this time, and I was very happy to be back on the water.

The 26'10" three-man Soling keelboat is the closest thing to a high-performance centerboarder that I've been aboard. It's exhilarating as a tactical boat on the wind. When it's blowing very hard, they tack in 70 degrees. Planing in these conditions on a spinnaker reach and surfing on the runs is equally thrilling. We found instant success with this boat and started a program toward the 1972 Olympics.

Bill Bentsen joined me again for the effort in 1972 on our three-man keelboat. Our middle man, Bill Allen at 210 pounds, scow sailor extraordinary, would be close at my side to aid in tactics. Billy Bentsen would continue his fantastic work with the spinnakers—reaching and running—preparing current and weather data, and joining with the programming and designing of the layout of *Teal.*

The first time the two Bills and I joined forces was at the C.O.R.K. Regatta in Kingston, Ontario, in 1970. On our hour-and-one-half sail to the starting line, we tried to tune as we went. The wind was blowing out of the southwest at 18 to 22 m.p.h., and we began to feel moments of good boat speed. By the time we arrived at the starting area, we felt we had the boat pretty well set up for the upcoming race. The feeling proved to be correct, for we arrived at the windward mark in second place after a poor start. We steamed on by and won going away. This pattern was followed for the remainder of the series and we won every race over the 59-boat fleet. This series was the last of the year. We put our boat to rest for the winter and returned to our beloved iceboating, waiting for spring to come, at which time we would launch an accelerated program in preparation for the Olympic Games in 1972.

A setback occurred on May 9, 1971. Melges Boat Works burned to the ground, losing 12,000 square feet of boat-building area. A crash program was put into effect to rebuild forms in order to get back into production as quickly as possible. During this time, we worked under adverse conditions—almost out in the weather. However, within six weeks after the date of the fire, the first 28-foot Class "E" was delivered off the new form.

It was not until late fall that we again ventured forth in the Soling, returning to Kingston for the 1971 C.O.R.K. Regatta and our first confrontation with Bruce Goldsmith. Bruce won the first race handily and then stayed tough with good finishes. We finished eighth and eleventh in the first two races. We got on track and won the last three. Our poor finishes in the first two races were too much for us to overcome Bruce's lead, and we finished second in the series.

On the drive back to Zenda we were enthusiastic, but obviously convinced that we had more work to do. The class in general was improving in overall performance, and we had to improve at a faster rate in order to achieve the berth on the 1972 team. A training program was put into effect for September, October, November, and December at Lake Geneva. Sailing by ourselves, we practiced tacking, jibing, boat handling, spinnaker sets, mark rounding, and all of the basics that I feel make for a smooth-working organization in a three-man keelboat. From time to time, our crew was complimented by our competitors for a smooth-working organization. I felt this was accomplished by our sailing alone—without another boat to use as a yardstick—in order to work on the fundamentals and also to set the sails on the spars as we thought best.

At Christmastime, Bill Abbott brought a boat to Lake Geneva. This boat was from a new plug and a new set of molds that Bill thought might have a slight edge over the present boat. Its shape was more in line with the European hulls, and we elected to go with this type of boat. Our new boat was delivered in January. I did the fitting out so that all controls were to the center of the cockpit in port and starboard consoles. Each speed adjustment could be accomplished with minimum crew movement, whether in light or heavy air. A flip of the wrist, and the jib luff camber could be changed. The Soling self-tacking device originated at Melges Boat Works under the direction of Gordon Lindeman and could be changed laterally from 7 to 12 degrees. To change the fore and aft adjustment, we had to move our wire jib sheet fore or aft on a multi-holed clew board arrangement. The third part aft in the console was the Cunningham adjustment for the main. Next came the boom vang, rear traveler, and backstay. Each adjustment offered sufficient mechanical advantage with the use of Harken blocks throughout and, without question, aided the smoothness of *Teal* and had much to do with her success. The rig was set up with fixed spreaders at 90 degrees to the mast. The lowers carried opposite the mast. The mast could be dropped over the bow of the boat when running free without the adjustment of shroud tracks. Again, this was a step toward simplicity. Our theme was to have a simplified boat so that maximum concentration could be given to developing speed through steering and sail trim.

281

At our first regatta in Miami, Florida, we again met Bruce Goldsmith plus the top sailors from all over the United States. We did quite well during the first half of the Miami Series. During the second half, we were overpowered by Bruce's speed and placed second. However, we came away from the Miami Series with a good feeling, for we had discovered that the boom vang, with our rig, was a potent piece of equipment. Conventional vanging on the Soling was a block and tackle from a point 32 inches aft on the boom to the base of the mast. By exerting fantastic pressure, we could move the mast forward in deflection. This, in turn, carried the draft aft in the sail and also freed the lower leech. In general, we found that 8 inches of mast bend in light-medium air developed the best speed for our cut of sails. We felt we had accomplished the proper tuning of the leech with the luff curve. Consequently, the deflection of the mast would tip the whole sail into perfect proportion for the best possible speed.

The other thing we found to be wrong with our rig and sail plan was the fact that the jib had too much draft aloft. Even though the jib leech is quite far in front of the main, it develops just as important a relationship with the main as does an overlapping jib. We called Zenda for a new jib that would have a much flatter upper one-third. The jib arrived in St. Petersburg in time for the start of the next series. S.P.O.R.T. was an entirely different situation than Miami. We had new speed and good control in almost all conditions—light, medium, or heavy. The drive home to Zenda was an easy one.

Our next series was to be the Texas Olympics. Again, we showed good speed using these new tuning techniques and general rig setup. The outcome was successful with several firsts. This time, we returned to Zenda just in time to meet the "Spring Rush" at the boat works.

The next series was the Midwest Trials. Even though we sailed on numerous occasions at Lake Geneva before these trials, I feel we became complacent. This showed in the results of the Midwest Trials. Bruce Goldsmith came on to win the last race and beat us because of poor boat handling on my part, some confusion regarding the point structure, and poor tactics on the race course—too much defense without enough offense. Hindsight is always better than foresight. In this case, the hindsight immediately after the series really got our adrenaline flowing to the point of anger. Both Bill Bentsen and Bill Allen were asked to write letters regarding the series and what we did wrong, what we did right, and how we could improve. We sat down, hashed over the whole program, and proceeded to get the boat ready for San Francisco.

We arrived at the final San Francisco trials with a calm confidence in our ability to win the right to go to Kiel. Bill Bentsen had our current and wind data down perfect. The hull was in excellent condition, having had every screw, every pin, and every bolt checked. All the leads were checked for proper alignment. The mast seemed to be in perfect order, and we were ready.

What happened in the first race is very typical of aggressiveness, putting one's head in the bag and failing to get a clear picture of the overall situation. Bidding with Bob Mosbacher for the pin end start, we misjudged the velocity of the current and just touched the mark. After rerounding, we found ourselves in the third tier starting the windward leg. Two tacks to the left side of the boat course cleared our wind, but put us away from the forward side of the course. However, our great boat speed started to show, for we arrived at the windward mark with the leaders and a chance for fourth place. However, we again misjudged the current—this time due to the fact that it was rolling at about four knots. The obvious happened—we missed the windmark, jibed around, came back up to get into the flow, were forced around early again, and missed it for the second time. Finally, we cleared in about eighteenth place. The two Bills went to work with the spinnaker, and we had an enjoyable two reaches. Our vang control to the center console was handled on these reaching legs by Bill Allen. Each time the Soling would become overpowered and want to go into a broaching situation, Bill would quickly pop the vang. This would, in turn, lift the boom and turn the leech completely free. *Teal* would track once more on a straight line while our competition was spinning out here, there, and everywhere. Apparently, they were not prepared for some of the sea and wind conditions of San Francisco Bay. We finished fifth in this race, and I was very pleased with the comeback and our apparent boat speed.

As we readied ourselves for the second race the next day, Bill Bentsen informed me of the best technique for weather prediction: "Read the *Stockton Morning News* for the temperature the previous day in the San Joaquin Valley." As Earl Elms put it: "The wind doesn't blow in San Francisco, the valley sucks." This was exactly the case. The day of our first race, the valley really warmed up. The second day when we went to the starting line, the wind was already piping in at 20 knots and still building at race time. We had a lovely first leg with fantastic boat speed. Rounding the windward mark in a tight race with Sam Merrick with boom vang hard set, backstay bent over maximum, and no freeing of the jib sheet, we found our mast to be faster than the hull as they departed company in abrupt fashion. Again, the calmness of the crew was evident. It was not disaster that struck, it was misfortune. We won our first race of the series—the race to Nils Erickson's spar loft to choose and rig a new spar. All was accomplished by 9.00 P.M. that evening, and the boat was set and ready to go for the morning's race. With minor adjustments on the course, we placed second in the third race. We won the fourth, fifth, and sixth races. Placing second in the last race won the right to represent the United States in Kiel.

When we arrived in Kiel, we were basically unknown, for we had not sailed in the world's championship at Seawanhaka the year before. Nor had we sailed at the European championships in Copenhagen. Instead, we elected to go in with the confidence that we were well prepared and had superior boat speed. We felt the latter was a great advantage as it would be a great shock to our competition to learn of it for the first time during the series. They would have no time to build up to our speed with adjustments. In the two tune-up races, Bruce Goldsmith and I finished first and second with very substantial margins over the European entrants.

The day of the first Olympic race did not bring typical Kiel weather. In fact, the whole series did not produce typical heavy-wind Kiel conditions. We jumped off the starting line in the first race at the pin end. Getting a bit of a header, we tacked across the entire fleet just beating the Swede—Stig Wennerstroem—to the windward mark and then sailing away to a seven-minute lead and a win.

Feeling confident that our boat speed was better than anyone else's, we elected to assume a defensive position in the second race. Consequently, we did not fight for the best start. Rather, we took the position on the line that would be close to Paul Elvstrom, David Miller of Canada, the East German (who had just come straight from the European championships with a victory), and the Englishman John Oakley only to find that these gentlemen had chosen the right-hand side of the boat course. This was not the way to go. Going left, we found the Russian and Stig Wennerstroem with a tremendous lead at the first mark. We found ourselves in tenth position. David Miller was in about fifth spot. Elvstrom, Oakley, and the East German were behind. Our pattern held true to form in developing offwind speed. We passed a number of boats on the two reaches and closed ground tremendously on the leaders. Starting the second weather leg, the wind dropped. We chose to keep the speed on and drive through the sea. To the right side a shift at the windward mark and a fantastic run of speed found us in second place behind Wennerstroem. However, he got away and we were unable to catch him. After two races, the two of us were tied with a first and second apiece. David Miller stood third with two thirds, having passed the Frenchman on the last beat to the finish line.

We decided to continue the same strategy—being more defensive—in the third race. We arrived at the windward mark in eleventh position; Elvstrom was in about seventh. Our offwind speed pulled us out of this hole for the second time in a row, and we passed Elvstrom and rounded the leeward mark in fifth position. We then went to work on the leaders. At this point, Spain was leading; Brazil was second. Upon preparing for the second beat, Elvstrom immediately tacked to the left side of the course, which was not the favored side as it had been in the earlier races. We found ourselves tangled up with Brazil in a tight tacking duel. No less than six times on this second weather leg, we tacked to clear our air only to have the Brazilian jump back on it. It wasn't until very near the windward mark that we shook his cover to move into third position behind Spain. Elvstrom, who'd gone to the extreme left and picked up a fantastic shift, had now moved into a comfortable lead. No one changed positions on the run. Although we closed on the last weather leg, it was impossible to catch either Paul or the Spaniard.

We stuck with our tactics for the fourth race. Playing it cool, we arrived at the windward mark in twelfth position. We picked up considerable distance on the two reaches, moved into fourth place starting the second weather leg, and closed ground on everyone. After the free run into the start of the second weather leg, we were in shooting distance of first place. The first half of this leg, people were just trying to sort out. It wasn't until the second half that we got hooked up. For a time, we passed the Frenchman and the Canadian. Feeling we had a shot at John Oakley, the leader, we elected to stick to the right side of the boat course hoping for a shift. This was our first gamble of the series, and it didn't pay. The wind backed instead of hauling, and we sailed a header back to the finish line. This put John Oakley clear on a reach and allowed the Frenchman to regain second place by passing both John and us. However, we felt that the gamble had been well worth it, as only David Miller gained points as a series threat. The other two had not beaten us in any of the prior races.

We went into the next day with a comfortable margin. As we conversed, we decided to pull the stops, get the favored start, and go all out to win the fifth race. During the rest days, we worked on the hull, checked all the fittings, and made two minor hardware changes which would give us better leads on spinnaker tending. We launched the night before the fifth race hoping for big air and the final confrontation with Elvstrom in the last three races.

Towing to the starting line, it looked as though the wind might pick up to 18 or 20 m.p.h. as the forecast had predicted. We elected to go with our heavy-weather main and our light-weather jib. We did what we had set out to do by winning the start. No one crowded us on the first leg. *Teal* rounded the windward mark with a two-boat length lead which opened up to a quarter of a mile on two reaches because of superior sail tending and confidence of the crew. We made some minor tuning adjustments in the second weather leg which really got the boat smoking and opened up a very comfortable lead. We were never challenged the remainder of the race and won by better than one-half mile. We now felt the pressure was on the others. We had to stay clear and not allow ourselves to become too relaxed. We also had to be aggressive at the starting line.

We went out for the sixth race on what appeared to be a lovely day. We started the race, locked up with Wennerstroem, and rounded the windward mark in seventh and eighth spots. If we stayed this way, we'd win the Gold Medal. The wind was dropping, we made some moves on the two reaches, and started the second weather leg in a comfortable position. Moving up the course nicely, we rounded the mark close on Stig's transom. A couple of jibes and a puff and we moved out ahead just before the wind went completely flat. Some new air came in from the right side, and we moved from fourth to eighteenth or nineteenth position. At the start of the pack, David Miller was leading the race. Wennerstroem, who was behind us a considerable distance, got into this new air, moved on up with the leaders, and we sat in the largest hole that I had ever seen. Finally, we got some air. We started to sail only to find that the whole fleet was going to be bogged down. At the bottom pin, a half-knot current made it impossible to make the mark. Soon the boats near the leeward mark started to drop anchor to hold their positions. Eventually, the race was called.

Towing back to land, we felt very fortunate. We felt even better about the fact that Paul Elvstrom would be exonerated. Paul, David Miller of

Canada, the Brazilian, and the Frenchman had all tangled up in the fifth race at a mark rounding. Paul and the Frenchman were thrown out. At the start of the sixth race, we had a general recall when the Frenchman forced Paul over the line and fouled him out. However the recall gave Paul a second chance. This time he wanted the pin end very badly. We elected to be very close to him, about two boat lengths up from him. We were in perfect position to see the Frenchman, sailing along the line underneath and coming up underneath Paul, force his boat into Paul's. Contact occurred, and Paul eventually left the boat course for the harbor. Later we learned that Paul Elvstrom had put his boat on the hook and had withdrawn from the series in a very upset state.

Going into the mouth of the harbor, we noticed the flags at half mast and learned of the killings in Munich. The next day was designated the Day of Mourning for the Munich massacre. We were towed to the starting line the following day to resail the sixth race. The fog was heavy and the wind very light. We played Frisbee with our Dragon counterpart and showed the rest of the Soling world this favorite American pastime. Finally, the race was called and we had won ourselves a Gold Medal. Even though this was only a six-race series, it would have been impossible for anyone to beat us even if we took a last in the seventh race.

As we towed to the line for the beginning of the last race (another try for the sixth race), we were feeling very jubilant, completely relaxed, calm and confident. We sailed the first windward leg in about fifth position. We lost two boats on the top reach and picked up four on the second reach. Shortly thereafter, on the second beat to windward, we moved into first place in front of Prince Harold of Norway. Winning our third race, we would also count our second and third place finishes and drop our fourth.

This covers my methods on scows, iceboats, and Olympic one-designs. However, it does not say anything about the most fantastic thrill of all—stepping up on the Number One podium and hearing our anthem played, knowing full well that we had made it possible to have Old Glory hoisted to the highest staff.

26. Piloting and Navigation for the Racing Skipper

Next to wind and water, I think that the Lord's greatest gift to the seafarer is the mariner's compass. This simple device is responsible for more of man's triumphs than would be possible to record in a good-sized library. Though the most important feature of the compass is its ability to point the way, for the racing man it has other functions as well.

Besides getting you home in a fog, the compass can show the favored end of the starting line; it can locate an elusive buoy; it can reveal hidden currents; and it can help to show whether you are sailing well. Therefore, I consider it one of the most important pieces of racing equipment in the boat. It should be constantly used in sailing to windward to determine if you have been headed or lifted.

Like most man-made things, the compass is subject to errors. These errors are magnified with a cheaply made instrument; for this reason, try to purchase the best compass you can afford. The features to look for in a mariner's compass are as follows:

It should have a large card that is easy to read; it should be sensitive; and it should have good damping action, so the card does not swing crazily with motion of the boat. There are many good compasses on the market, and choice is largely a matter of preference. For the larger boats, I like a spherical-domed compass because the plastic dome magnifies the card and makes it easier to read. The compass should also have a built-in set of variable compensating magnets so it can be adjusted without placing external magnets.

I prefer a compass that is graduated in both points and degrees. I was brought up with the point system, at a time when the degree-graduated compass was referred to as a "steamboatman's compass"—not without a note of derision. Yacht sailing is the last residing place of many venerable traditions, a heritage from the days when a rugged breed of men carried the world's cargoes and fought the nation's battles in wind-driven ships. Perhaps I will be thought overly romantic or nostalgic, but I think that the sailboat man should keep some of that tradition alive if it is not to become dead past—but not to the point of eliminating gear that adds to your racing competence or sailing pleasure.

Besides the historical implications, there is a practical value to a compass card graduated in points. Since they are larger, points are much easier to see. It is consequently simpler to keep the lubber's line of the compass lined up and a lot of sawing back and forth with the tiller is eliminated.

If you are a newcomer to sailing, be sure that you are thoroughly acquainted with the use of the mariner's compass and the meaning of and difference between the terms "deviation" and "variation." Any good elementary book on piloting, such as Chapman's *Piloting, Seamanship and Small Boat Handling,** or a course at the United States Power Squadrons or the Coast Guard Auxiliary, will teach the essentials of basic compass work. Be sure you thoroughly understand this subject, for it is absolutely indispensable to successful racing and cruising.

PLACING THE COMPASS

Whenever possible the compass should be placed on the centerline of the boat in a manner that makes it visible from both port and starboard steering positions. When this is impossible, it should be placed on a fore-and-aft line parallel to the centerline. Care must be taken that the lubber line represents the true direction of the keel, or serious errors will result.

I like to mount my compass forward in the cockpit, and high enough that it is within the natural line of vision when sailing the boat. I don't

---

* Charles F. Chapman, *Piloting, Seamanship and Small Boat Handling,* New York: Motor Boating.

believe it wise to take your eyes from the progress of the race more than is absolutely necessary, and if the instrument is below the line of sight, you must lower your glance constantly to check the course. For night sailing it is good practice to install a rheostat on the compass light, so the intensity can be varied to suit conditions and the preference of the helmsman.

Movable iron should not be stored within 7 feet of the compass or it will aberrate the magnetic field of the needle. Permanent iron is less critical, since it can be compensated for by adjustment. Unless you have had previous experience and thoroughly understand the technique, I would leave annual compass adjustment to a professional. Their fees are moderate and you can be sure that the job will be properly done. After the adjustment, run a series of courses, say four in each quadrant of the compass, using prominent landmarks that will not likely be subject to change. Record the readings on your chart, in a log book, or on a card, and file it away for safe keeping. Each year when your boat is recommissioned, and at other intervals, run the courses again and note whether there have been changes in the compass readings. If none appear, the instrument has not developed errors and can safely be used another season; if there is significant difference, the compass must be readjusted.

A compass, like any other precision instrument, must be carefully handled and properly maintained if it is to remain accurate. To protect the plastic dome from the sun's rays, a canvas cover should be kept over the compass and binnacle when the compass is not in use. A domed compass is made with a chamber to allow for expansion and contraction of the fluid under different temperatures. The appearance of an air bubble means that the expansion chamber diaphragm or the gasket has sprung a leak. Do not attempt to repair this yourself, and do not add fluid to eliminate the bubble. Return the compass to the manufacturer for a complete overhaul and accuracy check. When the compass is stored for an extended period of time, turn it upside down to remove friction from the jeweled pivot.

The Compass as a Racing Aid

The first thing the compass can do to help win your race is establish the best spot to cross the starting line. In theory, the race committee will try to lay out the starting line perfectly square to the direction of the wind. In practice, however, this is not always done. Usually the line is not at true right angles to the wind, and one end or the other will be the "favored" place to cross. Now your major concern will be to find out which end of that line is the favored end.

One simple and quick way is to place your boat with the head into the wind right on the starting line. Whichever end of the line her bow falls off toward is the favored end. A better and more accurate method is to establish the favored end by compass bearing.

To do this, bring the boat exactly head-to-wind; the compass reading at this time shows the true wind direction. Next, sail along the starting line on the starboard tack with your jibstay on the white flag on the committee boat and your backstay on the buoy flag at the other end of the line. At the moment when the fore-and-aft centerline of your boat is identical with the line from the buoy to the committee boat flag, take your compass bearing. Be sure that you are truly lined up with the white starting flag and not merely the bow or stern of the committee boat, because your start is observed from this angle only.

If too many competitors are in the area and the starting line is jammed, sail out beyond the buoy, line up the buoy flag with the committee boat white flag and while sailing directly on this line take your compass bearing.

Now, whichever end of the line is closest to the direction of the wind will be the advantageous place to cross.

For example: Using a hypothetical wind direction of north, if the bearing obtained when the flags were lined up was west, then it is obvious that the starting line is square to the direction of the wind. In this case, it is possible to cross anywhere on the line without losing advantage, since the distance to the weather mark is the same everywhere on the line.

Again with a wind direction of north, let us suppose that the bearing is west-by-north—or its reciprocal, east-by-south. In this case, we can see by consulting the diagram that the westerly end of the line is favored. Conversely, if the bearing was west-by-south—the reciprocal is east-by-north—then the favored place to cross would be the eastern end of the starting line.

If you have gotten out of practice, it is an excellent idea to go through simulated compass work at home. Use a compass rose with a pencil laid over it to represent the boat, and a cut-out cardboard arrow to represent the wind. Keep changing the direction of the imaginary starting line and work diligently until you can immediately call off the reciprocal of any compass bearing without hesitation.

There are other important ways that the compass can help you to sail a better race. For example, before the race starts, put your boat on the same heading as the second leg of the course and see if you will be able to carry a spinnaker and how well it will stand. This will save time and costly mistakes when you reach the weather mark. Similarly, for the third leg, which will probably be a run, use your compass to sail on the heading and see on which side you will carry your spinnaker. With this information you can rig spinnaker gear in advance and save many boat lengths over competitors who have arrived late or who have neglected this important preparation.

Your compass can also be a valuable tool for ascertaining whether you are getting the most out of the available wind. Frequently, when sailing on a large body of water with few landmarks, when there is light haze, or when the legs of the course are so long that the marks fall below the horizon, you must rely wholly on compass courses to raise the next mark. This is an ideal opportunity to use the compass to develop your "wind sense." Regularly check your heading; it is possible to tell whether you are being "headed" by the breeze, or if, perhaps, you might be getting the advantage of a momentary "lift." Playing the puffs this way can save you a tack and sometimes gain yards that might otherwise have been lost.

CHARTS

You should not fail to carry a local chart aboard even if you are racing in an area where you were born and brought up. It is rarely feasible to chart courses during a small boat race—they must be prepared beforehand —but nonetheless the chart should be aboard. After the race is over, you can mark on it places where you picked up a certain land breeze, or where you hit a dead spot. By doing this over the course of a season, you can compile a kind of wind pattern chart for your local waters related to objects inland and contours of the shore.

It is a job for an octopus to lay out a course on a large-scale chart while a small racing boat is heaving in a sea. The skipper usually doesn't need the chart except under unusual circumstances, in which case the first mate can find the reference for him. There is seldom a flat surface large enough to spread the chart out fully. To lay an accurate course is most difficult. A much better idea is to compile an indexed book listing every possible course for the waters where you habitually race.

I would like to pass on the system I have evolved over the years, and which has proved invaluable to me. Except for regattas away from home, our International races are usually held in Long Island Sound. We race in an area that can be contained within a rectangle roughly 10 miles wide by 30 miles long. In my spare time at home, I have laid compass courses to, from, and between every buoy, every lighthouse, every prominent landmark within this area. I then entered the courses in a loose-leaf book, cataloged by area and listed alphabetically.

This involves laying hundreds of courses, and although it seems like a complicated and cumbersome device, it isn't; it is just a matter of good indexing and careful preparation. For example, if I want the Guggenheim tower or the Glen Cove breakwater, these courses are cataloged from my Larchmont home buoy; I list them the other way around and cross-index them, too—from Guggenheim and Glen Cove breakwater to Parsonage Point buoy, Larchmont, etc.

I constantly thank my stars that I evolved this method, because it has constantly helped me in my racing. Here is a hypothetical example. You start a race sailing a course of east-by-south, but you find that because a competitor luffed you way out, or because you altered your course to pick up a new wind, you are steering a totally different course heading. If you cannot see the next mark, if a light haze or a low-lying fog makes up, you have no departure. You started off east-by-south, but now you are way above that course and you must determine how far up you are and what new course to set to reach that mark.

If there is any object that is marked on the chart—a flagpole, a water tower, visible on the shoreline, or a buoy, you can take your departure from that. You flip to the proper page of your book and select a new course that will bring you to the mark. If the mark you are searching for is not directly on the line of your new course, you can make a quick mental adjustment of a fraction of a point, but at least you will have a fairly accurate idea of where to head.

It is a blessing to have these courses laid out beforehand and not have to go through the throes of frantically plotting an emergency heading in the middle of a demanding race. This is just another one of those hundred little things that can mean the difference between becoming a champion or remaining an also-ran.

TIDES AND CURRENTS

It is important for the racing man to have a knowledge of the action of the tides. Not because the tides themselves are so important, but because tidal action bears an important relationship to currents. The currents we are primarily interested in are those called "tidal currents," because they are caused by the ebbing and flooding of the tide. Other currents exist, such as the ocean currents of the world, a result of the earth's rotation. These are of extreme importance to the ocean racer and many of them have fascinating histories and peculiarities. The Gulf Stream is an example of an important ocean current that is not caused by tidal action; it is a large factor in successfully competing in the classic Bermuda race.

The actions of tidal currents are of primary interest to the small boat racer; and unfortunately many small boat sailors are profoundly ignorant of this importance. I would venture to say that half the skippers at the starting line of any race have no idea what the current will be doing at every hour throughout that race. And yet current can make or ruin your start: it can win or lose the finish.

For the beginner in racing sail, I would again recommend thorough study of Chapman's *Piloting, Seamanship and Small Boat Handling,* to provide a basic understanding of piloting problems and techniques—including corrections for current. The book is a classic and should form part of the library of every sailor. Courses given by the United States Power Squadrons are invaluable, and they are given free of charge.

The chief techniques and factors that you should know about are: how to construct a vector diagram to allow setting of a compass course that allows for current; the rhythm of rise and fall of the tide and how it affects current velocity; the meaning of the terms *set* and *drift;* the difference between speed over the bottom as opposed to speed through the water; and the effect of leeway in making good a desired course. Let us now discuss the aspects of current that are of particular significance in sailboat racing.

Before you sail out to the starting line, you should have learned the times of current change (which are not the same as the times of low and high tides). From this information and the U.S. Coast and Geodetic Survey current tables you can figure the times of the tide change. If the C. & G.S. publishes a set of tidal-current charts for your area, you should certainly invest in them. With the aid of these tables and charts, make a small card that lists the current conditions at every half-hour throughout the length of time you might be racing. Don't overlook the possibilities that starts can be delayed, and that the wind can fall light, and that you may be out on the water past the time the race is scheduled to end.

In addition to the velocity of the current, be sure you have its direction firmly in mind. Remember that direction does not always merely reverse itself by 180 degrees from, say, flood to ebb, but often makes considerable deviations at half and maximum flood or ebb conditions. It is for this reason that the current charts are particularly valuable, as they graphically show the true direction of the current at any time. In any case, try to have a complete and accurate picture in your mind for each sailing leg of the course, including whether the current will be with you, against you, or at an oblique angle to your course.

The first occasion you will have to use tide calculations is at the start. You can always use a head tide as a "brake" or retarding force to gain time before the starting gun fires. On the other hand, you must take care that a fair tide does not set you over the line prematurely, or cause you to foul the committee boat. A fair tide can also set you in a position where you will become the burdened boat, and you will be without rights over boats that are to windward of you. So in every maneuver that you make at the start, be aware of the effects that tidal currents will have on your strategy.

We are all aware of current in light weather because it is so evident. As you go by a buoy, the committee boat, or any object that is anchored, you can see the current streaming by and it makes an impression on your consciousness. When the breeze is hard, even many good skippers will discount tidal currents, under the assumption that because the boat is moving fast, current is largely overcome by speed. This is a decided mistake. Current is just as much a factor to be reckoned with in heavy weather as in light.

With a little reflection it is easy to visualize the reason for this. Consider the current as a river, and think of your boat as sailing within a huge basin of water that is floating in this river. Now, no matter how fast your boat is sailing within this basin, the basin, boat and all, is being carried along by the flow of the river. This displacement, as it were, is constant for the velocity of the current and unaffected by the speed of the boat. Therefore, be sure you do not neglect to figure the effect of current even in hard sailing breezes.

When you are running out your time at the start, be sure that you have allowed minutes—either subtracted from or added to your running time— for the effects of adverse or favorable tide. No one can figure this margin by mathematics alone; there are too many factors involved. The best procedure is to make several practice runs and time the exact requirements of each leg with a stopwatch.

Here is an important suggestion. If the tide is favorable—that is, if it is setting you across the starting line, jibe back to the line after your run instead of tacking. By jibing, you will be able to cross at the precise spot that you had previously selected. If you tack instead, you will obviously be set to windward and unable to run the same course on your return.

Current and the Weather Mark

Your tactic, naturally, should always be to arrive at the weather mark as quickly as you can, and it is important to arrive there on the starboard tack. Tidal current as you approach the weather mark can make or break your race. It is unforgivably bad seamanship to overstand the weather mark because you have failed to allow for current. If you overstand, you will have donated hard-earned distance to your competitors and you can consider yourself lucky if there is a single boat in the fleet that you are able to beat. Tide or current must be a constant consideration both to windward and off the wind.

Lee-Bowing the Current

It will often be found advantageous to understand the weather mark. This can be done when the tide or current is flowing at an oblique angle to your desired course. Since the tide under the lee bow will move your boat to windward, it is possible to understand the mark, as the current will set you to windward. By playing the currents in this way you can gain immeasurable advantage over your less-knowledgeable competitors. It is simply a matter of obtaining a good knowledge of tidal-current action over the course throughout the racing day. Incidentally, when you are sailing an invitational race or regatta away from home, be certain that you invest enough time in study and that you understand tidal current conditions over the strange race course. If you do not, the local skippers will have a decided advantage.

Leeway

Every sailboat will have a certain amount of leeway when sailing upwind. That is, the boat will be displaced in a downwind direction. This caution is superfluous for veteran sailors, but do not fail to consider the effects of leeway when planning a smart arrival at the weather mark. The only way to measure leeway is by experience: no two sailboats are the same. The amount of leeway depends upon the underwater configuration of the hull and, of course, upon the manner in which she is sailed. The greater the area of lateral resistance, the lesser will be the amount of leeway. In actual practice, allowance for leeway becomes instinctive.

PILOTING AND NAVIGATION FOR THE OCEAN RACER

Navigational procedures in ocean racing become, in some respects, more simple than inshore racing, and in some respects much more complex. Celestial navigation, which is of no concern in day racing, is extremely important in ocean racing. However, the ocean racer carries a trained navigator, thereby relieving the skipper of this responsibility.

Cornelius Shields, Sr. and Jr., at the helm of *Do Do*.

27. *Passing on the Tradition*

For me, youngsters and yachting are synonymous; many of the finest times I have passed on the water were spent introducing boys and girls to the water and sailboats. Frankly, I am always fascinated by the miracle of a child's growing awareness of the world around him, and it is like experiencing youth again to watch this unfolding of a new personality.

I learned so many things about my own children, Aileen and Corny, while we were sailing together. I could see them absorbing the sights and sounds of sailing, I could watch their curiosity driving them to try and understand what was taking place, and I could share their pleasure when something delighted them. I am certain I would have missed all these wonderful revelations of character if I had not spent so much time sailing with them.

I have no doubt that introducing a child to sailing at an early age makes becoming a champion easier for him. There is so much to be learned, if one is to become a racing sailor, that the youngster who starts early has a distinct advantage. Perhaps the most important asset gained from being around the water at an early age is that children develop a love of the atmosphere of boats and the sea that will stay with them always. Most boys and girls are entranced by the water, anyway, so it is not hard to channel this natural inclination.

Investing time and money in teaching youngsters about yachting is not a one-sided proposition for those interested in yachting, for youngsters bring an immense amount of talent and enthusiasm to yachting. If we who love yacht racing want to see it prosper, we simply have to take pains to interest young people in participation. Many of the sailboat-racing champions who now represent the United States in international competitions are products of organized junior sailing programs.

In some cases, yacht clubs can recover from financial difficulty and avert failure by simply starting junior sailing programs. During the bad years of the 1930's, it was the juniors that saved the Larchmont Yacht Club. Although the story isn't generally known, it is an interesting one that shows how the youngsters can strengthen a club. E. G. Anderson will everlastingly be thanked for his institution of the first junior program on Long Island Sound at the Larchmont Yacht Club.

Back in the 1930's, as we all know, we were going through the worst economic distress the nation has ever known. Industrial firms, banks, clubs —in short, all types of enterprises—were either close to bankruptcy or had already gone under. Naturally, a yacht club is among the first hit because people economize on nonessentials first. I mentioned before that when I was newly married and just starting in business, I had to resign my Larchmont Yacht Club membership because I couldn't afford the dues.

So, during those depression years, the Larchmont membership had fallen to about 150 members. The annual dues were then about $150. I was a trustee of the club then, as I am now, and at one meeting we found it necessary to discuss the financial matters that threatened our survival. One of the officers suggested that we raise our dues to meet expenses, but I was very strongly opposed to any raise, since I felt sure that at such a time, when everyone was so hard-pressed, an additional expense would only reduce the membership further.

Some of the other trustees thought I was wrong at first when I was seeking a way to *lower* dues to attract more members. Luckily, just at that time I happened to look out the window and catch a glimpse of the club's beautiful swimming pool. "Why not," I proposed, "offer a swimming pool membership and charge only $60?"

Fortunately, the trustees approved the idea, and the results weren't long in coming. People flocked to take advantage of the swimming; the new members brought their wives and children, and it was the children who really got things moving.

At the time we had a rather meager program for juniors; but the youngsters in the swimming pool would watch their friends sailing the few boats we then had. When the parents saw how passionately and sincerely their children wanted to sail, many bought the $60 junior memberships and scrimped other places in their budgets. Soon we bought more boats for the program, and the junior club began to grow.

As the parents saw the facilities that the club offered besides the pool—the restaurant, the yachting, the social events—many of them became regular members and the families' summer recreation activities moved to the yacht club. I'll never forget how some fathers, fulfilling parental duty and full of righteousness for having given up the day's golf games, came down to watch their children's first races, wearing bored, patronizing looks. The following year these same fathers bought boats, their youngsters were crewing for them, and they were ardent racers. Within a few years, we had a fleet of fifty Lightning class boats at Larchmont alone, developed by A. R. O'Neal, Paul Forsman, Richard Carr, Roy Amy and Alfred Amy. They were all owned by people who had been lured to the club by the enthusiasm of their children. Larchmont has been a financial success ever since, and we have one of the most active and healthy memberships of any yacht club in the country.

After the youngster has successfully completed the junior sailing program, he can best improve his ability as a sailor by crewing aboard a boat in one of the active one-design classes, rather than by skippering his own boat. By crewing for an able and experienced skipper, he will have an opportunity to apply what he has learned under the actual pressures of highly competitive racing. If he is alert, he will absorb an infinite amount of new knowledge that will further prepare him for the day when he becomes a skipper himself.

I think it is a serious mistake to buy a youngster a boat of his own after he has just finished a sailing program. It is a mistake for two reasons: first, because he may be too young to truly appreciate the boat and he may come to feel superior to his companions who are still struggling to get aboard boats as crew members; second, because children often get bored if things are made too easy for them—the boy or girl could easily lose interest in the boat and sailing as well. If you buy a boat for a child too soon, you run the risk of his losing interest in a sport that can be a priceless benefit and source of lifetime pleasure. So for the sake of the child, exercise judgment, and don't give him a boat of his own until he has evidenced a deep and serious interest in sailing.

In my opinion, things should not be made too easy for children. They should earn and merit what is given to them. Anyone who has seen the living-room floor of a modern home on Christmas Day, piled with expensive presents for the children, and also noted the lassitude with which the children receive them, will agree that there is a responsibility inherent in gift-giving that we sometimes ignore.

It is a dreadful thing to me to see some world-weary little tot of nine or ten who has been showered with so much that there seems to be no excitement or novelty left that can arouse him. I often wonder whether the adults are giving to please the children or only to satisfy themselves. I suspect that there is a kind of selfishness involved here, and that the sentiment, "I'd like to give them all the things that I never had!" might constitute an almost criminal lack of sensitivity and awareness on our parts. After all, a child's great charm lies partly in the way his imagination transforms the commonplace objects of his play. We should leave some room for the exercise of that imagination. I have probably belabored this point, but I feel strongly about it, so in anything as important as giving a child his first boat, be sure that the timing is right.

To fully develop his talents as a sailor, therefore, a youngster should, by all means, spend a period as a crew man aboard the boat of an older skipper. In my own boat, I have always made an effort to have one or two children available as crew members—either my own, when they were young, or else boys or girls from around the club who were eager and interested in learning to race. Quite a few of these young people have now become champions in their own right. I urge the skippers of the competitive one-design classes to draw on these children for their crews wherever possible.

You needn't worry about their lack of experience, for a child will astound you by the speed with which he learns even the most sophisticated racing principles. It is a mistake to patronize or talk down to children, because they have an unerring instinct for knowing when you are not being natural with them, and they understand more than we realize. I have learned a great deal about racing from the youngsters in my crew.

I will never forget, for instance, one International race where I was out to hold my position against the wonderfully able skipper, Bus Mosbacher. We had a typical southerly breeze and I was fortunate enough to have picked up a little lead on the reach toward the finish. Young Corny, who was only about six years old at the time, was aboard the boat, and he came across the cockpit toward me and said in a serious way, "I think you ought to watch that fellow over there."

Aileen Shields Bryan.

I looked around and saw that Mosbacher had broken away from me and had gone out to windward. I went out after him and fortunately was able to maintain my lead. I couldn't believe that my son had that much understanding at that age, but he was right—I had gotten too confident about the lead I held. If he hadn't noticed the threat of that other boat, I would have lost that race. Here all the time I thought that the boy was just out there tying knots in my jibsheets and fooling around the boat!

One winter I was struggling with my racing dinghy; I couldn't, for the life of me, figure why that boat wasn't going the way she used to. It not only had me puzzled, it had me upset because I was losing races and not doing as well as I had in previous years. As I sailed dejectedly back to the dock from a race one day, my little daughter, Aileen, was waiting ashore where she had been watching the race. As I tied the boat up, she said to me, "You better do something about that mast."

Only half paying attention, I said, "What do you mean?"

"Well, it's got a funny big hook in it," she said.

A little impatient with what I thought was her lack of knowledge, and thinking she was mistaking the natural bowing of the mast for a defect, I grumbled, "Well, it happens I like to sail with a hook in it—it flattens the sail."

"No, not that," she replied. "It's almost 'V' shaped. I don't see how the boat goes with it." Then she walked away.

What she had said bothered me, and I looked the mast over carefully. The dinghies we were then sailing had two-piece masts that were made of aluminum and joined together with a sliding metal ferrule. I didn't think that the ferrule was long enough, so I had removed mine and replaced it with a wooden ferrule that was longer. I thought this would strengthen the mast and hold the two sections more rigid. Instead, what had happened was that the aluminum of the mast had chafed the softer wood as a result of the working of the mast. About an eighth of an inch of the wood had worn away, permitting the mast to sag toward the stern, distorting both the mast and the set of the sail. I replaced the wooden ferrule with a metal one and almost immediately began to win races again with that dinghy.

Since that lesson, I have never offhandedly dismissed the possibility of learning something about sailboat racing from children. They often can see the forest in spite of the trees.

28. West Coast Sailing Scene

BY ROBERT ALLAN, JR.

Bob Allen has looked to the future of sailboat racing throughout his career as a skipper-organizer of intercollegiate competition, participant in one-design and offshore racing on the West Coast, and as a father. Bob's two eldest sons, Skip and Scott, have both begun spectacular careers in racing. Skip was a helmsman aboard Fastnet and Transpac winners, and has won both the Congressional Cup match-racing series and the Kennedy Cup Intercollegiate Regatta. Scott won the Prince of Wales Bowl, the very important NAYRU (North American Yacht Racing Union) match-racing championship, and has been U.S. National Flying Dutchman champion as well as the 1972 Olympic helmsman in the FD.

Since his retirement as an extremely active and successful executive with Litton Industries and president of Cyprus Mines, Bob has devoted all his enormous energy to the promotion of intercollegiate racing, especially the development of the Shields class in college and university programs.

Along with George Griffith, Bob was the founder of the Lapworth 36 and Cal 40 boats, which placed Bill Lapworth at the head of the offshore-racing design field for many years. Bob was also a winning Star and Snipe skipper before his offshore career. He is the sort of man with a wonderful "take charge" attitude who makes an outstanding success of every activity he undertakes.

The development of West Coast yachting is worth investigating for many reasons. Because of its relative youth, formalized Pacific Coast sailing is an excellent barometer of present and future trends in American yachting. California tends to be an experimental area where things happen first, but not always for the best. The Eastern sailing fraternity looks upon California as a maverick, in spite of the fact that the San Francisco Yacht Club is one of the two or three oldest yacht clubs in the United States. Easterners may not realize that the race to Honolulu was started in 1906, the same year as the race to Bermuda. Yet West Coast yachting is still treated as an infant in many ways. For instance, it wasn't until 1952 that the NAYRU championships of North America were opened to yacht clubs that were "west of the Hudson River." This amazing situation was changed only when some of the Western representatives to NAYRU threatened to withdraw if not given full recognition.

The West Coast has some very peculiar problems for sailors. First, we have few areas good for offshore cruising and anchoring. Second, when you sail off the Pacific Coast you're in very deep water with normally strong, cold winds. I know the fog in Maine, the rough weather in the North Atlantic, and the sudden thunder squalls of the midwestern summers. The Pacific Coast, however, is primarily an area of all or nothing at all sailing. Sailors here are either blue-water ocean skippers or simply "Marina cocktail-bar owners who use their boats solely for entertainment," in the words of some yachting magazines.

The really amazing story on the West Coast is of the growth of sailing in general. I can remember sailing in Newport Harbor in the early 1930's and writing back East to ask if we could have permission to form a Snipe fleet. At the time, there were not more than 30 or 40 boats sailing out of Newport Harbor. Today there are over 11,000 registered sailboats there. In the boating boom of the past years, Southern California represents an atomic blast. Today, places such as Mission Bay in San Diego, Marina del Ray, Alamitos Bay at Long Beach, and the new 6,000-boat marina at Dana Point are ample evidence of the strength of boating in California.

The full impact of this growth hit me one morning shortly after sunrise. I heard a vast roar of motors and thought I was back in the Air Force hearing a flight ready for a dawn mission. I looked out the window and there were literally thousands of pleasure boats leaving the harbor in the roughest possible weather to go some 20 miles to sea to welcome the Queen Mary to her permanent berth at Long Beach, California. I heard later that the skipper of the Queen Mary saw the thousands of dots of white in the sea ahead and thought he was sailing into a squall of some sort. When he realized that it was practically the entire boat population of Southern California come to pay homage to the Queen, he was literally moved to tears and slowed his ship to give several saluting blasts of her great whistle. This encouraged the pleasure boats to approach despite the stormy seas, and the Queen Mary was imprisoned by an armada of small craft. The skipper was forced to maneuver the giant ship and use full speed to pull ahead of the fleet and make a normal approach into Long Beach Harbor.

The vast number of boats and the rapid growth of sailing have given California the opportunity to provide the finest facilities and racing-cruising programs in the United States. The problems encountered in meeting this challenge have also caused some of the most dismal stopgap measures to develop. Crowded, ill-equipped marinas and disorganized boating programs have accompanied the great accomplishments of the Pacific Coast boating world.

One of the most unusual success stories, at least as far as numbers, is that of the annual race to Ensenada from Newport Harbor on May 5 (*Cinco de Mayo*)—the Mexican holiday. The Ensenada Race attracts over 500 ocean-racing boats annually. The start is a sight that is not soon forgotten. I was a member of the original group formed to organize the Ensenada Race. Our goal was to simplify entrance into Mexico, which prior to this event required months of red tape and several hundred dollars of fees. We planned the first race hoping that 25 or 50 boats would enter. Instead, we had over 150 sailboats at the starting line. The festival atmosphere of this first race was to become a hallmark of future Ensenada ventures. For example, the race committee preceded the fleet to Ensenada and partied all night with the governor. They never did make it to the finish line, so the first 20 or 30 boats had no one to take their finish time.

I was race chairman for the second, third, and fourth races, and we tried using Phil Berg's beautiful 85-foot *Savatar* as a race-committee boat. We anchored her in the middle of a 2-mile-long starting line and had the boats start on either side of her. It worked out very well.

There have been a number of unusual incidents in Ensenada Races. I remember the foggy night that Humphrey Bogart radioed the committee boat to say he thought he was leading the race. There were 275 boats racing that year and Bogart thought he was about 2 miles from our position at the finish line. He asked if we would please give a blast on our horn, turn on our spotlight, and give a count on the radio to help him find us along the Mexican Coast, which is particularly barren of any navigational aids. We obliged and did as he asked. A few minutes later, Bogart was back on the radio with some of the saltiest language I ever heard. He had heard the radio, he had heard the horn, and he had seen the lights. He altered the course of his beautiful yawl, *Santana,* to round our committee boat, only to discover that what he had seen was a large Mexican produce truck on a dirt road along the ocean front. Bogart almost put the *Santana* right up on a hill and made it a permanent Mexican monument. (Despite his problem, Bogie finished in the top five.)

Equally unusual was the finish some years later when about 150 boats sailed into a calm a quarter of a mile from the finish line. Suddenly a blast of wind came down off the cliffs and 150 boats simultaneously tried to cross a finish line only 200 yards long. The race-committee chairman turned on his tape recorder and recorded for posterity the shouts, collisions, and noises of impact as practically the whole fleet smashed and crashed its way in a compressed mass across the line. No one was able to record the order of finish and it took days to unscramble the mess and approximate the results.

Even more impressive is the transpacific race to Honolulu. It starts on the Fourth of July and covers 2,250 miles of open ocean. My first Transpac was in 1947. Los Angeles Harbor was filled with naval vessels back from World War II. As we started they were all firing salutes. I was green enough to think they were doing it in honor of our fleet of ocean racers. Actually they were firing the traditional Fourth of July, 21-gun salute at noon. The Honolulu Race is one of the longest races in the world. There are those, particularly in the East, who feel that it is a very easy downhill slide. Having raced it, my opinion is just the opposite. Until you have followed a spinnaker for 10 or 12 days in 30 to 50 knots of wind and weathered squalls, planing and surfing before huge waves, you have not really learned one of sailing's ultimate skills nor experienced one of her greatest thrills.

I served as a weather officer in World War II and brought to the 1947 Honolulu Race the single-station synoptic-map forecasting techniques that we could use on the boats while we were sailing, thereby avoiding sailing into the calm center of the Pacific high-pressure area. This technique helped produce a series of record-breaking passages in the following years.

The most fantastic finish in Honolulu Race history, in my opinion, was between the famous Herreshoff ketch *Ticonderoga* and the equally well-known *Stormvogel*. *Ticonderoga* had broken out of a rain squall 100 miles from the finish to find *Stormvogel* less than 50 feet astern. The two boats raced to the finish line at 14 knots down the great roaring seas of Molokai Channel. The *Ticonderoga* made a full flying jibe like a Star boat across the finish line to edge out the *Stormvogel* by several hundred yards after almost 2,400 miles of open ocean racing. Both boats broke the record. Our 19-year-old son, Skip, brought home a short section of amateur film that he took between turns at the helm of *Ticonderoga*. Those two majestic ocean racers fighting like small one-designers had to be captured on film to be believed.

Even more historic was the more recent 1971 race when the famous *Windward Passage* set an all-time record to Honolulu of 9 days, 9 hours, 6 minutes, and 48 seconds to win overall and on corrected time. *Windward Passage* was literally sailing in a race not only with the fleet but also with hurricane Denise. *Windward Passage* had broken the record in 1969 but was disqualified in a luffing situation at the start. She had made contact with the man-overboard pole on one of the smaller yachts.

The man-overboard pole is no insignificant item, for a number of people have gone overboard in a Honolulu Race. There have even been fatalities aboard the vessels. One of the great stories concerns the Hollywood cook who joined the Hawaiian crew on the schooner *Lady Joe* in 1947. When the weather became rough 30 miles off Catalina and the Hawaiians would not turn back, the cook simply put on a life preserver and jumped overboard. The Hawaiians, being made of sterner stuff, continued the race leaving the cook in the ocean where he was later picked up by some sympathetic spectator boats.

The case of Ted Sierks precipitated the rule that made the man-overboard pole a mandatory piece of equipment. Ted fell overboard from the 85-foot sloop *Lapache,* and was in the water for two days. No one could find him. A whole squadron of destroyers joined the fleet of sailboats in the search. After two days, they gave up the search, and as the last destroyer turned away at sunset, a sailor on the stern happened to catch sight of Ted. They swung back and picked him up. The problem was that without a pole, he was almost invisible in the water.

There has been a steady increase in class racing on the West Coast.

Bob Allan, skippering the Cal 40, *Holiday Too,* to a fourth-straight ocean-race win in YRU off Catalina Island.

The National Midwinter Regatta has been held every February for the past 46 years. This regatta used to be held at Los Angeles Harbor, but now, due to the number of boats, it is held simultaneously at five different harbors. Fifteen yacht clubs organize the event and there were 87 classes racing in February 1973.

The same growth is evident in ocean racing. Some years ago, Chuck Ullman, Barney Huber, Dick Stewart, George Griffith, Bill Lapworth, Porter Sinclair, and I met to discuss what we could do to improve the sailing and ocean-racing turnouts. We came up with the idea of a high-point series and set up a series of races, calling it our championship. The Southern Ocean Racing Circuit in Florida was developing a similar format in the late 1940's and the early 1950's. Our series became known as the Whitney Series. Walt Elliott was going to put up the trophy originally, but he passed away. I asked Lou Whitney if he would be interested, and he provided a beautiful replica of the America's Cup, a fitting tribute to the winner of the series.

The Southern Ocean Racing Circuit has become unique, a real commercial showcase for the finest of new equipment. The Whitney Series has evolved as one of ten or twelve other high-point ocean-racing series, each out of a separate harbor in California. These include one out of San Diego, the Danforth high-point series out of San Francisco, the Overton series of Marina del Ray and the Ahmanson series out of Newport Harbor, to name just a few. The point is that there are enough people to put 50 to 100 ocean-racing boats in each of these series. Recently, with the increasing problems of getting IOR measurements and the complexity of the new measurement rule, many of these boats are being transferred over to the Performance Handicap Rating Rule. This rule was based on the bare bones of the CCA or IOR rule but modified slightly by the performance of a large number of boats of any one type. It is not truly an arbitrary handicap based on performance, such as in bowling or in golf. In other words it is a rule based in part upon measurements and in part upon performance. The fee for a rating is only $5.00 and you don't have to have your boat measured since the boats are classed by the general specifications of their sister ships. As a result, there are nearly a thousand boats measured in racing under this rule in Southern California alone.

Some wonderful new designs have originated in California. The Cal 40 is probably the most renowned. It was designed by Bill Lapworth and won the Bermuda Race, the Southern Ocean Circuit, and the Honolulu Race three times. The Cal 40 proved that a yacht could be an all-around cruising and racing boat as well as a family boat and was probably the most successful fiberglass boat of its kind. California skippers have also raced the Erickson 39, Newport 41, the new C. & C. Redline specials, as well as some very unusual and wonderful designs. Among these are the world-famous 73-footer *Ondine, Improbable, Windward Passage, Kialoa II,* and the 12-meter *Easterner,* now known as *Newsboy,* which still races without an engine as a virgin 12-meter, strengthened and converted for ocean racing.

The West Coast has produced many fine skippers. Forty-odd years ago Darby Metcalf won the Snipe World Championship and Hook Beardsley and Walter Hubbard won the Star World's Championship. The trend

311

has continued right up to the present, as exemplified by Lowell North's Olympic gold medal and Bill Ficker's America's Cup win. Warwick Tompkins, Skip Allan, Ben Mitchell, and Bob Grant have been on boats that won the Fastnet Race, the race to Jamaica and the Bermuda Race. Some of the young stars of the future are coming off the college campus. These include Tim Hogan from U.S.C.; Argyle Campbell, All-American at U.S.C.; young Dave Ullman, who emerged from the Snowbird class to become world champion in three different competitions; and Burke Sawyer, a real ocean-racing star, to name just a few. Some of the famous West Coast trophies originated with Sir Thomas Lipton. On one of his trips, he left some beautiful sterling silver cups at San Diego and San Francisco, which are still coveted challenge cups.

More recently, the Congressional Cup series sponsored by the Long Beach Yacht Club has received worldwide recognition, not only for the caliber of its competition but also because of its unique format. In the Congressional Cup, the boats are assigned by drawing lots and each skipper engages in a series of match races, rotating boats until he has raced with every other skipper. In my humble opinion, this type of match racing is a more definitive test of the skipper's skill than any other kind of race. It is certainly most exciting for the spectators. Admittedly, starting in 30- to 500-boat fleets takes a great deal of skill, and the problem of maneuvering to clear a large fleet takes patience and experience. But there is nothing quite as demanding as the match race. To adjust yourself and tune your crew and sails to compete on a one-to-one basis demands the utmost sailing knowledge. Using identical equipment puts the emphasis on tactics, the heart of competitive racing. This kind of match racing has been used for years to tune up our own boats for ocean racing. I have personally seen the difference this practice has made in the Cal 40 class.

Match racing should be used by every yacht club to sharpen the skills of their junior and senior skippers. It think it could be an invaluable part of Olympic training. After the top four or five men in each class have been selected, there should be a series of match races to determine boat speed and to improve each man's tactics. Those who are the best match racers usually prove to be the best fleet racers.

The West Coast has long been happy and willing to follow the direction of the North American Yacht Racing Union, even though prior to the late 1950's members of the western area yacht clubs were not ap-

Soling class sloops rounding a mark on the Olympic course outside California Yacht Club at Marina del Ray during the 43rd annual Southern California Yachting Association Midwinter Regatta, 1972. A total of 940 boats raced in 74 separate classes. This has become the world's largest annual regatta, involving fifteen yacht clubs.

pointed to positions on the NAYRU committees. Thank God this situation has been corrected. Jim Michaels of San Francisco is now the head of NAYRU. This has helped to unify the West and East Coasts in seeking answers to problems and in planning more meaningful programs. The growing pains of Western sailing add new insight and a fresh approach to the common difficulties of the NAYRU. The West Coast had recent experiences with the problems of rapid growth, pollution, the right and wrong way to have a marina, commercialism in ocean racing, the need for adequate safety precautions, the need for newspaper coverage and distribution of racing results, and the ever-increasing problem of high taxation on boats without relief from the shoreside politicians.

One of the most productive meetings of the NAYRU occurs at the annual Tinsley Island rendezvous in the fall. Many prominent members from the East come to San Francisco to attend the fall ocean-racing series. Following the races the group sails up the Sacramento River to Tinsley Island. Over camp fires, problems are discussed in a more relaxed manner than is possible at the New York Yacht Club in the formal January NAYRU meeting. Another favorite West Coast meeting spot is Catalina, the only island that is available for easy mooring within one day's cruising range of most Southern California ports.

In the 1930's we introduced sailing to colleges on the West Coast and finally formed a Western college sailing association. It was primarily Stanford racing against University of California. Dick Lough, one of the finest skippers ever, was the captain of the Berkeley team and consistently beat us at Stanford. It didn't seem to bother Dick that he was unable to walk. He was in iron braces from an attack of polio. Knowing him taught me that sailing was not only for those who were young and strong, but also for those unable to participate in most other competitive sports.

After World War II, I approached Len Fowle and the Eastern collegiate establishment to encourage the development of a national Collegiate Racing organization. In 1950, California held its first National Collegiate Sailing Championship. It was a memorable series with a nail-biting finish. The Western team was from the University of California, Berkeley. The skippers were two young men named Lowell North and Bill Ficker. They raced against unbeaten Bobby Monnetti of Yale and a youngster by the name of Dick Carter, now a famous naval architect. The Yale team won the 44-race series by one point. Len Fowle as chairman turned to me and in the finest New England tradition said, "If you'll excuse me, I would like to give one small cheer for the Eastern team." I didn't have enough lung power left to offer even a weak protest.

In recent years, though, the Western college teams have pretty well swept the boards, winning not only the National Championship but also the Sugar Bowl at New Orleans, the Angston Big Ten races in Chicago, and frequently the Kennedy Cup at the Naval Academy. In 1967, personal pride was involved when our son, Scott, won the Collegiate Championship and was named the outstanding sailor for performance and good sportsmanship. The same year his brother, Skip, won the Kennedy Cup for yawls and the famous Honolulu Race later in the season. While developing this college program, it became apparent that we needed other than just dinghies for racing. Corny Shields decided to develop boats that would fill this need. He commissioned his old friend, Olin Stephens, to design a boat and he came up with a modified 5.5-meter design. The finished product was a beautiful boat that could sail in any weather, easily steered and driven, with plenty of room in the cockpit.

At this time we had a Western crew sailing the *Columbia* in the America's Cup trials. *Columbia* had belonged to Corny Shields' brother Paul, and the present skipper was Walter Podolak. Walter's wife Charlotte was on the spectator boat with Corny. She told him of our efforts to promote college sailing in the West. Corny offered a personal donation which allowed us to buy more boats, including some of his new 30-foot Shields class boats. Understand that Corny at no time benefitted from the sale of these boats. He was donating his own funds, often in memory of his brother Paul. The money was used to promote college sailing and to purchase a few of the new Shields class boats which Corny rightly felt would be perfect for our use.

The first four or five of these 30-footers delivered to the Coast were distributed to the University of California, Irvine, to the University of Southern California and to Stanford University. The Stanford boats were given mooring facilities at the San Francisco Yacht Club in return for shared use, but we had a helluva time finding a home for the Irvine and U.S.C. boats. Newport Harbor was over-crowded. This situation led to an all-out battle with the local authorities to find some area in the Bay that was both available and accessible to the public. We finally found a 400-foot stretch of land destined for future development. It was the last piece of waterfront on the bay, so we nicknamed it the "Bay Window."

During the next four years we took turns attending public hearings, writing letters, sending in plans, and generally trying to be as constructive as possible in oiling the political machinery that would finally enable us to build a college sailing center at Newport Harbor. The progressive planning of the San Diego Harbor Commission enabled the colleges in that area as well to secure a spot in San Diego Bay. At a later date Santa Barbara made available a college sailing area. It is unfortunate, however, that Los Angeles, Monterey, and San Francisco have never done the same.

The Shields sloops at Newport Harbor are still being used seven days a week for training, classroom exercise, recreation, and of course for racing. The University of California at Irvine Training Program has trained as many as 1,800 potential sailors in one year. In addition to student instruction, U.C., Irvine, provides an afternoon and evening program for the parents and younger members of the family. Anytime of the day you can look out on Newport Harbor and see four or five Shields boats in training maneuvers. They have worn out suits of sails, lines, and blocks, but the hulls are as strong as ever and they race regularly. During the recent championships, the oldest boat, sailed by Joe O'Hara, former champion of Long Island, came out on top decisively, proving again the lasting value of a true one-design.

An uncanny coincidence occurred during these years of fund raising and donations. Following my doctor's advice, I was relaxing in the seclusion of the forest at Carmel. While walking slowly through the wooded area at our home, I was startled by two large dogs chasing a small fawn. I was using a golf club as a walking stick and instinctively skidded the club in front of the dogs to prevent them from killing the baby deer. The dogs were well-trained and stopped immediately, but when I went to pick up the seven iron it was bent. At the Pro Shop a few months later, I asked for a replacement for my wife's bent club. The only similar one available was in the bargain barrel. I bought it for $3.00 without bothering to examine it closely. That evening at home, I discovered up under the handle the name of Mrs. Cornelius Shields. I immediately called Corny and told him I had his wife's seven iron in California. He and his wife were dumbfounded. They had never been to California.

Somehow that club had been misplaced in the East and ended up in California—to be found by me.

These one-design boats are used not only by the colleges but also by high schools. There is a very active group of Western high-school sailors racing regularly for interscholastic cups.

Recently we formed a Navy sailing squadron whose members use our boats for small-craft training. The U.S. Navy, whose stock-in-trade is boats and the sea, often seeks the advice and aid of lay yachtsmen to develop sailing programs. Both Corny Shields and I joined the Fales Committee at the U.S. Naval Academy in the mid-1960's. Other members included Ev Morris; Harry Anderson, then Secretary of NAYRU; Richard Latham of Chicago, and Albert Faye of Texas. This group first convinced the Navy to sell their fleet of wooden boats and purchase an equal number of modern fiberglass craft. The Navy had been spending millions of dollars each year on the maintenance of outmoded wooden hulls. We obtained the free use of modern ocean racers such as *Ondine, Maradea* and *Rage*. We also sought cash donations to replenish the Navy sail locker and cover expenses for a crew to sail a Cal 40 in the Honolulu Race. In a few years, the Fales Committee helped the Naval Academy bring its sailing reputation from an all-time low to a new high. Admiral Sheldon Kinney, Admiral Bob McNitt, Admiral James Calvert, and Captain Jake Vandergrift contributed greatly in achieving the present quality of the Navy sailing program.

The development of Western collegiate sailing would not have occurred without the help of people like Jim Webster, Dick Sweet, David Grant, Dr. Norman Watson, Carter Ford, Glenn Waterhouse, Jack Wood, Chancellor Dan Aldridge, Dr. Norman Topping, Brooks Maue, Andy Graham, Dick Fenton, and Cy Gillette, to name just a few. It is not generally known that Humphrey Bogart, who portrayed the tough man on the screen and in public, was a dedicated sailor. At his funeral, the only thing on the altar in the church was a full model of his yawl, *Santana*. I can now reveal that when I started raising funds for college sailing after World War II, Humphrey Bogart called and offered me the sum of $8,500 to buy a fleet of International 14-foot dinghies for the University of California at Los Angeles with the condition that no one know that he made the donation. This is typical of the cooperative spirit of the sailing fraternity that helps to compensate for the more "newsworthy" shortcomings such as the bickering over rules and measurements or the seemingly unsportsmanlike attitudes expressed during the America's Cup series.

College sailors have graduated from dinghies and larger keel one-designs to the large ocean racers. We now have several college teams entering the Honolulu Race. Unofficially, a number of collegians have done well in the Bermuda Race and in the Whitney series. Leslie Messenger, a blonde coed from the University of California at Santa Barbara, was team manager for the All-American team that won 17 of 22 events to bring home the Lipton Cup from England.

Collegiate sailing has an unlimited growth potential, but it is unfortunate that there is no central headquarters to coordinate the regional programs. The North American Yacht Racing Union should make a college headquarters available as it did for the ocean-racing fleet. Such central coordination would not only aid in the growth and financing of collegiate sailing and assure its proper direction, but prepare collegians for future leadership in the NAYRU.

29. Maintaining Your Boat

About half the pleasure of sailing for me has been maintaining the boat. When I was a boy, I could never sail until I had cleaned her up and polished all the brass. It would take me close to an hour to polish all the cleats and winches, and after a half-hour's sail the salt spray made the brass just as dull as ever. I didn't consider that work futile, because I had the satisfaction of seeing the fittings shiny and sparkling in the sun.

To my eyes there is something beautiful about boats, and I love to spend hours just looking at them. I am very demanding in my standards of maintenance, and I can't tolerate seeing a boat in a run-down condition. I think that even minor neglect reflects on the character of the owner. In my opinion, he doesn't deserve the joy of owning a boat if he will not properly maintain her.

PAINTWORK

Caring for paintwork is a fussy, time-consuming chore, but fortunately it is the kind of work that the owner can do well himself. Shipyard costs come high these days, so after the yard has applied the initial fitting-out painting, the owner should do routine touching-up and varnishing.

I wonder if there will ever be a foolproof paint for use on boats. When wood is exposed to water, many actions and reactions occur. Paints that are successful in one place under certain conditions sometimes fail when used in another location under different conditions. When I present the shipyard with the annual work list, I generally specify the brand of paint I want used and do not leave the choice to the yard's discretion. I don't know exactly why, but a brand that works well in one part of the country is sometimes unsuitable in another. Probably the chemical composition of the local atmosphere and waters have a great deal to do with this variation.

When you discover a boat in your area with a beautiful finish that you admire, ask the owner what brand he is using. Also ask how well it stands up, for a coating that looks good only during the first week after leaving the yard can be an expensive disappointment.

TOPSIDES

Nothing looks so beautiful as smooth, gleaming topsides, which show the natural lines and curves of the freeboard to good advantage. The secret of smart-looking topsides is time and care spent in preparing the surface before painting. The seams must be smooth, and any nicks and gouges should be carefully filled with a hard-curing trowel cement.

There is a knack to applying trowel cement. It should be put on with a very flexible, wide-bladed putty knife. Best results are obtained by applying several thin layers rather than one thick one. Allow the cement to dry thoroughly between each coat, and brush lightly with a fine open-coat garnet paper. Try to get your topsides to look as if they were molded of one piece rather than made up of many strakes of planking. By rubbing your fingers over the hull, you can feel bumps and unfairnesses that might not be apparent to the eye before the hull is painted, but that would show after painting.

For topsides, I prefer a glossy paint rather than a semi-gloss paint, even though greater care is required to get a smooth finish with glossy paint. It is true that semi-gloss doesn't show laps as much as gloss, and that hull irregularities are more easily hidden, but I think that the greater beauty of the glossy finish is worth the extra labor involved.

THE UNDERBODY

If your boat is to win races for you, it must have the smoothest underbody obtainable. One of the factors that slows a sailboat is skin friction of the water flowing past the bottom surface. Any bumps or irregularities increase this friction: the smoother you can get the bottom, the faster your boat will go. It is interesting to note that tank tests have shown that wax does not improve the surface of the bottom. Certain detergents, however, are effective in this regard, although they, of course, are soon washed off. Both *Columbia* and *Sceptre* used detergents in this way during the 1958 America's Cup races.

William E. John, chairman of the International class, contacted scientists at the Stevens Institute, hoping for a definitive answer to the question of what exactly is the fastest bottom finish. He was told that the speed variation between bottom finishes in the modern racing boat was less than one-half of one percent, or hardly enough to be significant. In addition to its physical effects, keeping the boat's bottom clean and free of unfairness will help keep you psychologically at ease, and this is important in winning races also.

A bottom finish must also be antifouling if you race in salt water. Any hard finish, such as epoxy, serves well for a racing dinghy or any boat that is dry sailed. But if your boat stays in the water any length of time, or if your class rules limit the number of times you may haul during the season, then you will want your bottom finish to have anti-fouling properties. Since different local waters have different marine organisms that foul the bottom, it is best to find out what finish the racing men in your area have discovered to be most successful.

Even after only a comparatively short time at the mooring, a coating of slimy algae can accumulate on the bottom of your boat. At least once a week I swim under the hull and wipe the bottom with a towel to remove this growth; it is surprising how much drag algae can create—especially after the middle of the summer. Since aqualungs have come into general use, many of the International skippers have bought them for this specific purpose.

DECKS

On my boat I prefer to keep a glossy deck without anti-skid compound mixed in the paint. Bleached teak decks, of course, are very beautiful, but when decks are canvas covered, I like to see them shine. I even go so far as to lace my deck paint with varnish to build up a mirror-like finish. Many racing men think that decks should be coated with an antiskid agent to help prevent crew members from falling overboard. Personally, I don't like this treatment of the deck, since it is so difficult to keep clean. "Topsiders" or even wet socks will make for surefootedness even on the glossiest decks.

When antiskid compound is added to deck paint, it is well nigh impossible to keep decks looking really smart. Dirt and harbor-film lodge in the little valleys formed by the added particles, and no matter how diligent you are with your washing down, the surface always looks dingy. If pumice is used as an antiskid agent in the paint, decks become like a huge sheet of sandpaper: clothes will wear out and knuckles are skinned with regularity. If ground-up rubber particles are added, the paint coating wears off the tops of the little bumps first; your deck soon has a "salt-and-pepper" look and must be repainted.

Try your best to maintain the water-tight integrity of your decks. Fresh water from rain or snow promotes the growth of mold and rot fungi quicker than anything else. Where shrouds or stays run through holes in the deck, put rubber stoppers in the holes when you leave the boat at the mooring. White rubber sink stoppers from the hardware store can be cut with holes of slightly smaller diameters than the shrouds or the stays. The stoppers can then be trimmed to fit and shoved into the deck holes, and the shrouds or stays can be threaded through the stoppers. This will keep a lot of water from seeping below.

Interior

Keep the interior of your boat's cabin as dry, fresh-smelling and clean as possible. There is no reason for the interior to become fetid or musty-smelling and therefore unpleasant. To avoid this, keep the cabin well ventilated and the bilges scrupulously clean. When sailboats are left at the mooring, they are generally wind-rode, that is, they lie with the bow facing into the breeze. This, in effect, creates a forced draft that can be utilized to ventilate the cabin.

A patent cowl ventilator, which permits air to enter but excludes water should be fitted as far forward as possible. For racing, a deckplate can be installed in the deck with a screw cover, permitting removal of the ventilator to keep the deck clear. The companionway slide can be made with louvered vents and covered with a plastic screen to let air through but no insects. The breeze will enter the forward ventilator and exhaust through the louvered slide, providing a constant flow of fresh air. When you leave the boat for any length of time, open locker doors and drawers slightly to permit fresh air to enter freely.

Don't allow rope, wiping rags, or other gear to accumulate into sodden piles at the backs of lockers. Fit hooks and shelves to hang life preservers and rope neatly where air can circulate through them. Make sure that all nonstructural bulkheads and partitions that divide the cabin into restricted areas have patterns of ventilating holes bored into them. Proper ventilation is extremely important if you would keep your boat's cabin pleasant and livable.

Most of the International class members prefer a lustrous white or slightly off-white paint in the cabin. It brightens up the interior. Don't use a dark color. Not much light penetrates into a small boat cabin, and darker colors have little cheeriness.

Sometimes, despite adequate ventilation, mildew will grow on cabin surfaces. A fungicide added to the paint will prevent mildew from forming. Most of the major paint manufacturers produce effective fungicide additives under different brand names. Incidentally, check all hidden spots—such as underneath the deck, or behind clamps, knees, etc.— for fungi.

BILGES

Be sure that the cabin sole floorboards are fitted so they can be easily removed for inspection and cleaning. If your hull is ever holed, you want to be able to get down into those bilges quickly to ascertain the damage and stop the leak. I have been aboard boats where all the cabin furniture was securely screwed to the floorboards, and others where the boards were either swollen so tight or fastened down with so many screws that it would have taken a day to pry them loose.

Cleaning the bilges regularly must be a part of routine maintenance. It is inevitable that dust and dirt will drop down to lodge there. A weekly cleaning with a good detergent followed by a rinse with fresh water, which is then pumped overboard, will prevent foul bilgewater odors and help insure a long life for your boat. A long-handled bathroom brush is ideal for scrubbing out the bays between the frames.

In most boats, the limber holes are not large enough. Sooner or later they clog up with debris and fail to drain bilgewater to the pump intake. Take a rat-tail file or wood rasp and enlarge the openings to a generous size. While you are down in the bilge, use a small oil can to squirt Cuprinol into the limber holes and the ends of the frames, for this is a favoraite place for dry rot to start.

If your boat does not already have one, rig a limber chain through the holes to clear them. A limber chain is merely a brass chain of small diameter that is threaded through the limber holes fore-and-aft and attached by one end to a spring. When the chain is tugged the holes are cleared of debris and drain freely.

PLANKING

Inspect your planking frequently for unfairness and breaks in the paint. Paint that is cracked in a long fore-and-aft line usually indicates a check that has opened in the wood. Unfairness is an indication that fastenings have either pulled out or wrung off in drying. Pulled-out fastenings are usually the first sign that ribs have developed dry rot in the way of the screw. Hairline checks can be filled and repainted. Small seam openings can be recaulked with some of the new synthetic compounds. These compounds expand and contract as the planking dries during storage ashore and require no specialized skills to use.

FRAMES AND FASTENERS

Frames should be inspected àt the turn of the bilge, as improper shoring-up during storage will sometimes cause transverse cracks. Dry rot seems to affect oak ribs more frequently than it affects other structural members, so include them in a regular inspection program. A good preventive measure is to paint ribs with one of the copper-naphthenate preservative-fungicides. If ribs are badly damaged, sister frames can be installed alongside the defective ones. Unless you have near-professional skills, however, this is a job for the shipyard.

Occasionally, in an iron-fastened boat, rusting of a fastener head will cause the wooden plug over the fastener to obtrude. This can be cured by removing the plug, chipping off the rust, daubing the head with several coats of red lead or Rustoleum, and putting in a new plug with water-proof glue. If many plugs are raised, something is wrong with the fastening method, and a thorough inspection should be made to determine the cause. If large numbers of the fastenings are bad, refastening of the

324

complete hull may be necessary; this too is a major repair job and should be done by a yard.

TIE RODS, KNEES, AND BRACES

Sometimes when a racing boat is built with too light scantlings, the designer finds it necessary to support the mast partners, the shelf and clamp in the way of the mast partners, and parts of the hull with bracing, strapping, and tie rods. Quite often these members will be made of galvanized wrought iron. Now wherever iron passes through wooden timbers, especially if they are oak, a rust problem arises. It is essential that ferrous-metal components be maintained carefully to prevent failure under stress. Keep iron well painted and use an oil can to drop a light fish-oil rust preventive wherever iron contacts wood and cannot be painted. Whenever feasible, iron members should be replaced with bronze or monel, if replacement does not involve tearing the hull to pieces. Sometimes insulating the iron part from faying surfaces with a rubber or tarred-felt gasket will stop excessive rusting, but this too generally requires major carpentry.

HARDWARE

When installing hardware, be sure that you place padding blocks under the deck and on the inside of planking to help distribute the strain upon the fastenings. The blocks should be smeared with a luting compound on the faying surfaces. Especially, never install seacocks or scuppers through the planking without padding blocks.

If it is necessary to change the locations of cleats, fairleads, or other hardware, make certain that you plug the old fastener holes. Do not use common dowel sticks, but use the same kind of wood as that to be plugged: dip the plug in waterproof glue before driving, and it will never fall out.

MAST

The racing yachtsman must pay great attention to the proper maintenance of his mast. Any failure will surely cost him not only a race, but a loss in overall fleet standing as well. The International class boats have Sitka spruce masts, and Sitka spruce has a tendency to splinter when it is not protected from the effects of weathering. Be certain that you get some paint or varnish into the mast groove where the bolt rope of the sail slides. Some skippers use neither paint nor varnish in the groove, but wax it so the sail slides up and down easily. If you use wax, be sure that the surface of the interior of the groove is well covered with wax, and keep waxing the bolt rope and the sail stitching at the luff throughout the season.

If your boat uses sail track instead of a mast groove, the track must be securely fastened to the mast to withstand the twisting strain of the gooseneck. Since Sitka spruce is soft, the track should not be fastened directly to the mast, but to a hardwood batten that is glued and screwed to the mast. Several through-bolts should be driven through the bottom of the track, at the region of the gooseneck fitting and at the top of the mast. Do not use bolts of overlarge diameter, however, or you will seriously weaken the mast.

Where spreaders, jumper-strut pads, or tangs are secured to the mast, be sure that a bedding compound is used beneath the metal parts. Moisture has a habit of collecting in these locations, and they are ideal places for rot to start. Always use a bedding compound that will maintain its elasticity and not dry out with time. While you are working on the upper mast, it does no harm to brush Cuprinol beneath the hardware.

One section of the mast that frequently causes trouble is the base. Unless precautions are taken, dampness here promotes dry rot. Every hollow mast and the mast step itself has drain holes to allow condensation and accumulated water to escape. These drain holes must be kept open and cleared of obstructions. Use a long, stiff wire to clear the mast and mast-step drain holes before the mast is stepped at the beginning of the season. While you are at it, take this opportunity to apply Cuprinol to the base of the mast and the mast step. It is a good idea at this time, also, to fit a metal collar around the base of the mast to protect the butt when lowering and stepping the mast. This collar should ride on bronze or stainless steel straps secured to the mast step.

BOOM

It is seldom that a boom not fitted with a boom vang causes trouble. However, when a boom vang is used, tremendous strains are exerted as the vang is bowsed down. We had a great deal of trouble with broken booms in the International class until we found and remedied the cause. The vangs formerly consisted of a wire that led through a hole in the boom near its center. The concentration of strain at this hole was causing the booms to break. Now we use long monel straps to distribute the strain, and broken booms have become a rarity. It is most important that your gooseneck track be thoroughly reinforced on the mast. The thrust of the boom when the vang is set is enormous.

Incidentally, do not let the boom bang across in a hard breeze when the vang is set, since the boom can be broken.

RIGGING

Rigging failure is the greatest cause of racing-sailboat breakdown. Despite this well-known fact, the rigging is usually the last item to receive attention. I would no more think of entering a series without a thorough rigging inspection than I would of entering without sails; frequently it amounts to the same thing.

Wire rigging is usually 1 x 19 stainless steel wire rope. Though stainless steel withstands loading and weathering well, it reacts poorly to vibration. With constant vibration, stainless steel fatigues; the metal crystallizes and the strands break. For this reason you must keep a constant check on your rigging for broken strands. By running your hand down the full length of a shroud of stay, you can immediately feel a broken strand. Stainless steel, incidentally, is not completely stainless; it will rust somewhat. It is necessary, therefore, to lubricate wire rigging with light machine oil from time to time.

Patent fittings, which have all but replaced eye splices, often cause rigging failures. There are any number of them on the market; most of them utilize the principle of swaging under pressure. This operation is usually done at the factory and requires specialized machinery. If a fitting is improperly swaged, damage to the fitting sometimes results. All fittings should be carefully inspected under a magnifying glass for imperfections or hairline cracks, and if any are found, the shroud should be removed and sent to a professional rigger for installation of a new fitting. If these patent devices are made of stainless steel, they too are subject to failure from metal fatigue. Patent fittings are usually designed with a large built-in safety factor, but this is no reason to neglect them.

Patent fittings should be sealed with a rubber sealant where the wire rope enters the fitting. This should be done before the rigging is put into use; if the sealant is run in after use, it only traps moisture already present, and rust will develop. If the rigging has been used, do not employ a sealant, but occasionally run oil into the fitting to prevent rust. Wherever rigging wire terminates in sockets, clevises, or toggles, pay close attention to maintenance; these often cause trouble.

327

It is best to avoid the use of turnbuckles aloft, because they are difficult to service. If a turnbuckle aloft is necessary, use silicon bronze rather than stainless steel; it is less subject to vibration fatigue.

My comments on maintenance in this chapter are mainly limited to wooden boats. I have included them because these techniques I've used over the years might prove helpful to traditionalists who, like myself, prefer the aesthetic qualities of wood. The practicality and economy of fiberglass is obvious, but the joy of admiration and accomplishment gained from the care of a wooden boat is lost to many modern sailors. Every bit of work involved is more than rewarded in the beauty of the hull and brightwork of the properly maintained wooden sailboat.

The newer materials for hulls, masts, and booms also require proper care. There are numerous books available on the maintenance and repair of these materials, and manufacturers are always willing to supply owners with guidance.

30. A Helmsman's Tipsheet

Many of these tips may be elemental and familiar to more experienced sailors, but there is so much for all of us to enjoy learning that everyone, when this is realized, becomes a beginner. In my own case, I've sailed all my life, only to find out how actually little I know. The wonderful fascination of sailing is to realize that every time you go out, there is something new to learn, or something that you've learned but forgotten.

The fly on your shrouds (black thread or wool, not ribbon) is the golden key to sailing your boat properly. Keep your eye on it constantly.

Tape all pins both aloft and below to protect your spinnaker.

Prior to the start of your season, lay off compass courses between all marks in your racing area.

Include any reference marks indicated on the chart—bridges, buildings, water towers, chimneys, etc. Bearings of this nature are invaluable in determining your course to an unseen mark in hazy weather. Cross index in a book for immediate availability.

Carry a government chart of your racing area and a pair of parallel rulers.

Carry rip-stop tape for spinnaker rips.

Helvetia will beautify your teak.

If you sail in salt water, wash your boat with fresh water after every sail to protect the paint and varnish.

A tiller strap of shock cord leading directly to the cockpit floor simplifies making the mooring when sailing alone and makes for more accessibility in the cockpit than a thwartship lanyard. The latter does not give the rudder freedom and causes wear on the key in the rudder post.

Fiberglass battens are the most durable and will permit the sail to take its natural shape, especially aloft.

Be constantly aware of what direction the tide or current is running. Even in your pleasure sailing, know how it is affecting you.

⚓ *Know the Racing Rules!*

Check halyard sheave pins in the spring and fall. Check swage fittings for cracks in the barrel regularly during the season, using a magnifying glass. Also examine shrouds for broken strands in the areas of fittings.

Should you upset a centerboarder, neither you nor any member of the crew should leave the boat.

Have an accurate compass. Check your new course after each tack to determine lifts and headers of that particular board.

Stow your anchor clear of the compass.

⚓ *Look at the fly.*

Make it a rule that no mediocre swimmers go off your boat when you are anchored in current unless you have aboard 30-40 feet of line streaming with a life preserver attached.

Practice man overboard procedures by throwing over a life preserver and attempting to recover it.

Exercise your powers of observation to the fullest degree. You will be astonished at the amount of knowledge you will acquire. Observe the tactics and the sail trim of your successful competitors. Observe the weather, the characteristics of the winds, the tidal and current flows.

Make certain the bottom of your boat is free of slime. The best of tuning, sails, and good helmsmanship cannot overcome this handicap.

To show no respect for a thunderstorm is a sure sign of inexperience. Don't try to pose as a hero in a treacherous squall.

Practice making your mooring in a seamanlike manner. A skipper can be judged by how he handles this department. Tide and sea are important factors to be considered.

Keep your boat immaculate and shipshape. You will enjoy her more.

⚓ *Know the racing rules!*

Look at your barometer morning and evening. It is very important in estimating the wind velocity and direction.

Unless you operate your boat on a very extravagant basis, a drifting genoa is an unnecessary inventory item. It is more practical and economical to put this amount of money in a light weather jib. Drifting genoas are good in theory but the actual distance gained over a regular light-weight jib is negligible. It must be taken off when the wind increases to two or three knots, and if there has been any advantage it will probably be lost, with added time consumed in changing to a heavier sail.

Theoretically a large spinnaker through the presentation of a larger area should be a faster sail than a small one. This, however, is not true except in fresh breezes of 18-20 knots and up. A big sail will not stand as well, especially in disturbed water, because it does not dispose of the wind as readily as the smaller spinnaker. A smaller spinnaker should not contain too much draft. We conclusively proved in the Twelves time after time that the small, relatively flat sail was faster in light to moderate breezes dead before the wind. On reaches, the larger sails are definitely faster but only when the apparent wind is 12-14 knots and up

If necessary be sure and firmly demand your right of way when it exists.

Don't race or cruise offshore without a spinnaker net. When this sail turns around the headstay a textile machine couldn't wind it any tighter. It can take hours to clear it. There are various types of net that are satisfactory. One is quite simple that can be quickly set. It involves a rope halyard set next to the jibstay with the device that is used in self-furling jibs secured to the foot and a swivel at the head. Four or five lines of ¼ inch nylon lines secured equidistant up the net halyard lead off to a foot line for setting. When the self-furling device is released the net rolls off like a curtain. The net has the profile of a conventional working jib. The foot or trimming line is placed where the clew of the jib would be.

A well-designed, staunchly built light-weight genoa is decidedly advantageous over a sail a few ounces heavier. The difference can actually be sensational. For example, in the Twelves, we learned that a five-ounce genoa could be carried in a breeze up to approximately 12 knots' strength of wind. Previous to this it was our practice to put on an eight-ounce sail in seven or eight knots. We proved that the lighter weight sail was very much faster until the wind reached the sail's upper limit of 12 knots. It is therefore recommended to skippers of open and cruising classes to put more emphasis on lighter weight jibs in their sail inventory.

Don't take chances at the start, crossing on the port tack, bearing off and tacking too close. Laxity in rule observance can only bring the same result as all other forms of carelessness. It is far better to be conservative in this regard, rather than to be disqualified in one race which could be most costly in your season championship standing.

In maneuvering for a downwind start in a centerboard or a keel centerboard boat, make certain your board is down. This will permit you to fully control your boat in close quarters.

After you have tested the starting line for the favored end, you and all crew members should constantly watch to make certain the Committee launch has not moved the flag end, or that the Committee has not rendered 40 or 50 feet more scope on the Committee boat causing a material change in the line. Too, see that the white flag of the starting line on the Committee Boat has not been changed.

Check course signals again at the time of the preparatory and enter it in your daily log. Don't trust to your memory.

Have a crew member assigned to the binoculars for a recall signal on the start. All crew members listen for your number. At the beginning of each leg, all the crew should call out the next mark.

⚓ *Don't overstand the weather mark.*

Constantly anticipate possible changes. If the spinnaker is set, be prepared to get it off and set the jib if the wind draws ahead. Be prepared to set the spinnaker if the wind draws aft. Boat lengths of profit can result if you are alert in this regard.

The same preparation must be made for changing to light and heavy sheets. It may not sound too important, but costly panic parties can occur when the crew is unprepared for these minor changes.

Don't carry your spinnaker too close to the leeward mark. The little you gain will be lost if you are unprepared to properly and quickly trim for the windward leg.

If you set your spinnaker and find the wind is too far ahead to carry it, get it off immediately. Don't fight your error.

Free up your jib and main in the lulls of breezes that vary in strength.

Move your jib lead out when the breeze is strong and the main luffs.

If necessary, change your sail trim on each tack for the different angle sea.

Don't fight for either end of the starting line. If you lose (especially the leeward end), it is much too costly. However, be sure to be on the line, and of course endeavor to have your wind free with full way. Select your starting point and plan your start accordingly. Don't flounder and hope to find a clear spot. Constantly keep your boat moving at good speed after the preparatory.

⚓ *Know the racing rules!*

Lower the main halyard a few inches on all light-to-moderate weather reaches and runs.

If you are leading, make certain you cover the second boat, and if possible the third. Under no circumstances get in a position where you are not between them and the weather mark.

Don't overstand and give away hard-earned distance to windward. Plan to approach the weather mark on the starboard tack.

Don't be harassed by power-boat swells. More harm to your boat's speed can come from the distraction than is lost by the swells. Let your competitors do the shrieking and complaining. If they do, you may well convert the problem to a gain.

No matter how secure your position may be in the race, permit no relaxation in your boat. Constantly expect the unexpected.

Don't cry about bad breaks. They come to all members of the fleet. If you moan about them, you can do yourself more harm psychologically than the bad breaks can do you. Dismiss them from your mind immediately and sail your boat.

A Helmsman's Tipsheet

⚓ *Minimize your tacks.*

Unless there is a good reason, such as ability to lay the windward mark, try to avoid tacking under a competitor's lee bow. If you do, you are locked (unless you are close enough to back-draft him) with no flexibility. Better to cross or go under and tack clear of his weather quarter. You are then in control.

In a large class, avoid luffing matches even if it costs you a place. At best you can win the battle but lose the war.

To prevent your boat from rolling to windward in a fresh breeze, dead before the wind, trim the spinnaker sheet as hard as possible.

⚓ *Don't overstand.*

In light weather, search for new wind constantly. Indications can be seen on other sailboats, fixed smoke, flags, and of course, in the appearance of wind on the water.

⚓ *Don't take your eye off the fly.*

A boom vang set up very hard will produce the same effect as a wide traveler, and will trim your sail aloft. It is recommended that you sail to windward in fresh breezes with the vang set very taut. If the vang is not set as you approach the weather mark, set it while the mainsail is trimmed. Be sure to ease your vang as wind strength diminishes. The boom or gooseneck fixture may break if caution is not exercised in hard breeze jibes.

Similar to the vang, the traveler, when positioned to a wide trim, flattens the upper part of the mainsail and permits the sail to be trimmed considerably wider, 12 to 15 degrees on a reach, thereby providing more power. Be sure you obtain this advantage, as with the vang, and slack the sheet to the maximum. In reaching, the problems associated with the traveler are not so difficult to deal with; but in windward work, the traveler presents many difficulties. Great delicacy is required for obtaining the correct positions for this point of sailing. Considerable judgment and patience are necessary in the skipper's experiments for the proper positions in various strengths of wind, for the shape of the mainsail is the most important factor. In light weather, for example, the sail should be trimmed from a midship position; as the breeze increases, a wider trim is required for trimming the upper part of the sail. A mainsail with a high clew should use little traveler, whereas a low-clew sail with moderate-to-full draft must be eased well over on the traveler to trim the upper area—even in light weather. The traveler is not an easy device to master, but it is a worthwhile one when properly employed.

⚓ *Don't permit a lee-bow current to cause you to overstand.*

Don't tack to leeward unless the wind is dead aft and light.

On the wind, allow your boat to have her head. Don't force her higher than she can sail. Let her sail herself. She can do it better than you. Merely guide and trim her properly. There is no mysto-magic touch of the helm that so many seem to think exists—especially some winners. It is a combination of various efforts that wins races. In a one-design class, it is the tuning, the bottom, and the helmsman's ability to select a good crew, to organize the boat, to start well, to be composed, to know how the sails should be trimmed in all conditions, to know where to go on the windward leg, to get out of trouble and not waste time crying about his bad breaks or gloating that the favorable breaks are his good judgment. Most important of all (unless sails are one-design and drawn by lot) are *sails*. The latter are, in my opinion, 75 percent of the factors that make a boat successful.

Don't trim your jib too flat, even in hard weather. This is a common failing about which you must be cautious. You deprive the jib of its power. It is a sign of tautness on the part of the skipper and crew. They believe this will make the boat point higher. The reverse can be true.

Make certain you call *mast line* when it is achieved.

Steer your boat from the windward side in moderate and hard breezes. It is more pleasant and comfortable, and you will see the breeze better. Also of great importance, you will have a better look at the seas and in consequence be able to work her through them more effectively. Of some consideration, too, your weight will be to windward. From this position, sail her by what you can see of the jib and, of course, the fly. Disregard the luffing of the mainsail in this strength of wind.

Feather her through the strong puffs. Keep her on her bottom. Never let the lee rail get in the water. Ease the main a few inches if necessary to prevent this.

The crew must concentrate 100 percent on sail trim during runs and reaches.

A HELMSMAN'S TIPSHEET

⚓ *Watch the fly.*

If you have a sufficient lead at the leeward mark, split the difference with the following boat—that is, hold a tack for one-half your lead, then tack to place your boat between the competitor and the weather mark.

At the leeward mark, start your turn away from the mark so you will lose no distance to windward in the turn.

⚓ *Complete concentration throughout the race is vital.*

Permit no undue excitement in your boat; yelling, scolding and tautness will immediately permeate the atmosphere aboard the boat, and performance is bound to suffer.

The head of your jib is not normally seen from the cockpit. If it is not standing, attempt a correction through moving your leads forward.

Persuade an experienced helmsman to come aboard and watch you steer your boat to windward. Ask him to comment on your ability to hold her high enough without being too fine—or perhaps he will find you are inclined to sail too wide. Also let him comment on how you work her through the seas. If possible, have him observe your tactics throughout an entire race from a power boat—or better yet, by sailing with you. Assistance of this kind from an interested friend is priceless guidance that could provide a shortcut to skills that otherwise might take years for you to acquire. Merely use the same procedure that the golf professional uses with the golfer, and the football, baseball, and tennis coaches use with aspirants in those sports.

Select a class to race in that has a large number of competitors. You will learn more, and faster.

Constantly study the racing rules. The appeals are most instructive. Robert N. Bavier's book, *The New Yacht Racing Rules, 1973–1976,* is excellent.

⚓ *Don't take your eye away from the fly.*

Constantly anticipate necessary changes and maneuvers.

Do not waste your time attempting to tell your friends and competitors why you did not win. No one is interested, and you will soon learn that you are talking to yourself. It is much better to ask questions of the more experienced, then *listen*—you will be surprised how much you can learn.

⚓ *Don't lose your concentration—*
   no matter what position you are in.

Do not be discouraged by serious blunders. Your competitors are making them, too. The one who makes the fewest usually wins. The greatest mistake you can make, however, is not to learn by your mistakes.

After you have gained a top position in your class standings, seek opportunities to enter open championship series in other boats. Do not give up your own class, but occasional broadening out will be instructive. You will learn to sail other types of boats and meet new competition. It is fine to be a big frog, but prove your ability in a larger pond. It may eventually be the means of getting you on an America's Cup boat.

To be successful in racing as in other sports, you must be intensely interested, anxious to learn, and constantly thinking, and you must fiercely want to win. As in practically any endeavor, you can accomplish almost anything that you really want to do.

⚓ *Don't take your eye off the fly.*

Have your anchor and line stowed in a convenient place for immediate use in an emergency.

In very light drifting weather, slack the jib halyard sufficiently to eliminate the draft curl at the luff.

Learn to pick up a tow in a seamanlike manner.

In light drifting weather, set the windward sheet slightly to produce better contour to the jib.

In the spring, before your season starts, sail your boat in severe weather to test your rig and gear. This is very important for you psychologically. It will give you complete confidence to sail her hard when heavy weather is encountered during the season.

Check wooden spreaders at both ends for dry rot, keeping them protected with sufficient paint.

Racing in dinghies will teach both the beginner and the experienced sailor more in a shorter period of time than any other form of racing. Here he will learn that indefinable "feel" of his boat, develop concentration, acquire a knowledge of tactics, rules, starts, sails, etc. And if he isn't alert, he will also soon realize the importance of being able to swim.

Get to the starting area early. Abandon any crew member who keeps you waiting more than once.

Make certain you and your crew all know the course.

In any series always endeavor to obtain a good average position in each race. Don't take "long shots" to win. Stay in company with your closest competitors. You don't have to finish first in every race to win a series.

31. We Sail a Race Together

While sailing out to the starting line, or before, the skipper should check the current tables so he knows the state of the tide at the start and during the race. It is as important to do this when there is a real sailing breeze as it is in light weather, which is when the majority is aware of the way the tide is running because it is more apparent then. The state of the tide must at all times be included in your calculations. A skipper who neglects it may find at the start that a fair tide will put him over the line before the gun or that a head tide will make him late in crossing. Also, if he doesn't figure tide or current in his windward work, he may overstand or under-stand when he tacks for the weather mark. On runs and reaches, consideration of the tide is no less important. If in doubt about the state of the tide, place a bottle or chip alongside the starting buoy or an anchored boat to obtain the direction and speed of tide or current.

No keen racing skipper would consider sailing without a compass, but many, especially on small boats, either do not carry one or fail to make full use of it. Yet a compass may be of inestimable value in determining the tactics at the starting line and during the race. For example, before the start you should sail the reaching leg on a compass course to decide if a spinnaker may be carried. The course for the run should also be tested to determine which jibe is preferable. A shift in the breeze may subsequently necessitate a change in your strategy, but nevertheless you should plan ahead.

Everyone on board should observe the signals on the committee boat, and the course to be sailed should be logged with the date so there is no possibility of confusion. Depending on memory alone is not enough. At the preparatory gun, every crew member should again look to see if the course has been changed.

THE START

The start can be the most important part of your entire race. It is most difficult to regain ground lost at the start. The starting line should be square to the wind, but it may not be, and the skipper must therefore determine which end of the line, or which spot, will be most favorable for a windward start. There are two methods for doing this.

The quickest and simplest method is to place your boat head to wind in the middle of the starting line. Her heading will be closer to the favorable end.

The more exact method is as follows:

1. Luff your boat head to wind, take the *exact* compass heading to obtain wind direction.

2. Sail on the starboard tack on the starting line. Line up the flag end with the white flag on the committee boat, through the headstay and permanent backstay. Read the *exact* compass bearing. If you are unable to get on the line due to the starting activity of other classes, line up the buoy end with the white flag on the committee boat from either end of the line—in other words, make an extension of the starting line. In this case there is only one bearing to be taken. Whichever end of the line is closest to the direction of the wind will naturally be the preferable end on which to start. For example, if the wind were due north and the bearing of the line were east by south (west by north) the easterly end would obviously be favored. If the reverse were true and the bearing of the line were east by north (west by south) the start would then be made at the westerly end to gain the advantage of the one-point differential. A little practice is required for those unaccustomed to using the compass regularly, but it soon becomes automatic.

If the committee has set the line square properly to the wind, you may start anywhere on the line without disadvantage. The position will be determined by where you have elected to go on the weather leg.

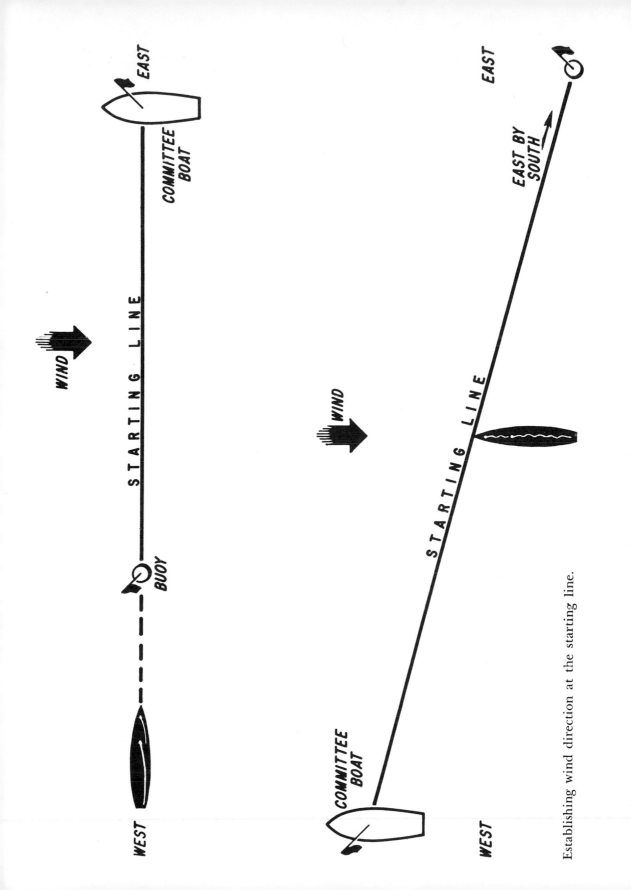

Establishing wind direction at the starting line.

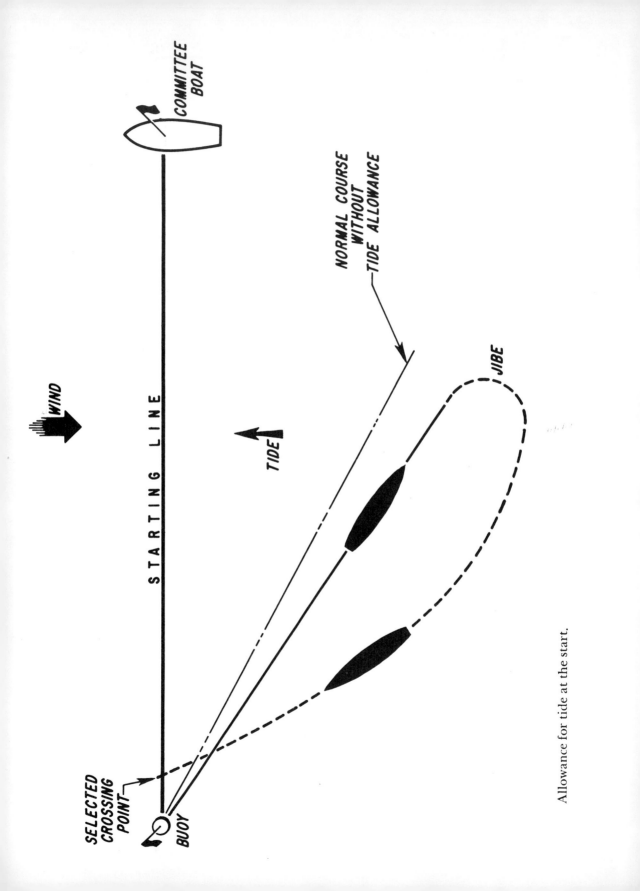

Allowance for tide at the start.

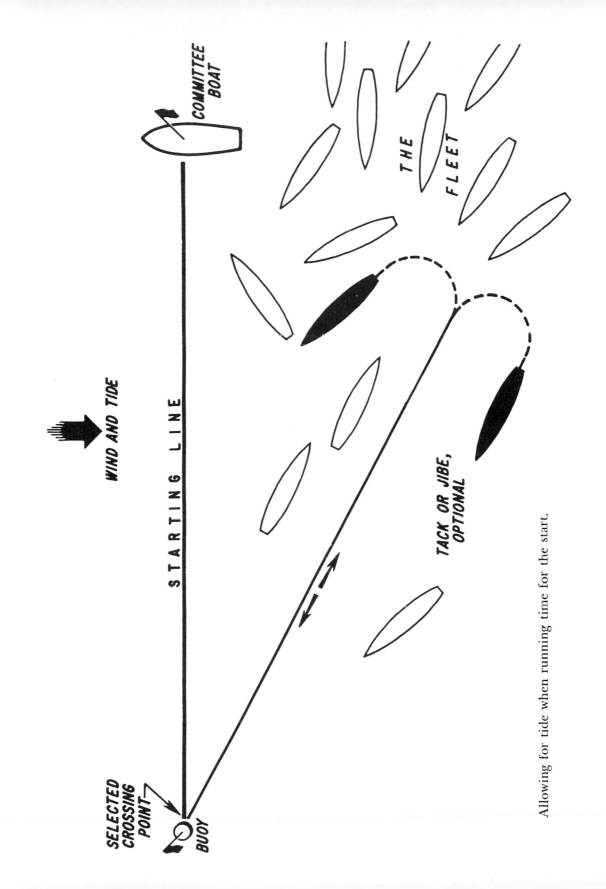

COMMITTEE BOAT

THE FLEET

WIND AND TIDE

STARTING LINE

TACK OR JIBE, OPTIONAL

SELECTED CROSSING POINT

BUOY

Allowing for tide when running time for the start.

For those unaccustomed to a quick reading of the compass, it is suggested that a compass rose be used for practice ashore by placing a pencil on the rose representing your boat and practice lining up the wind. Keep changing positions of the simulated starting line and become proficient in various bearings—that is, learn that the reciprocal of N/W is S/E, that of northwest by west is southeast by east, and so forth.

Having decided previously exactly where you want to be on the line at the gun, here is a suggested procedure for running time at the start. First, with your stopwatch, determine your tacking and jibing time from reach to reach. For a moderate-size boat (25 to 35 feet), I recommend that the normal run from the line back to the line be two minutes. It may be seen readily that if your total running time were one minute, you would meet the fleet heading for the line while you were endeavoring to tack or jibe for your return to the line. In boats 50 feet or larger, it is suggested that the total run be a minimum of four minutes, because of greater speed, longer tacking times, and need for maneuvering.

Presume your tacking time is ten seconds, reach to reach. You will be on the line, at the spot where you have chosen to cross, exactly two minutes before the starting signal, reaching (on the port tack), and you will continue on this reach for exactly 55 seconds. Then you will tack or jibe (ten seconds) reach up to the line for fifty-five seconds, and cross with the gun.

Naturally tide and sea must be taken into account in your runs. It is, therefore, vitally important to make several practice runs to learn what allowances should be made. A jibe is often preferable to a tack in returning to the line, especially in a fair tide. In this way you avoid a "barging" course. Furthermore, a jibe places your boat in a position to sharpen up and maintain rights of the leeward boat. In starts on the line away from the buoy or committee boat, the skipper must anticipate being smothered by weather boats on his approach as well as at the line itself.

It is also advantageous to have a tabulation for odd times in the event you are not free to leave the line at exactly two minutes before the start. For example, if you left your designated starting spot at a minute and 50 seconds before the actual start, your total seconds would amount to 110. With ten seconds allowed for tacking, your runaway would be exactly 50 seconds. With the various times tabulated on a card, the skipper will not have the problem of leaving his planned starting point at exactly two minutes before the gun, a difficult matter in a large class.

A few seconds can be life or death on a start. How often have we wished to speed up the committee's official watch when we are in the so-called coffin corner with too many seconds to dispose of. It is either over the line ahead of time, jibe and then be under the entire fleet on the port tack, or the third awful choice of hitting the committee boat. Walter Bowes, always a quick-witted sailor, found himself in this dreadful spot with eight or ten seconds to kill when sailing a 6-meter in France at Cannes. When he realized he was faced with the three equally unhappy alternatives, he observed a French sailor aboard the committee boat getting ready to pull the lanyard on the starting cannon. Bowes started a loud chant, "Cinq, quatre, trois, deux, un—Au feu!" As the sailor yanked the lanyard, Bowes crossed at the favored end of the line with a nice lead on the fleet.

SAILING THE COURSE

On the weather leg, the skipper must be continually alert to the trim of the sails. As a general rule, both the mainsail and the jib should be trimmed in flat, but take care that the jib is not so flat that it has insufficient drive. The jib *must* have lift and draft to pull the boat, especially in disturbed water. Skippers and crew are too often inclined to trim the jib too hard, subconsciously feeling this will make the boat point higher. The reverse is usually true.

One of the most vital items of racing equipment is the wind fly, or tell-tale, tied on the upper shroud, the one farthest outboard. Narrow pieces of ribbon are most frequently used, but ribbon flutters too much. My preference is for black thread, black being easier to see than white. However, if you haven't top vision and have difficulty seeing thread, use pieces of dark yarn—it doesn't flutter. The importance of the fly cannot be overemphasized. The keen helmsman will never let it out of his sight. *Absolute concentration* on this little guide rates A-1 in the list of must requirements for the skipper. It is also of equal importance off the wind and especially in light weather.

Of course the trim depends on conditions of wind and sea. If in a hard breeze the boat is burying her lee rail or carrying too much weather helm, ease the mainsheet a few inches. She must be sailed on her bottom. Adjustments should be continued as necessary. Always be sure the lee rail is not under and that sails are *not* trimmed too flat in rough water. Do not be too concerned about a luff in your mainsail. Remember that if the boat is overpowered, the mainsail must be eased to keep the boat on her bottom and the rail out of water.

Different tacks may require changes in the trim of the sails to meet wave conditions. On one tack you may have the sea at a better angle than on the other, with the result that the boat will foot well with the sails trimmed in hard on one, but not on the other. On the latter, it may be necessary to ease the sails to give them pulling power to drive her through the seas. Changing the trim of the sails on different tacks is overlooked much too often.

When the breeze increases, attempt to feather your boat through the hard puffs. In other words, sail her a little finer as the puff strikes. This will keep her on her bottom, she will point higher, and she will actually not lose speed. Feel is a prerequisite for skillful feathering. The patient struggle through light weather is good fun and requires consummate skill, but for me there is no greater joy than sailing a well-tuned, well-equipped boat to windward in a very hard breeze.

On which side of the boat the helmsman should sit, whether to windward or to leeward, is another much debated subject, but I doubt that it will ever be resolved, for either side may be the right one, depending on conditions. In a breeze I prefer to sit to windward; it's the natural place and the more comfortable. When you are seated to windward your weight is where it will help the boat most, and you can see the wind on the water before it strikes. Watching the seas, working her through them so they do not slow your boat down, is of great importance. Even when sailing before the wind, the skipper and crew should, in a good breeze, stay to windward, to keep the boat on her designed lines and ease her helm.

You must realize that you cannot force your boat to do the impossible. Merely guide her. Let her sail herself. Don't for example, try to sail her closer to the wind than she is capable of. You will sense and anticipate just before she is about to luff. You will similarly realize subconsciously that she is being sailed too wide. In disturbed water you will immediately feel that you are not giving her the necessary opportunity to get through the seas to her best advantage. Just remember that she can do it herself if you don't deprive her through poor handling.

Plan your approach to the weather mark long before you reach it. By all means be on the starboard tack if possible. Few maneuvers can be more costly than finding yourself on the port tack and meeting a solid wall of starboard-tack competitors. Never make the unpardonable mistake of overstanding the weather mark. Precious hard-gained distance you have earned is thrown overboard if you do. On the contrary, you may be able to improve your position by under-standing, especially if there is a current or tide setting you up to it. Whatever your tactics at the weather mark, you should be in a position to come in on the starboard tack or know you can cross ahead of the boats approaching with right of way.

The main halyard should be lowered a few inches on a run or reach to permit the headboard to be in the same plane as the sail. This will produce more draft in the upper part of the sail and is of great importance, especially in light weather. Slackening the tack downhaul is of secondary importance; it helps the lower but not the upper area. In drifting weather, the outhaul may also be slackened to advantage, and this is vitally important if your sail is flat. In light weather, when sailing to windward, you can use the spinnaker boom topping lift to take the weight off the main boom, thereby giving more draft to the sail. Off the wind, use the jib halyard when the spinnaker is set. Do not haul the foot of your mainsail beyond normal bounds; it merely distorts the sail, and gains no additional area.

A reach or run becomes, on some boats, a form of rest period, but very often it is these two legs that offer real opportunities for ground-gaining. On a reach, head no higher than the next mark, and if possible, steer to leeward of it so you are in a position to gain speed by reaching up. Again capitalize on the tide or current.

Everything must be set to hoist the spinnaker as you are approaching the weather mark, and by the time the spinnaker is two blocks it should be drawing. On many boats the spinnaker pole is set at the proper angle beforehand, and the sheet can be gradually trimmed in as the sail is hoisted. Be careful not to trim too fast, for if you do the spinnaker will fill and be difficult to hoist.

The great value of the boom vang is demonstrated on this leg. It should be set up before reaching the weather mark. The boom vang makes the sail and boom swing as a door, or, in other words, holds the sail in one plane. The sail can therefore be eased further off than would otherwise be possible. Without the downward pull of the vang, the mainsail will luff aloft first, and the entire sail must be trimmed to accommodate this condition. With the vang down, the luff occurs simultaneously along the entire hoist. The vang should be used with caution in light weather.

With the wind dead aft, and especially in light airs, a skipper should be aware that some advantage may be gained by tacking to leeward, by reaching up approximately a point or two to gain speed, and then jibing over at the proper moment to maintain the equivalent course on the other jibe. In this way he also has a better chance of avoiding the fleet and keeping his wind clear.

At all times, whether on a run or on the windward leg, an alert skipper must make every effort to keep clear of his competitors. Avoid luffing matches on the runs even if to do so you must sacrifice your position. In the final score and in a large fleet, this precaution usually pays off. This also applies to private scraps on windward legs.

As in so much of life, there is really nothing new in sailing. Something appears to be new only because it was previously unknown. I have found that the more I learn the more I realize how little I know. Thus sailors who have had little or no experience in yacht racing may find more of interest in my comments than old timers will. As far as the experienced racing skipper is concerned, I can only hope that I have reminded him of at least one thing he knew but had forgotten. I hope that by applying that one new-old idea, he may win a race that otherwise he might have lost. I wish, too, that the ardent enthusiast starting to sail will some time give me the benefits of his learning. A great deal of my best instruction has come from juniors and beginners.

Index